in **SEARCH** *of* **HAPPINESS**

ANGUS DEAYTON AND LISE MAYER

in SEARCH *of* HAPPINESS

MACMILLAN

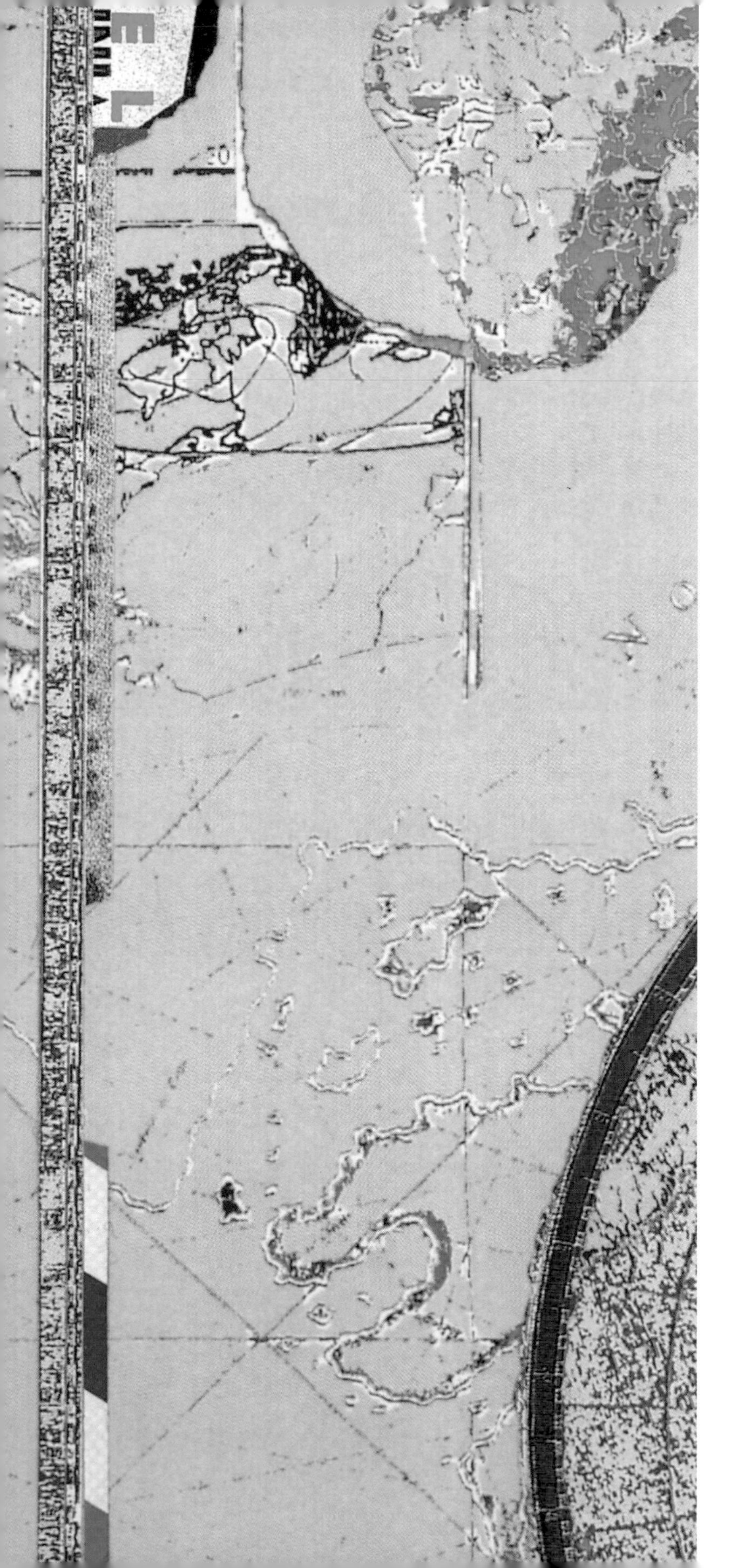

First published 1995 by Macmillan
an imprint of Macmillan General Books
Cavaye Place, London SW10 9PG
and Basingstoke

Associated companies throughout the world

ISBN 0 333 63061 0

The publishers gratefully acknowledge the following for the use of copyright material:

'All I Have to do is Dream' by Bourdleaux Bryant. Copyright © 1958 House of Bryant Publications, USA. Acuff-Rose Music Ltd., London W1. Used by permission of Music Sales Ltd. All rights reserved.

'Art for Art's Sake'. Words and music by Graham Gouldman and Eric Stewart. Copyright © 1975. Reproduced by kind permission of EMI Music Ltd., London WC2H 0EA.

'Can't Buy Me Love'. Words and music by John Lennon and Paul McCartney. Copyright © 1964 Northern Songs. Used by permission of Music Sales Limited. All rights reserved. International copyright secured.

'I Am the Walrus'. Words and music by John Lennon and Paul McCartney. Copyright © 1964 Northern Songs. Used by permission of Music Sales Limited. All rights reserved. International copyright secured.

'Love is the Drug' by Bryan Ferry and Andy MacKay. Used by permission of EG Music Ltd and BMG Music Publishing Ltd.

'People'. Words by Bob Merril, music by Julie Styne. Copyright © Chappell-Styne Inc. and Wonderful Music Inc., USA. Warner Chappell Music Ltd., London W1Y 3FA. Reproduced by permission of International Music Publications Ltd.

'Sex and Drugs and Rock and Roll . . .' by Ian Dury. Used by permission of Ian Dury.

9 8 7 6 5 4 3 2 1

A CIP catalogue record for this book is available from the British Library

Colour reproduction by Aylesbury Studios, Bromley, Kent.

Printed and bound in Great Britain by BPC Hazell Books Ltd
A member of The British Printing Company Ltd

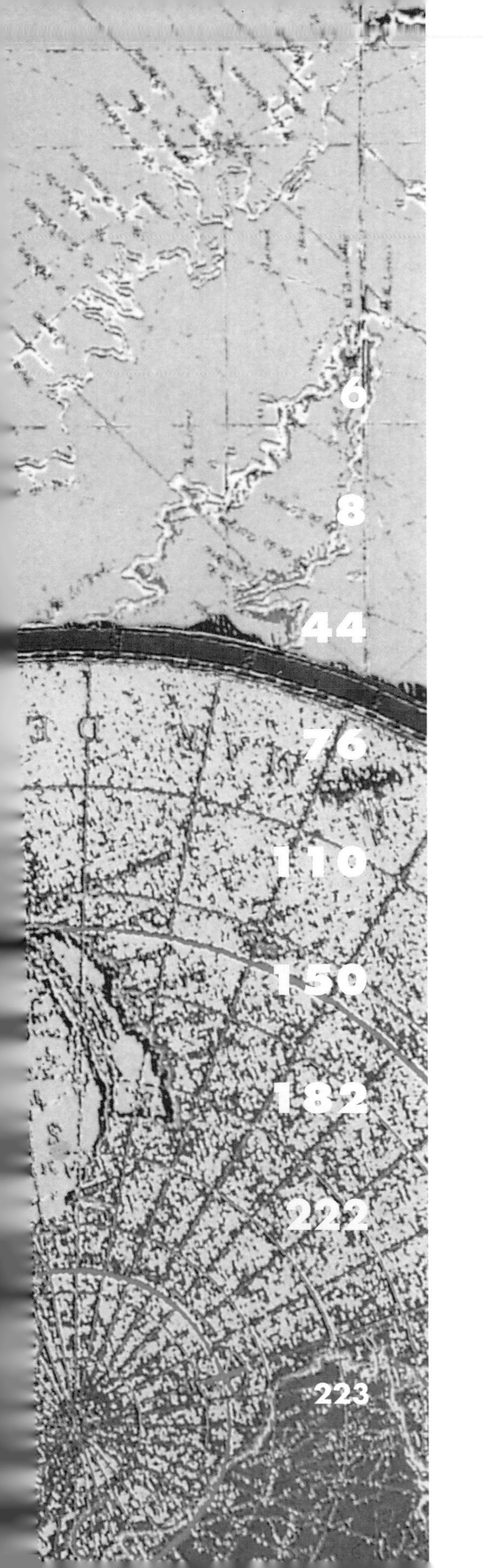

CONTENTS

FOREWORD

'Happiness is a warm gun', 'Happiness is egg-shaped', 'Happiness is a thing called Comfort' – or is that softness? In any case, happiness obviously means different things to different people, depending on whether you're John Lennon, an advertising copywriter or a spokesman for the Egg Marketing Board. Or indeed a Hungarian, where Hapeinos is a type of household bleach.

So what exactly is happiness? How is it defined? And what are the chemical components that bring it about? These are just some of the questions we've avoided, and instead have concentrated on topics like: 'What's the quickest way to get happy?', 'How much does it cost?', 'Is it legal?' and 'Will I still be able to cross my legs afterwards?'

Interestingly, the word 'happy' comes between 'haply', meaning chance, and 'hara-kiri', meaning suicide, in the dictionary. So what does this tell us? It tells us, for a start, that for some reason my dictionary seems to have chosen to omit the word 'happen'.

Obviously happiness is a subjective thing and the routes to people's happiness are many. To some it may mean watching André Agassi and Pete Sampras on Wimbledon Centre Court with a bowl of strawberries in your hand, to others it may mean watching André Agassi and Pete Sampras in the showers with a Polaroid camera in your hand. And to the surrealists amongst us it may mean watching a bowl of strawberries and a Polaroid in the showers with André Agassi in your hand.

The book breaks down into six chapters – a manufacturing defect for which I apologize. Each chapter, numbered one to six for the sake of numerical simplicity, deals with a different aspect of my search. Is Love the key? I answer that one in the chapter entitled 'Love'. Is creating your own Ideal World the key? I answer that one in the chapter entitled 'Ideal Worlds'. Or is changing some vital element in your life the secret of true and lasting happiness? I answer that one in the chapter entitled 'Is changing some vital element in your life the secret of true and lasting happiness?' And so on. You'll soon get the idea, as the hours drag by.

In conducting this torrid twelve-month search,* I've come of across an abundance of fascinating facts and personalities, some

* You may think that this book is a mere spin-off a documentary series, but actually the TV programme is just a blatant attempt by the BBC to cash in on the book.

of which are contained in this book, and some of which aren't – just in case there's a sequel. For example, there can be very few of us who would guess that the happiest nation in the world, according to statistics, is Switzerland, although there can be very few of us who wouldn't have wagered good money on the most miserable of all being the French. Equally startling is the revelation that according to scientists the unhappiest profession is that of farmer. Conversely, the happiest profession is that of vicar. And in the gender/marital-status stakes, married men without children score higher on the Happy-ometer than single men or married men with children. (Single women, you will be completely unsurprised to hear, are statistically happier than the married ones, whether they have children or not.) So if you come across a Swiss vicar with a wife and no family, expect him to be beaming from ear to ear; he is one of the most felicitous beings on earth.

So why should you read this book? Well, for a start you've just bought it, or at least been given it by some well-meaning friend or relative you wouldn't want to offend. Secondly, you might just hit upon the one path to permanent bliss that you'd never hitherto considered, but which could change your life for evermore. (And believe me, if you think you've thought of everything, just turn to page 101.) And finally, once you've read it, it might just prove crucial when you come to need something exactly this thickness to wedge under that wobbly table-leg in the kitchen.

LOVE

Makes the World Go Wrong

Love is the sweetest thing.
Peter Skellern

Love, love, love – all the wretched cant of it, masking egoism, lust, masochism, fantasy under a mythology of sentimental postures, a welter of self-induced miseries and joys, blinding and masking the essential personalities in the frozen gestures of courtship, in the kissing and the dating and the desire, the compliments and the quarrels which vivify its barrenness.
Germaine Greer

Love is a many-splendoured thing. Love makes the world go round. Love is in the air. Love is all around. All you need is love. Love loves to love love. Love's a bitch. Love me, love my dog . . . There is nothing that hasn't been written, said, sighed, sung and probably even dribbled about love. Four in five adults surveyed rate love as 'important to their happiness'. Likewise, when people are asked, 'What missing element would bring you most happiness?', the most frequent answer is, 'Love.'

But, then, what exactly is love? Definitions vary considerably. For some love means security and contentment, while for others it's all romantic longing and knee-trembling desire, characterized by the rapid beating of the heart, dizziness and shortness of breath normally associated with a mild coronary seizure. Love can come as suddenly as a thunderbolt or as slowly as a Network Southeast commuter train. It can last a lifetime or until she sees what you look like first thing in the morning. The ancient Greeks distinguished between *eros* – romantic love – and *agape* – spiritual love; the *Oxford English Dictionary* defines love as: 'warm affection, strong emotional attachment, sexual passion, devotion, self-sacrificing goodwill' (so think twice before you tell a lexicographer that you 'love' your pet Alsatian). George Bernard Shaw said love is 'a gross exaggeration of the difference between one person and everybody else'; H. L. Mencken said love is 'a state of perceptual anaesthesia'; and Englebert Humperdinck said, 'Love is all.'

But for the majority of people, love, if all goes well, means A Relationship. Statistically, people in stable relationships enjoy greater well-being than their solitary brethren. Surveys in the USA and Britain have unanimously produced the finding that married people are happier than single or widowed people, and considerably happier than those who are separated or divorced.

Bronzini's *An Allegory with Venus and Cupid*: the 16th century equivalent of a Madonna video.

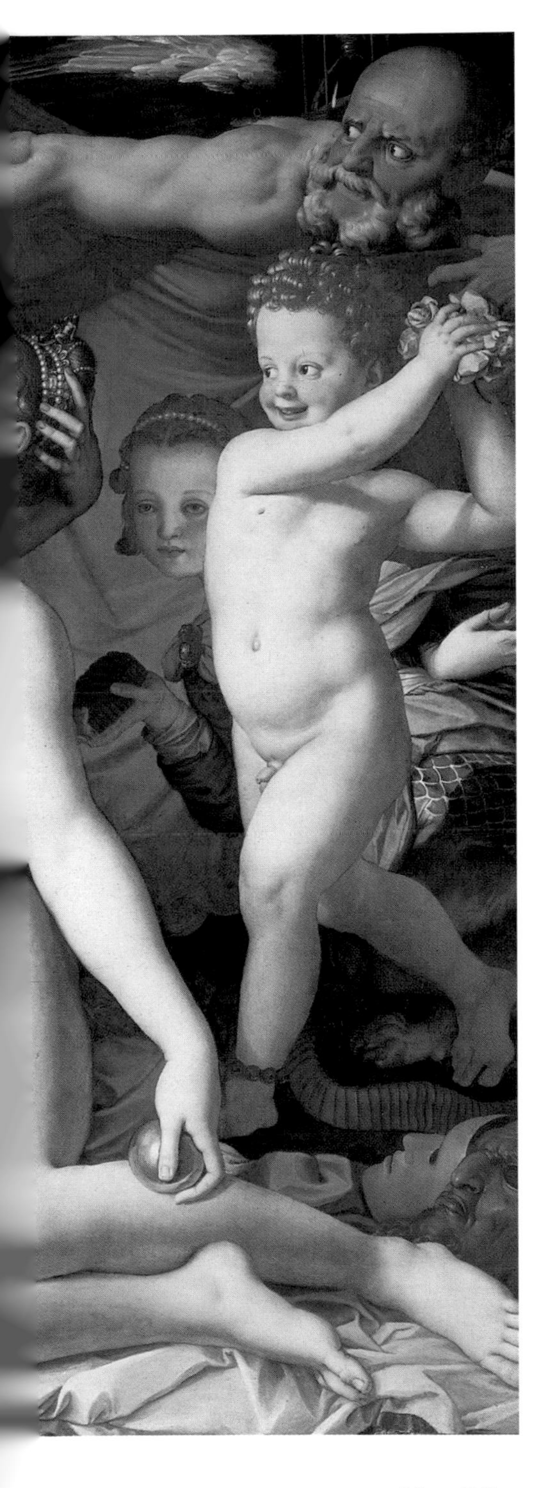

Bridgeman Art Library

(This would indicate that most people would prefer a spouse to die rather than divorce them, which possibly comes as a surprise to almost no one.) In one particular survey, 66 per cent of married couples claimed that their marriage was 'very happy', 75 per cent said that their spouse was their best friend and 80 per cent agreed that they would marry the same person again. However, whether those findings would have been the same if they had interviewed people when their partner wasn't in the same room, I don't know.

Not unsurprisingly, married people are more likely to enjoy an enduring, supportive, intimate relationship, and are less likely to suffer loneliness. They also gain status in society by having a recognized role. The one unanswered question is, does marriage make you happy or are happy people more likely to get married?

Of course, marriage, or a relationship *per se*, is no guarantee of happiness. Unlike flattery and male genitalia, quality is more important than quantity, and an unhappy relationship is almost always worse than none at all. These days between 40 and 50 per cent of marriages will end in divorce, with first marriages standing a slightly better chance of success than subsequent endeavours. There are many theories about the rise of divorce: some say that people are now making higher demands on a marriage than they used to and are more concerned with their own pleasure than with the well-being of those around them. Others argue that past generations simply didn't have the choice and remained trapped in miserable relationships because society and the law made it hard to do anything else. Getting divorced is like dogs licking their privates. They do it because they can.

Whatever the truth of the matter, the pursuit of love is still a major, perhaps *the* major, human preoccupation. Box-office returns from 1993 showed that love and romance is still more popular with cinema audiences than guns and biceps, and Hallmark notched up one million sales of Valentine cards in Britain alone. And, after all, fifteen million Mills and Boon readers can't be wrong.

JUST
MARRIED

MARRY AT LEISURE, DIVORCE IN HASTE

1. Jamaica: Love and Marriage

To love is to place our happiness in the happiness of another.
Gottfried Wilhelm von Leibniz

We don't refer to it as 'rain', we call it 'liquid sunshine'.
Sarah of Sandals

Sandals: more bodily fluids are being exchanged in broad daylight than at 'Virgin Night' in a Transylvanian disco.

It's worse than a Saturday morning at Sainsbury's and a Sunday afternoon at IKEA rolled together. Even a suburban garden centre on a Bank Holiday Monday has nothing on this place. Everywhere you look there are couples. There are couples holding hands at the beachside barbecue, couples smooching in the swimming pool, couples canoodling in the candlelit bar and couples snogging under the coconut palms. In the pool, sporty couples are batting pink balls to each other with heart-shaped paddles, while under the palm trees in the tropical garden, more bodily fluids are being exchanged in broad daylight than at 'Virgin Night' in a Transylvanian disco.

I have come to Jamaica to visit one of the increasingly popular Sandals' couples-only resorts. On this island alone there are now six separate luxury-hotel complexes which cater exclusively for romantic twosomes aged eighteen and over. If you are single, gay, have children or live in a *menage à trois*, don't bother even trying to make a booking. The couple rule is so firm they wouldn't even let Mel Gibson in without a partner. On the other hand, if you're after a dirty weekend with your chiropodist, no questions will be asked.

The previous week in London, I suffered the indignity of sitting through a meal in an ill-fitting jacket and soup-stained tie after being greeted at the door by the *maître d'* with a curt, 'Is sir unfamiliar with the dress code of this establishment?' (All very well – but at Pizza Hut?) Accordingly, as I arrive, conspicuously alone, at the hotel reception desk, I am fully expecting to have an ill-fitting, soup-stained woman forced upon me by the concierge before they allow me to check in. Luckily, I am given special dispensation to enter the hallowed halls of coupledom in my bachelor state, although the words thumb, sore, out and sticking all immediately spring to mind. As it says in the brochure:

Sandals is created for romance. There are no worries, no kids, no inhibitions. Nothing to come between the two of you. You can share the excitement of doing it all. Or bask in the pure bliss of doing nothing at all. Here there are romantic gardens where you can stroll. Wander through palm groves, with slender trees swaying overhead and island music serenading you in the distance. And discover very secluded hammocks and love baskets, conveniently built for two. From the moment you arrive, you'll discover a tropical hideaway where romance is a twenty-four-hour-a-day adventure designed for couples only . . . Meet other couples from around the world at the friendly swim-up pool bars. Here you have all the privacy you wish, or all the excitement you desire. At dusk, we salute the end of another day in paradise with a picture-perfect sunset. Choose from one of our gourmet restaurants as you savour a deliciously romantic dinner for two. Then gather in the intimate atmosphere of the piano bar for festive sing-alongs. Or dance the night away at the pulsating disco. Finally, as you walk back to your room under a canopy of stars, the moon lights a silver trail that leads straight to romance. And the rest is up to you . . . If this is love it must be Sandals.

'All WeddingMoons™ include a justice of the peace or clergyman and special touches such as tropical flowers, Caribbean wedding cake, champagne celebration dinner and wedding-day video. Other WeddingMoon™ options include private island cruises, massages, manicures, pedicures, Calypso band or classical violinist and personalized candlelit dinners' . . . Or you can have your wedding gatecrashed by a BBC 2 quiz show presenter.

I can't help thinking that it must be a disappointing job for all the young, single barmen, windsurfing instructors *et al.* No wet T-shirt competitions or clamping an orange between the buttocks at *this* hotel. The majority of the couples here are content to pass their days basking in the hot Caribbean sun, their evenings sipping giant paper-umbrella-bedecked cocktails served in hollowed-out coconuts and pineapples and their nights listening to the gentle lapping of the waves on the beach, the chirp of cicadas and the rhythmic creaking of two hundred sets of king-sized bedsprings.

'From the moment you arrive, you'll discover a tropical hideaway where romance is a 24-hour-a-day adventure designed for couples only.' It's called your bedroom.

Also, an increasing number of customers are opting to display their affection in a more public way. A further option, and a more extreme version of the all-inclusive holiday concept, is to combine a romantic holiday with that most romantic of all activities, a wedding. No doubt in a few years' time wedding/honeymoon packages will seem old hat as we trek off around the globe for combination holidays involving childbirth, surgery and probably even funerals:

A three-piece suit and full wedding outfit is the perfect choice of clothing for the Jamaican summer.

After a sumptuous buffet breakfast on the palm-fringed terrace of one of our premier resorts, you may wish to scatter your loved one's ashes on the golden sands of the nearby beach, to the accompaniment of a local steel band. In the afternoon, complimentary windsurfing lessons will help take your mind off the tragic passing of your kith and kin . . . guests who would like something 'just a little bit different' from our usual cremations and interments may wish to send off for our 'Crocodile Dundee' brochure featuring funeral destinations as diverse as the Florida Everglades and the lower Amazon basin . . .

Dawn and Dave and Julie and Graham and Denise and Anthony and Debbie and Paul and Christopher and Samantha are just ten of the brides and bridegrooms who, instead of a traditional wedding in Britain, have chosen to tie the knot in Jamaica or, as Sandals would have it, invest in a 'redefined destination wedding' catchily entitled a 'WeddingMoon™'. And, after all, what could be more romantic than to put on a morning suit and full-length white wedding dress in 90° heat and wobble across the sand in high heels to say your vows in front of a bunch of gawping strangers in swimming costumes?

The promotional literature (strange how junk mail likes to describe itself as though it were part of an A-level set text) eulogizes thus:

All WeddingMoons™ include a justice of the peace or clergyman and special touches such as tropical flowers, Caribbean wedding cake, champagne celebration dinner and wedding-day video. Other WeddingMoon™ options include private island cruises, massages, manicures, pedicures, Calypso band or classical violinist and personalized candlelit dinners.

More importantly, although they omit to mention it in the brochures, getting married in foreign climes means *no relatives*. That means no fights over whether to invite the second cousins twice removed, no worrying about whether his family will notice that the champagne is sham and the caviare cod, or worrying about how to keep Uncle Donald away from the bridesmaids and Auntie Margery off the Scotch . . . Obviously, judging by the increasing number of Britons getting hitched abroad, this is a powerful incentive for many couples who wish to make it to their wedding night on speaking terms.

So, what do Dawn, Dave, Julie, Graham, Denise, Anthony, Debbie, Paul, Christopher and Samantha think of the experience? Mysteriously, they all seem to have disappeared up to their king-sized bedrooms. And on a lovely sunny day like this.

'Meet other couples from around the world at the friendly swim up pool bars. Here you have all the privacy you wish, or all the excitement you desire.' And unlimited opportunity to play paddle-tennis using two foam-bats with hearts on them.

2. Tucson, Arizona: the Divorce Machine

Stand by your man and tell the world you love him . . .
Tammy Wynette

Our D.I.V.O.R.C.E. becomes final today . . .
Tammy Wynette

Go, and never darken my towels again!
Groucho Marx

Here in Britain, as we hurtle towards the millennium, the white heat of technology has revolutionized the lives of everyday men and women up and down the land. We have in-car stereos, we have CD ROM, we have the National Lottery. And we have vending machines. We now have machines that dispense food, cash, rail tickets, cinema tickets, even dry-cleaning. You put in your 30p, out comes your chocolate bar. (Or, in most cases, you put in your 30p, out comes nothing, you hit the dispensing machine, a few people stare at you, you hit the dispensing machine harder, your train arrives, you depart chocolateless and 30p poorer.) Of course in the United States, home of the brave, frozen yogurt and car-jacking, they have, as ever, gone one better. Not only do their vending machines sometimes work, but there now exists a machine that dispenses divorces.

All you have to do is pop into the civic offices in downtown Tucson, Arizona, and you can get the quickiest of quickie divorces. About fifteen minutes, to be precise. This is providing you are willing to bear the indignity of responding in public to questions like, 'Is your spouse pregnant?' 'If yes, are you the father? If no, do you have any idea who the father might be?' List the names in alphabetical order . . .

You would think that one of the great advantages of getting your divorce from a machine would be that you wouldn't have to divulge all your personal details to some complete stranger. However, in the way of these things, the Arizona authorities have decided to try to make their divorce machine more 'human'. To this end, a computerized face appears on the screen and quizzes you about your broken marriage in a booming, humanized voice.

In the UK, the latest vending machine can give you a cup of lukewarm coffee with lumpy bits of powdered milk. In the US, it can give you a divorce.

'Has your marriage irretrievably broken down? In other words, are you absolutely certain that your marriage cannot be saved?' shouts the machine as soon as you switch it on. 'Touch *yes* or *no*.' A few people turn to watch as they make their way across the linoleum floor to the child-benefit counter. 'Divorce can be emotionally difficult for all members of the family, and can involve complex legal procedures. Conciliation services, legal advice and other free help is available. If you want a print-out of these services, touch here. If you want to file for divorce, touch here. If you want to respond to a divorce started by your spouse, touch here.' By now, a small crowd has gathered to watch you.

Deciding that my marriage is definitely on the rocks, I start to tap in all the heart-rending details. 'If you want to receive maintenance from your spouse, touch here. If you want to pay maintenance to your spouse, touch here. If you don't want any kind of spousal maintenance, touch here. If you would like to forcibly insert something up your spouse's bottom, touch here.'

The divorce machine now asks the petitioner to decide, on the spot, which of the children, pets and house contents they wish to claim. No need to spend weeks arguing over who gets to keep the Rick Astley albums, it's all done with the press of a button. 'Select *yes* for the appropriate chattels: "Microwave . . . TV . . . contents of bedroom one . . . contents of bedroom two . . . that strange coffee table made out of deer's antlers . . . etc." This mechanized divvying up is about as painless as a person could hope for, providing you don't have a sore finger.

Half an hour later I have amassed a dossier the size of the *Encyclopaedia Britannica*, a watching crowd who could almost fill Madison Square Gardens and a sore finger. Most importantly, I have an official document from the Arizona State Department granting my divorce from Meryl Streep, with whom I have nine children, and citing Alan Titchmarsh as the third party. I kept the car, the house, the business and all the furniture but, in the end, I decided to let Meryl keep the Rick Astley albums.

3. Albuquerque, New Mexico: Ring-Bashing

Mutual love, the crown of all our bliss.
John Milton

By the time you swear you're his,
Shivering and sighing,
And he vows his passion is
Infinite, undying,
Lady, make a note of this –
One of you is lying.
Dorothy Parker

With this swing let freedom ring.
Lynn Peters

Don't mess with Lynn Peters: 'I've become very comfortable with a 4 lb sledgehammer.'

When we arrive at Lynn Peters's bungalow on the outskirts of Albuquerque all the paraphernalia for the ceremony has already been laid out in her garden: rows of red-canvas director's chairs, a table with champagne on ice next to a red rose, a second table with a red cloth on which sits an anvil and a heavy sledgehammer – red, naturally. Lynn comes out to greet us wearing her self-styled ceremonial dress – an apron (I forget which colour) depicting her own logo of a couple in wedding dress, with their backs to each other, each holding a gun against the background of a no U-turn road sign. The symbolism is not exactly understated, but then, this ceremony isn't about subtlety.

It's a beautiful day for a divorce. The guests arrive in Lynn's small backyard in dribs and drabs, and are handed a welcoming drink by Lynn and her uniformed assistants – a Ring Carrier and a Hammer Beater. The atmosphere is certainly as cheerful as any wedding I have ever attended (possibly because they rarely serve alcohol in British parish churches) and everyone mingles happily. Most of the guests have grisly divorce stories of their own to tell and, being Americans, they tell them.

As we wait for whatever the divorce equivalent of a bride is, Lynn explains the genesis of her unusual but increasingly popular celebration. 'My own divorce was in 1988. I kept looking at my wedding ring, it was sitting around, I didn't know what to do with it. I was never going to wear it again in the form that it's in, and I wanted to do something positive with the metal. That's how it developed.'

By 'it', Lynn means her 'ring-bashing' ceremony, the climax of which is the point at which a divorcée calmly, rationally and publicly beats the shit out of their wedding ring with an extremely large sledgehammer. But like marriage, ring-bashing isn't as easy as it looks. 'I didn't hit it the first time, it took three attempts. It was a very thin ring, 14-carat gold. I'm a better shot now – I've become very comfortable with a 4lb sledgehammer.' Not the kind of skill you advertise in a lonely hearts column, but Lynn swears by its therapeutic properties. 'When I got my divorce decree I felt like there was no conclusion. I called up my divorce attorney and said, "Is this it?" The ceremony brought closure for me. It bashed my past, but not in a negative way. It was fun to do something physical, it was a celebration, a transition, a ritual and it also made me realize I could turn the ring into something that I could wear today in a different mode.'

'I'm hoping to franchise. I hope to have a divorce chapel of some kind, hopefully to offer a quickie divorce service to move on with your life. I also have a ring-bashing kit that's being developed. It's almost ready to go.'
Lynn Peters, divorce priestess and entrepreneur.

After twenty-two years, one month and twenty days of marriage, Priscilla Corteva leaps at the opportunity to beat her wedding ring into an unrecognizable pulp . . .

Lynn's own wedding ring is now a lapel pin. Conveniently, Lynn is a graphic designer and jeweller, so after helping you to beat your wedding ring into an unrecognizable pulp, she will help you to redesign it. Lynn prefers to make the old rings into something as frivolous as possible. Tie-pins, golf tees, key chains, ear-rings and charms are all popular items. She also specializes in the 'freedom ring', bearing her special no U-turn logo, or a loving epithet like 'I miss my husband/wife, but my aim's getting better'. Lynn describes this transmogrification of that band of gold as 'turning lemons into lemonade'. And, like many American inventions, she is anxious to point out that it's not only fun, but good for your health. 'The wedding ring really is a very symbolic object. It represents a big commitment when you get married and usually a big disappointment when you get divorced.' Whatever the secret, Lynn's ring-bashing ceremony has become hugely popular. Her back garden now sees dozens of rings being bashed each month (two-thirds of them belonging to women) and her furnaces are always stoked.

There is a momentary hush as the guest of honour arrives. As far as possible, Lynn's divorce ceremony mirrors the wedding ceremony, except that the centre of attention is an individual rather than a couple. Today, the individual in question is Priscilla Corteva, who looks radiant in a pair of jeans and a cotton shirt.

'Dearly enlightened, we are gathered here today to celebrate the new life of Priscilla Corteva, who after a period of twenty-two years, one month and twenty days is hereby released, renewed and freed. You, Priscilla, are charged with the following duties: to have and to hold anyone you damn well please, to experience the pleasures you've hereto only dreamed of, to recover emotionally, financially and sexually and to remember that being naked does not mean being alone. Now place the ring on the anvil and repeat after me . . . "I, Priscilla, will adopt a positive outlook, and will pursue any and all opportunies to enjoy life . . ." Now take the hammer. With this swing let freedom ring. One, two . . . Whooo!' Not a moist eye in the yard.

As the champagne corks pop and the strains of Tammy Wynette waft across the suburbs of Albuquerque, Lynn allows herself a moment of self-congratulation. 'They're not only happier at the ceremony, but sometimes they call later and tell me, "I don't know what happened – I felt a release,"' she says proudly, then hastily qualifies her statement. 'I'm not saying that this is the answer, it's not. It's simply part of the process of going through divorce.'

And what does Priscilla think? Was it as good as the wedding? Was it worth the money? (Between $150 and $700 depending on the item of jewellery selected.) 'It's absolutely therapeutic. It's fun. It's laughter. It's cathartic. It's a reason to move on. A reason to discuss your divorce. A reason to get your friends together. A reason to do something tangible.'

So as a satisfied Priscilla goes off into the sunset to have and hold anyone she damn well pleases, how does Lynn Peters see the future of her one-woman divorce industry? 'I'm hoping to franchise . . . I hope to have a divorce chapel of some kind, hopefully to offer a quickie divorce service to move on with your life. I also have a ring-bashing kit that's being developed. It's almost ready to go.' Perhaps Lynn should get in touch with the management of Sandals. Before you know it thousands would be flocking to the Caribbean for a luxury all-inclusive singles-only 'DivorceMoon™'.

. . . The resultant pulp.

SHAYDIE SORI

The Woman Who Will Teach You How To Steal Any Man You Want From the Arms of Another Woman For Only $200

The silliest woman can manage a clever man.
Aldous Huxley

In love all women are professionals and all men are amateurs.
François Truffaut

Men have died from time to time and worms have eaten them, but not for love.
William Shakespeare

In the city of New York, where a woman's chances of meeting a single heterosexual male are considerably lower than the likelihood that she will be mugged within two blocks of her home, it comes as no surprise that Shaydie Sori's business is flourishing.

Shaydie gives me some tips about how to steal my best friend's husband.

Shaydie is a self-appointed 'Love Coach' (not that anyone else could appoint you, as far as I am aware), and she makes a comfortable living instructing the dissatisfied maidens of the metropolis in the ancient science of man-catching. She is happy to work with clients on a one-to-one basis, or you can sign up for her succinctly entitled course, 'How To Steal Any Man You Want From the Arms of Another Woman or Just Keep the One You Love'. Shaydie's basic thrust, if I can call it that, seems to be teaching her clients to enact variations on the 'treat 'em mean, keep 'em keen' theme, but such is her dedication she has managed to eke this out into a philosophy, a way of life and, most of all, a business.

My first encounter with Shaydie takes place in the self-help section of an uptown bookstore the size of Harrods. Women Who Love Too Much, Men Who Have Forgotten How To Be Men and Women Who Have Forgotten How To Love Men Too Much are only some of the customers browsing these well-lined

bookshelves, and two feet above my head is the smiling face of Anthony Robbins, inviting me to *Awaken the Giant Within* (see Chapter Three). This is only one of the venues that serve Shaydie as office, consulting room and lecture hall. 'That's the best thing, you know, no overheads.' Like any self-respecting woman of the nineties the first thing Shaydie does upon arrival is to change her shoes. Her boyfriend, it turns out, used to own a shoe store, and she claims to own more than a hundred pairs. Hence the change of footwear every half-hour, and the huge rucksack to carry them all. Shaydie herself is a New Yorker born and bred: perky, upfront and super-confident. She expounds her theories lucidly and persuasively, accompanied by lots of hand movements. One day, surprise, surprise, she'd like to be an actress.

Shaydie is quick to point out that she is not a therapist. 'I'm not a therapist. I don't ask you to love yourself in a heartbeat, you know what I mean. I just get to the heart of things.' Her aim is to tell clients *where* they are going wrong, not *why*. 'My job is to teach them how to get the person of their dreams and how to move through the bad stuff of relationships very quickly.' There is no doubt that Shaydie is enthusiastic about her work. 'It's like a map. I see everything like a puzzle, or playing chess. The object of the game is to win, OK. And the puzzles of a relationship are usually fun, it's a great game for me. I let them see what the pieces are and I say if we put this piece here this is what's going to happen, and if we put that piece here that's what's going to happen. And the object of the game is to be happy.'

Although she is only twenty-six years old, Shaydie says her credentials lie in her own track record, the proof being that she herself has never experienced any insurmountable problems in her relationships. But then, she is only twenty-six years old. She also thinks that many women benefit from an objective eye. 'Sometimes when you are emotionally involved in a relationship you can't see what works for you. If you have a problem it's better to have someone look at it more clearly from the outside.' Shaydie claims an additional advantage because, she says, she thinks like a man. 'Men are free – they don't have all these major, major hang-ups. Women are far too emotional. I don't have a lot in common with the way women think. Sometimes when my friends get upset I just think: What's the problem? Fix it later, let's have fun now.'

Much of her knowledge of men, Shaydie says, she picked up from observing her father – 'Probably the biggest womanizer in the world.' You might not think this was an instant recommendation but Shaydie feels differently. 'I saw how he could get people in the palm of his hand, and I would say, "My God, he's not very honest, but I'll be damned, everybody likes him, and there's something charming about his ways." He was a good bad boy and every woman wants a good bad boy.' And to think that all these years I thought what every woman wanted was a tall Noel Edmonds.

The oldest woman to enlist Shaydie's services was seventy-five; the youngest was sixteen, and was brought to Shaydie by her parents, who wanted to start her off on the right track. 'I see all types of people, all ages, all religions, all nationalities. You know, you might have a girl sitting next to you who's a stripper, sitting next to a woman who has a million dollar co-op. But basically they're all there for the same reason, they can't get it together.' For a mere $200 a session, Shaydie soon sorts them

To remain incognito, Shaydie will even feign interest in a Jeffrey Archer novel.

out. 'I break things down for them, I give them homework, I tell them, "OK, we have to fix this area here," or, "Let's take this away from him, 'cos he gets a little bit too much candy here." Often the women are initially reluctant to take Shaydie's advice. 'However, they always want to prove me wrong, so they're going to do whatever I tell them to do.' As soon as Shaydie is proven right (which, she claims, is always the case) the women are willing to place themselves in her hands. 'They think, "Like, wow, she really knows what she's talking about," which is true, I do.'

Shaydie won't help a woman find a man: she is there to help her to secure the affections of one she has already met, slept with or even married. And, unlike most psychotherapists or counsellors, Shaydie is not prepared to hold her clients' hands for ever. 'Once you get it, I disappear, my job is done. I'm not going to be in your life for ever. I don't have a family or a country home to pay for, so I'll give quick results . . . I walk in and I walk out very quickly.'

Although the majority of her pupils are women, Shaydie has had one or two men seek out her professional services too. Usually he will be the sort of man whom women claim is 'too available', a man of whom they say, 'He just doesn't have that Indiana Jones feel to him.' So how does she go about turning a man from Bobby Crush to Bobby De Niro? 'It's usually a case of toughening them up a bit, teaching them when to say no and not letting them be so taken in by her.' However, experience has taught her to be slightly less blunt with them than she is with her female clients. 'Men don't like to be criticized, you know, their egos are a little more sensitive.' It also seems that the male of the species has a problem in facing the truth about where we might have gone wrong in our wooing. 'Women demand brutality, they like you to tell it the way it is, but a guy is like – "Well, tell me the way it is sort of . . . but not too much."' Usually, she says, the trouble with these guys is that they're being too nice. 'I'm not saying treat a woman like a dog, but I tell you, if you say you're going to call give her something to argue about.' So is it true what they say – all women love a bastard?' Shaydie considers. 'A nice bastard.'

As well as the bookstore, Shaydie meets and treats her clients in venues all over Manhattan. Favourites include Isabelle's on Columbus Avenue and, weather and muggers permitting, next to the lake in Central Park. She also favours the cafeteria in the Natural History Museum, which is where I agree to meet her the following day for more tips on relationship success. I find myself seated near a number of models showing the evolutionary stages

in the development of mankind. Behind me is a glass case displaying a couple of our hairy, naked forebears huddling together in front of a primeval landscape. A party of schoolchildren burst into the hall, take one look at *Homo apallachus* and cry, 'Look at the tits on that!' Of course, give them ten to fifteen years and they'll be back at the bookstore poring over the 'self-help and gender issues' section like everyone else.

A couple of primitive specimens of the missing link chat in front of a case containing some gorillas.

'If we can learn bad habits we can learn good ones,' proclaims Shaydie. 'The real trick is knowing when not to get crazy and emotional about stuff.' The most common complaint she gets about men is their reluctance to commit: 'If you want to marry him don't talk about it,' says Shaydie. 'Don't have a conversation about for ever and the marriage and "when are we going to do this, when are we going to do that", because he's going to say "soon", and "soon" will never come.' As an example of the correct technique she tells a story about herself and a former boyfriend. 'We were driving along and I said, "The traffic is really heavy, why don't we go and get married?" And he said, "OK, sure."' The marriage never took place, but only because Shaydie herself had second thoughts. A few years later, when she wanted to move in with her new boyfriend she found him less than enthusiastic. 'So what I did was I went down to my landlord and told her that I had to move out, then I called him up and said, "Honey, I have something to tell you, I've been evicted." He's, like, "Oh my God, I don't believe it." I got off the subject very quickly, I didn't want to have this big pity party on the fact that I got evicted, 'cos obviously I didn't. I said, "Look, here's the deal – how about it if I move in to one of your spare rooms, just as a guest, and the longest I'll stay is three months? I'll put all my things in storage till I can get back on my feet." And he felt really bad, so he said yes. I already had my things packed, I already called the movers, 'cos I figured if he says no I'm goin' to show up anyway. Well, it's been four and a half years and I didn't move out.'

If you want to move in with a man, but find the idea of giving up your own place too drastic, Shaydie proposes another option. Plan B involves gradually moving your possessions into the man's place of residence. 'That way you don't have to have a conversation about it.' But what if this dim-witted man-person should perchance happen to notice? 'If you see that he's not really quick on the idea of you moving in then you move everything out. But if you move everything out now, he realizes that a large part of you was living in his house because now it's bare. And now he wants you to come back because he feels like half his life is missing.'

Once you've succeeded in moving in with your designated male, you may start worrying that he's not paying you enough attention. Shaydie has plenty of advice in this area. 'First of all, you should always remain a challenge for men. Men love the chase, they love the hunt. That's what keeps the spark going. Once they know they have you, what's the point?' How about intimacy? Contentment? Sitting in front of the telly in your underpants not worrying about that pot belly? No. Shaydie believes in Mystery. 'Keep the spark going and do something that makes him notice you. Whatever you do has to be short, sweet, drastic, out of character and insane – those five things, and it has to, like, give him a pow, right in the face.' Once your beloved has recovered from the nosebleed, he will be putty in your hands. 'Women should be naughty and nice to their men,' says Shaydie, conjuring up the spectre of Dick Emery. 'No one ever gets passionate about something that's humdrum. But I really believe, and maybe I'm just a little romantic here, believe it or not, that you could be in a relationship for ten years and still have magic.'

That is, of course, until another of Shaydie's clients enlists her help in stealing your husband. 'Nobody belongs to anybody,' says Shaydie. 'Even when they're married.' She has no qualms about helping women who are involved with married men, but she says she does try to warn them that they probably won't want him once they've finally succeeded in getting him. 'The mentality of a woman who gets involved with a married man is totally different than the woman that wants a man . . . ultimately it's going to fail.' A happy exception is a former client whom Shaydie helped to steal a bridegroom from the very altar of the church where he was getting married to someone else. 'This girl I knew met someone who just happened to be getting married. He loved the girl he was marrying but he wasn't in love with her. On the night before he was supposed to be getting married she was really depressed about it.' So depressed, in fact, that she turned to Shaydie for help. Somehow, the subject of movies cropped up in conversation. 'The funny thing is that one of her favourite movies was *The Graduate.* So I told her, I dared her to do it, and I guess out of desperation and hysteria she said yes. I really didn't think she was going to go through with it, but I drove her up to the church in my car. She ran in there and I was sitting outside going, "Oh my God, this is nuts." I waited for what felt like for ever, but from what I understand it was about ten or fifteen minutes. Then they both ran out of the church together, jumped in my car and I just sped off going, "Oh, my God!" And they're still together.'

Most guides to the perfect relationship give high marks to qualities like friendship, understanding, giving and sharing problems. Shaydie's top three tips for what to bring to a relationship are: 'Spontaneity, separation and an air of selfishness.' And when I gently suggest that some of her methods are not dissimilar to those of an animal trainer, Shaydie shrugs. 'Everybody manipulates everyone. We do calculating things that *don't* work. Now I'm asking you to do all the little things that *do* work.' (And, funnily enough, it seems that they really *do* work.) Out of those who had embarked on her How To Steal Any Man You Want From the Arms of Another Woman or Just Keep the One You Love course, she claims almost 100 per cent success. They are all out there, busy stealing, keeping, marrying and moving in with the newly house-trained men of their choice. And, according to Shaydie, this is good for everyone. 'The main thing is there's nothing more satisfying than a very happy man, because if he's feeling good it's going to come right back to you because he's going to want to be with you and he's going to be more giving because you make him feel good.' Great. Let's just hope that none of Shaydie's former pupils ever takes a shine to *her* boyfriend.

ONE'S COMPANY, TWO'S A CROWD: VIVIENNE DOUGHTY

The concept of two people living together for twenty-five years without having a cross word suggests a lack of spirit only to be admired in sheep.
A. P. Herbert

The critical period in matrimony is breakfast time.
A. P. Herbert

When Vivienne Doughty's divorce came through, the first thing she did was to go and buy herself two pairs of woolly tights, one red and one purple. On the face of it not that anarchic, but after years of wearing nylons and high heels to please her husband, it was a declaration of freedom. 'He used to like sexy clothes and I tried to please him. I was compromising so I couldn't be myself.'

Vivienne has now been divorced for twelve years. And it doesn't seem a day too long. She lives with her daughter in Ely and says she's happy doing what she wants to do. You won't find

'The whole of marriage is a compromise. You can't just be a person in your own right because you're half of something else.'
Vivienne Doughty, happily divorced for twelve years.

◀ One of the joys of being single – the freedom to throw your woolly tights up in the air in your back garden, whenever you want.

Vivienne signing up for one of Shaydie's courses or booking a WeddingMoon™ in the West Indies. In fact, you're more likely to find her reading, gardening, painting, looking at Victorian architecture or even tap-dancing in her kitchen. But marriage – never. Now that she has tasted the joys of single life, she says she cannot imagine ever wanting again to be part of a couple.

'The whole of marriage is a compromise. Your individuality and his individuality are lessened. You can't just be a person in your own right because you're half of something else.' Vivienne now studies the behaviour of married people with the same sort of detached cynicism with which an ex-prime minister regards his or her successors. 'One of the quaint hobbies of married couples is to go out – I call it "coupling", going out for dinner in

▼ 'When you're a single person you can do so many more things. I tap-dance. I paint. I write. I read a lot. I have got a big garden that I look after. I'm a tourist guide. I also dress up as Saint Etheldreda, which is part of the tourist guide thing. And I go Toulon hunting.'
Vivienne indulging in one of her more conventional pursuits.

couples on a Saturday night. You go to a little trendy restaurant somewhere and you have to go in a foursome.' Sounds all right so far. 'My ex-husband was a passionate golfer.' Maybe not. 'So all of his friends were golfing friends. If you go out with a golfing couple you're not necessarily going to get on with the wife, just because the two husbands are going to talk golf all the time. I'm more of an arty person, I paint and do photography and things like that, so my friends tend to be more arty types. My husband wouldn't necessarily get on with them, and quite often when we came back from one of these coupling evenings I used to think: What a waste of time. I wish I'd been sitting on the settee reading a good book.' Provided it wasn't *The Observer Book of Great Golf Courses*, that is.

'The worst Christmas I ever had was when I was married, and we watched golf while we were eating the turkey. You wouldn't imagine golf was on on Christmas Day, it must have been from Australia or something, and we sat eating our turkey and watched the golf.' Unbelievable behaviour, especially when you consider that any rational human being would be watching either re-runs of *The Two Ronnies* or, for the fifty-eighth time, *The Great Escape*.

But the horror of coupledom doesn't end with Christmas telly and Saturday-night double dinner dates: 'You go to the supermarket together and feel the tomatoes together and all that sort of stuff, which I find very depressing,' remembers Vivienne. 'Sundays especially you have to have a Sunday dinner and you have to be peeling potatoes and then you have to go, "What shall we do? It's Sunday afternoon. Shall we go to a garden centre or take a drive to the seaside?" I just don't like things like that.'

Of course, now that Vivienne is single she can put the horror of those tomato-fondling days behind her and get on with the things that are really worthwhile. Like squeezing avocados. 'When you're a single person you can do so many more things. I tap-dance. I paint. I write. I read a lot. I have got a big garden that I look after. I'm a tourist guide. I also dress up as Saint Etheldreda, which is part of the tourist guide thing. And I go Toulon hunting.'

So, just what exactly is a Toulon? Do you hunt them on foot or on horseback? Is there any cruelty involved? Will you encounter Toulon hunt saboteurs? I put all these questions to self-confessed huntress Vivienne. 'Samuel Toulon was a Victorian architect. I first became interested when I discovered that he was the architect of the house that I've lived in for the past eight years. Then I became interested in looking for other buildings by Toulon. Now it's become a real passion and I just go out most weekends Toulon hunting.'

Now, you might, if you were that way inclined, think that this was not the most exciting of weekend pursuits. You might almost begin to yearn for a good golfing conversation. Well, almost.

Vivienne's home – a 'Toulon'. It's tall, good looking and has no interest in golf.

Toulon Hunting

It is Sunday and Vivienne and I are in a quiet Suffolk village, walking purposefully up a hill towards our quarry. As we approach the designated spot, you can almost cut the tension in the air.

Vivienne has started to fizz. 'Now, when you can't quite see it yet, and you're coming round the last corner, this is when you get the tingly feeling,' she says nervously. 'It's like when you go out on a first date with a new man, the same tingly feeling.' I ask her if she has ever been let down by a new Toulon, or led up the garden path, as it were. Vivienne ponders. 'I was disappointed in one which had been completely covered in pebbledash,' she says. 'It was still very nice, still a very good looking building. But it was like a very attractive man wearing a shell suit.' We round the bend, and there it is in all its glory. A house. But Vivienne is glowing. 'It looks really nice,' she enthuses. This Toulon is obviously like a very attractive man wearing nothing at all.

Vivienne leads a life jam-packed with hobbies, interests and activities. She no longer has to go Saturday-night coupling, or talk about golf or prod soft fruit in Sainsbury's. But in the dark of night, or when she's got the flu or even when she hears a joke that she'd like to share, does Vivienne ever wish she was still married? 'There are some things that you miss. You miss the sex and the companionship and the money. Because a single wage doesn't go as far. But that's the only three things.' She grins. For Vivienne Doughty, the advantages of the single life and the happiness she derives from the freedom to pursue her own interests far outweigh the drawbacks. 'Once you get away from a man you bloom. You become an individual again. I'm sure it's possible to be like that and be married but I think it's very unusual. Most marriages are not like that. Most marriages are "we". "We" like to go for an afternoon drive, or "we" like roast beef for dinner. It's never "I". You can't say "I" in marriage, and I'm a person who likes to say "I".'

MY HUSBANDS AND I: CLIVE, KEITH AND GEORGIA

Marriage is a wonderful invention: but then again so is a bicycle-repair kit.
Billy Connolly

Matrimony . . . a sort of friendship recognized by the police.
Robert Louis Stevenson

In married life three is company and two is none.
Oscar Wilde

'I don't know who the second-best girl in the world is, but we've got the first.'

There was no big white wedding or Caribbean honeymoon for Georgia Lang. She got married on 31 December 1958 at Marylebone Register Office, wearing a green skirt, a black polo-neck sweater and an old suede jacket. And, unlike most people, newly wed or no, she was back at work on New Year's Day. Nevertheless, she reckons her marriage is one of the happiest in human history. 'I mean, with due respect to everyone who has white weddings, they can turn out wonderful and it's a lovely day for them, but I don't personally think it's a good basis for a relationship. A piece of paper or a big wedding means nothing compared to what's in the heart.'

So what factors have contributed to the success of her happy thirty-six-year marriage? 'We've got the same sense of humour, the same likings in food, social life, everything . . . we seem to just blend into one.' What Georgia doesn't bother to mention is that her highly compatible 'other half' is actually her 'other two-thirds'. In other words, Georgia Lang has two husbands. 'Well, technically I only married one of them.' She grins. 'But I would have married both of them if I could.' Clive and Keith are twins, identical twins, so alike that even after all these years Georgia sometimes gets them confused, especially on the telephone. Recently, she says, she was at home with one twin when the other came in wet from the rain, so she fetched a towel and accidentally started vigorously rubbing the hair of the dry one, occasioning much hilarity.

It was the summer of '58, as some song probably goes. Clive and Keith, aged twenty-six, had just come out of a stint in the Merchant Navy, and were 'tanned and handsome with bright blond hair' when Georgia first caught sight of them. They lived with their mother in the basement flat below a firm of solicitors where Georgia, then only twenty-one years old, was working. 'One morning they stopped to talk to me. It must have been a hot day because I was struggling to open a window, and they offered to help. An hour later the phone rang – I'm not sure which of them it was – and he wanted to know if I wanted to go downstairs for lunch with "us". That evening they met me from work and we went for a walk in Hyde Park. From then on I saw them every single day. I was completely infatuated.'

It never occurred to Georgia to prefer one twin to the other. 'They were so alike that it was just sort of an extension, it was just one person as far as I was concerned.' At first this took a little getting used to. 'I admit I was a little taken aback by them to begin with. They had this way of doing things simultaneously. If one of them lit a cigarette the other would light a

Clive and Keith . . . or is it Keith and Clive?

'It would be impossible to fall for one and not the other,' says Georgia. 'They are the same, from the same egg. One cannot bear having something the other hasn't got.' . . . Even when it comes to a wife.

cigarette, when one started a sentence the other would finish it.' To this day the twins have an uncanny knack of mirroring each other. They automatically dress in the same clothes without having to discuss what the other is planning to wear, they get sick at the same time and if one hurts himself the other feels pain. 'It would be impossible to fall for one and not the other,' says Georgia. 'They are the same, from the same egg. One cannot bear having something the other hasn't got.' Even, it would seem, when it comes to a wife.

For a while Georgia and the twins were just good friends, but soon they became lovers. 'I think it was Clive first, then Keith later that same day,' recalls Georgia. 'Perhaps it's part of my make-up that I didn't think it was unusual, but, then, don't forget it was the late fifties, early sixties, a time when everybody did their own thing and nobody took any notice.' Nobody except for the Lord Chamberlain, the Hay's Code on Public Morality, J. Edgar Hoover, Senator Joseph McCarthy and a young Mary Whitehouse, that is. After all, it was in the early sixties that the publishers of *Lady Chatterley's Lover* were taken to court for obscenity, and the word 'bloody' was first passed by the British Board of Film Censors in 1963.

'It just happened,' says Keith, or is it Clive? 'We just met Georgia, and both of us fell in love with her.' Although the twins had had separate girlfriends in the past, there was somehow never any question of that once Georgia came along. 'I don't know who the second-best girl in the world is, but we've got the first,' they boast.

'It just happened,' says Clive. 'We were passing Marylebone Register Office one day and we said, "Oh, they do special licences, shall we get one . . ."'

'". . . and then go and ask Georgia if she'll marry us?"' Keith neatly completes the sentence.

Talking to the twins is like watching a particularly thrilling rally at Wimbledon in the era before the power serve when there still were particularly thrilling rallies.

'If we both could have married her officially, we both would have.'

'But we couldn't.'

'We did in a way, I suppose.'

'Clive married her.'

'But it could just as easily have been Keith.'

'We don't have jealousy, it doesn't exist in our make-up.'

'It's not there.'

Deuce.

Georgia says the marriage proposal came completely out of the blue. 'I was in the office one day and they both came up and said, "We were passing Marylebone Register Office and we've bought a special licence – can we get married tomorrow?" And me being a typical woman said, "But I haven't got anything to wear." It didn't cross my mind that I could only marry one of them, that it would be illegal to marry both.' It was only when they got to the register office that she saw that the name on the licence was Clive's, but despite the legal technicalities she considers them both equally her husbands. 'I bought a very wide wedding ring and had it cut in half. I didn't want to buy two wedding rings because that's, like, separate and because I married the one person I bought the one wedding ring and had it cut in half. So they've got half each.' After the ceremony they all went and had sausage and chips in the Globe, the pub on the corner. 'We knew everyone there, so it turned into quite a party.'

Luckily, they have encountered very little hostility in reaction

▶ Suntans fade . . .

▶ . . . fashions change . . .

▶ . . . but one's husbands are for ever.

to their somewhat less than conventional relationship. 'Sometimes people used to joke about it,' says Georgia, 'you know, you've got two husbands and the usual sort of rude jokes and so on. But basically everyone accepted it, and it was quite normal to me.'

It's time to don a neck brace as the twins chime in: 'Some of them might have a bit of a shock about it, but I think most of them know, especially by now.'

'We say to some people, "Yes, we've got one wife . . . we share a wife."'

'Or we introduce her and we automatically say, "This is our wife."'

'And people sometimes are taken aback, but generally speaking they're OK.'

'Anyway,' says Georgia, intercepting at the net, 'we always walk down the road holding hands and things like that, so I suppose everybody can see how happy we are.'

Perhaps naturally, the most common reaction tends to be a certain curiosity about their sex lives. So what about sex? 'Yes, that happens,' smiles Georgia. 'But it's easy to misinterpret our relationship. Let's just say that it's not about orgies, or about one of them getting some voyeuristic thrill by watching the other. I always divide my attentions equally, but I never have sex with them both at the same time.' Mainly it's just about wanting to be together as much as possible. 'Even when we lived in a two-bed flat, there was an empty bedroom,' says Georgia. 'We sleep like three sort of grown-up kids: we joke and laugh and chat . . .' Sure enough, the Langs' bedroom looks like something straight out of *Goldilocks and the Three Bears*, with three single beds all in a row.

'One night,' says a twin, 'we woke up to find our two cats, Charlie and Susie, fighting.'

'So the three of us got up to sort them out . . .'

'And we always sleep in the nude anyway . . .'

'And then we said, "Let's see what it's like in a nudist colony with them dancing, shall we see?"'

'And then I tapped Georgia on the shoulder, I said, "It's actually an excuse me."'

'And we were dancing naked in the hall at three or four in the morning and we were hysterical.'

'It was fabulous really, and so we said, "Cor, this is fun, I wonder how many other homes are doing this at this moment?"'

'In the end,' Georgia says, 'the reality is that Keith, Clive and

I are like any ordinary happily married couple. Sex happens when it happens. And sometimes it doesn't happen at all.'

In fact, most 'ordinary married couples' would be hard pressed to seem half this head-over-heels after thirty-six years of married life. As far as general soppiness goes, this threesome take a delight in each other's company usually only associated with teenage girls and Häagen-Dazs commercials. 'They're very romantic, they always send me cards,' says Georgia. 'They have to change them, of course, because you can't get one to "our wife", so they get one to "my wife" and then cross out the "my" and put in "our". Because I work longer hours than they do there's invariably a meal waiting for me. They've always done everything for me, they really are very, very good to me.' In return Georgia massages them, cuts their hair and even makes them face-packs. 'I'm always touching them and kissing them and telling them I love them,' she says. 'Every day they phone me up to tell me that they love me and ask me if I'm all right. And when I walk home from work I come round the corner and they're invariably hanging over the balcony waiting to wave to me. Sometimes they'll pop into where I work and I see these two faces come to the door, beaming, and I go, "Ooooh, it's them again."'

Unfortunately, Hallmark don't yet make cards for *ménages à trois.*

The twins seem equally smitten. Keith to serve: 'We get on very well. We don't have jealousies. We just automatically give to each other.'

'Our philosophy in life is to make each other happy and make life easy.'

'It's a lovely relationship. You feel content and very, very happy talking about it.'

'You feel a lovely feeling when she appears, it's funny, you can't explain it . . . after being all these years together, we miss her when she's not with us.'

Game, set and perfect match.

So, do Georgia and the twins think that being a threesome is a positive advantage in having a happy relationship? 'I do think having the third person takes the tension off,' says Georgia. 'It's better, because it's like having friends.' She also thinks that the 'extraordinary love' Keith and Clive have for each other is an important factor in their harmony.

'We can't argue, it's impossible,' says Keith.

'If I argued with him it would be like arguing with myself,' agrees Clive.

Georgia adds, 'We're very sort of happy-go-lucky people, and I suppose if you've got that kind of nature you don't go nit-picking for things to argue about. They make each other laugh, they make me laugh, I make them laugh.' (Once, apparently, they made her laugh so much she had to be taken to hospital with an asthma attack.) 'I hear people talking about their relationships. Even the ones that are happy have their down sides. One partner doesn't pull their weight and all these kinds of things, and I think we're really lucky because we don't go through all that turmoil.'

'We're almost like triplets in our disposition and the way we get on.'

For a while, after they were first married, Keith got a job which took him away from Clive and Georgia, sometimes for weeks at a time. It was such an unhappy experience for all of them that they agreed never to repeat it. For many years they lived in Spain, running a small hotel, but a few years ago the threesome returned to London. Now Georgia works in a museum and Keith and Clive got a job with a telephone firm which means they can be together all the time. 'We don't need anybody. We're a threesome and we're our own company,' says Georgia.

Clive, not unusually, concurs. 'It's frightening in one way, but you could actually brick up the flat and I'm sure we'd be content with each other. We're in our own little world and it's so lovely.'

Keith adds, 'Lots of twins part. They marry separate girls and they go off on their own, we've met many. But we wouldn't want to live if we were separated.'

If the ingredients of a happy marriage are consideration, give and take, common interests, sense of humour, emotional intimacy and ability to talk about everything, the Langs' shopping basket is full. Plus, like Coca-Cola, they have a mystery trade secret, the extra ingredient that only they know about. I need hardly ask them if they consider themselves to be happy, but I do anyway. Georgia replies first.

'I think it's immeasurable how happy I am, because I really am contented and happy and sometimes you can't put that into words . . . I love waking up every morning and seeing them, of course, and I always look forward to coming home from work and seeing them and even while I'm working I tell myself how lucky I am and how happy I am.'

In unison, the twins lean forward, grin at their wife and continue. 'We didn't plan all this, it just happened. It's a wonderful thing that happened in our lives. We both met Georgia, we love her, she's wonderful. We love her more each day, and then there's us too.'

'I bought a very wide wedding ring and had it cut in half. I didn't want to buy two wedding rings because that's like separate and because I married the one person I bought the one wedding ring and had it cut in half. So they've got half each.' Keith, Georgia and Clive, hand in hand . . . in hand.

'You've got to pinch yourself sometimes. We're lucky.'

'It's not conventional, I know that, but it's worked out wonderful. We get happier each day, you know we're more in love with each other every day.'

'Tomorrow will be better than today, so we're lucky. It is lovely really. Very fortunate. It's lovely, lovely.'

So, would it work for everyone? Should we all go out searching for a pair of gorgeous identical twins? 'Oh, no,' says Georgia (shattering a million lifelong fantasies). 'It wouldn't work with female twins. Women would never be able to share one man.' I can't help feeling the Marquess of Bath would disagree.

So, married, single, divorced or just browsing, love does seem to be for most people the single greatest cause of happiness – and unhappiness. Whether your philosophy is nothing ventured nothing gained, once bitten twice shy or the more the merrier, somewhere in the world there's a special cliché just for you . . .

MONEY

Lucre – Filthy But Fun

There are much more important things in life than money. Trouble is, they all cost money.
Anon.

Art for Art's sake, money for God's sake.
10CC

The sixty-four-thousand-dollar question has always been: can money buy you happiness? And if, as the songs claim, it can't, why on earth do most people spend a great deal of their lives trying to acquire as much of it as possible? According to surveys, the bulk of the population believe that money leads directly or indirectly to an increased sense of well-being or, to be more precise, most people think that they would be happier if they had more dosh. And to most people, sixty-four thousand dollars would do very nicely. But just because the man in the street thinks that money can buy him happiness doesn't mean he's right. After all, he might be the the same man who bought a Sinclair C5 in 1985.

There have been many studies about the links between money and happiness, and sociologists, statisticians, psychologists, economists and pollsters have all been paid good money to conduct them. Good money that you or I might have had instead. Money that might have bought us a microwave oven or a new car or a holiday in Florida. Money that might have made us happier. All these studies have resulted in numerous astounding theories and equally fascinating statistics.

Some Fascinating Statistics

Statistics show that an increase in income of 10 to 20 per cent only seems to affect the happiness of people who are very poor.

Having a *secure* income seems to contribute more to happiness than having a *high* income.

Research shows that the inhabitants of rich EC countries like Denmark may be statistically happier than the inhabitants of poor countries like Portugal, yet the Irish are both the poorest and the happiest of the lot. A statistician couldn't tell you why – although perhaps a publican could.

A survey of forty-nine of the wealthiest Americans – all of whom had a net worth of over $100 million – proved that the extremely rich are just as happy or unhappy as everyone else. Either that, or they're better liars.

The most expensive confetti in the world – the £2 million pictured on the previous page is reduced to dust by the Royal Bank of Scotland.

It seems that very rich people worry about money as much as, if not more than, anyone else. Even the super-rich may experience great anxiety about losing their ill-gotten gains.

Studies show that when people suddenly acquire money they may experience a sudden surge of increased happiness, but the chances are they'll soon revert to normal. Here in Britain a study of 191 Pools winners reported that despite certain obvious benefits, their windfalls had also brought new causes of unhappiness: hostility and envy from old friends and neighbours, begging letters from complete strangers and rejection and snobbishness from the not-so-*nouveau riche*. Worst of all, things which had given them pleasure in the past soon lost their thrill. Everyday pleasures paled in comparison with the once-in-a-lifetime thrill of winning the jackpot, and new-found delights, like yachts and swimming pools, soon seemed humdrum and ordinary. After a while, all they really wanted was to win the Pools again so that they could buy a bigger yacht and a longer swimming pool.

Where money and happiness are concerned, the keeping-up-with-the-Joneses factor comes into play. Research indicates that a person on £20,000 a year living in an area where most people earn around £10,000 a year will be more satisfied than a person on £30,000 a year with neighbours earning around £40,000 a year. Being loaded isn't enough: you have to be more loaded.

The average American is twice as rich today, in terms of buying power, than he was in 1957, when one in three people interviewed by pollsters described themselves as happy. There are now twice as many cars *per capita*, not to mention colour TVs, VCRs, faxes, CD players, microwave ovens, air conditioning systems, personal computers, Gameboys and lights that turn on and off when you clap your hands. Nevertheless, when a similar poll was conducted in 1991, one in three people described themselves as happy – exactly the same result as over thirty-five years ago. So, this would appear to indicate that in the long term, provided you have enough money to fulfil your basic needs, money is going to make little difference to whether or not you are happy. (Or else it indicates that polls are as useless and inaccurate as they've always been.)

Money, it turned out, was exactly like sex: you thought of nothing else if you didn't have it and thought of other things if you did.
James Baldwin

What's so great about being rich anyway? I mean apart from the big houses and the swimming pools and the yachts and the designer clothes and the great big diamonds and meals at fancy restaurants and holidays in exotic locations, what can money really buy? Well, for $120,000 Neiman Marcus in Dallas will supply you with a life-size dinosaur, and a mere $200,000 buys you an electronic toy Ferrari. (Might it not be cheaper to buy a real Ferrari?) An organization called Short Cuts, which caters

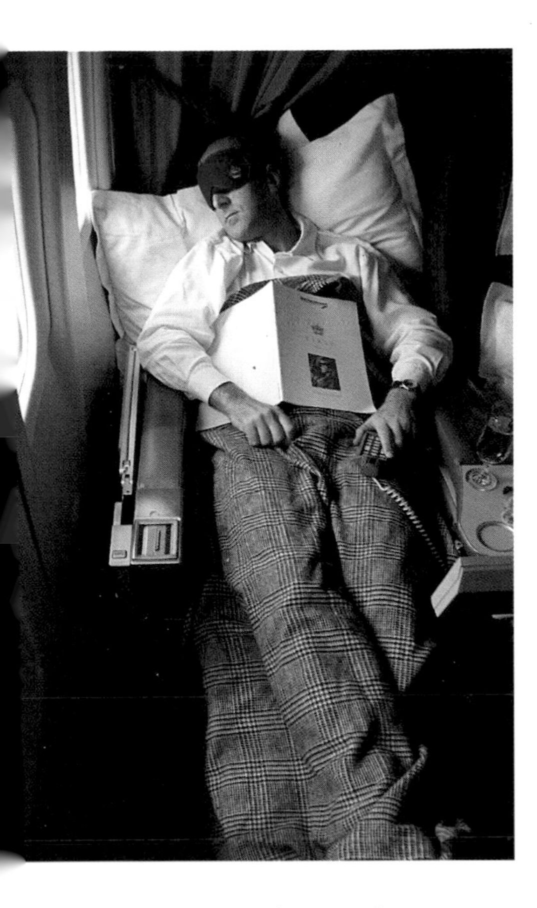

For only ten times the economy fare, you get to sit at the front of the plane and force down as many free drinks as you can regurgitate into your free first class airline socks.

for the whims of the very rich, reports that some of the requests they carried out last year included making and delivering a hand-made suit of armour to Hong Kong for a fancy dress party, driving a Second World War tank to someone's house for his son's sixth birthday party, and flying fifty mountain bikes to Jamaica and four boxes of cream crackers to a boat in Antigua.

Of course, as the cream crackers incident illustrates, it's only when you're really rich that you can start to afford the simple things in life. Getting back to Nature can prove very expensive, and not only because of having to import so much bottled water. Wealthy people in search of true simplicity might consider purchasing a thatched cottage in Devon or an old barn in Normandy, while for an even greater sum they could become the proud owners of a log cabin in Colorado or a beach hut in Barbados. Once you've got back to Nature, there's always the danger that Nature won't do exactly what you want it to. Hence, if you go somewhere hot, you must spend even more money on air conditioning, and if you go somewhere cold, be prepared to fork out for a dead rodent or two to drape around your fashionably bony shoulders. Legendary TV producer Aaron 'Dynasty' Spelling once had a ton of snow delivered to his California home on Christmas Eve so his kiddies could have a white Christmas, while Pia 'She's in the Attic' Zadora is reputed to have bought an £18,000 floor-length chinchilla coat for her five-year-old daughter. Presumably when her daughter grew out of it after six months she had it retailored to fit the dog.

Exotic holidays are always a good way of disposing of any surplus cash that might be scuffing the lining of your trouser pockets. Among the most popular of rich people's destinations is the romantic city known to tour operators as 'The Venice of Italy' and to Dutch people as 'The Amsterdam of the South'. You can fly to Venice in a couple of hours, but for a lot more money you could spend three days getting there by train. If you are forced to fly, the rich person can always travel first class, where, for only ten times the economy fare, you get to sit at the front of the plane and force down as many free drinks as you can regurgitate into your free first class airline socks. And if that's not worth a few grand, I don't know what is.

SEMINARS AND SAUSAGE ROLLS

Roy Diaper and the Workshop for the Wealth Adjusted

Money is like manure. If you spread it around it does a lot of good. But if you pile it up in one place it stinks like hell.
Clint Murchison Jnr, US industrialist

So if money can't actually buy you happiness, can it bring you unhappiness? Is the poor little rich girl a myth or is she our future queen? Research shows that people who inherit their wealth, as opposed to those who have earned their money through work, are more likely to admit to feelings of loneliness, isolation and aimlessness.

Of course, if you are one of those unfortunate people who suffer from being just too rich for comfort, you can take yourself off to the jet-set resort of Aspen, Colorado. There, high in the Rocky Mountains, you can rub shoulders with local residents like Jack Nicholson, Martina Navratilova and John Denver, while numerous elegant hotels, exclusive shops and fancy restaurants will all help to relieve you of vast dollops of your unearned cash. Afterwards, if you're still worried about having too much money, you can get your chauffeur to drop you off at the Aspen Institute, where for a paltry $825 you can enrol in the annual 'Workshop for the Wealth Adjusted'.

Yes, there really is a self-help group for people with too much money, or for the 'wealth impaired' as they are known over there. Each year twenty-five people who have inherited fortunes worth from $1 million to $500 million can come together for a 'participatory workshop' where they discuss their problems among other like-walleted people. 'They're not going to get much sympathy from most people,' says organizer and investment consultant Myra Salzer. 'In my programme they can relax and be themselves, because everyone has the same problems.'

But aside from the obvious dilemmas, like where to buy the new summer house or whether to get the Mercedes in silver or black, what problems? 'A lot of people who come into a

Sporting Pictures

Aspen, Colorado – where better to find a self-help group for people with too much money, or the 'wealth impaired' as they're known over there.

great deal of unearned money – whether they inherit it, marry it or win it in a lottery – have problems dealing with it. They frequently feel guilty about having it. They feel like a target for money-grubbing acquaintances. And above all, they often drift through life, having neither purpose or self-confidence.'

These are problems you may think you'd rather like to have a go at dealing with, but working with inheritors has its own particular disadvantages. Myra finds that being unused to the concept of normal work schedules, many of her clients are bad at keeping appointments: 'Time does not have the same meaning.' Myra says that those who have had wealth thrust upon them can often seem immature – a statement the Marquess of Blandford would no doubt hotly dispute by throwing bread rolls at you. Problem solving is a constant weak spot: 'Because they can buy themselves out of any difficulty they never learn to resolve conflicts.' When one of Myra's clients was having trouble with the landlord of her apartment building, her solution was to buy the entire block of flats.

Myra says that many very rich people have low self-esteem, become secret and mistrustful and are constantly afraid that people are trying to take advantage of them. She relates the story of one man who attended last year's conference. For nine months of the year he lives off the money he earns as a college professor, telling nobody about his wealth, but every summer he slips off to his villa on the French Riviera where he lives the life of a millionaire. Another man took part-time work at an office, just so that he could tell people he had a job. 'One of the biggest fears is going to a party and having someone ask, "What do you do?" Somehow, saying, "I manage the money that was given to me," doesn't cut it.' Myra hopes that her workshop will help her clients to be more confident with their riches. She still thinks many of them might be happier if they had refused to accept the money in the first place, but this theory is hard to prove, as she has yet to meet anyone who has done so – and if anyone did, they would probably be enrolled in another sort of clinic.

▲ Of all the games he's seen, Roy cites the England versus Australia Rugby International in 1991 as one of the most enjoyable – if only Will Carling could have agreed with him.

A budget is a method of worrying before you spend instead of afterwards.
Anon.

According to some expert's theory, it's not how much you've got but how you spend it that makes the difference. Roy Diaper is fifty years old, single, unemployed, lives in Swindon with his widowed mother and gets £45 Income Support per week. Yet Roy Diaper says he is extremely happy. A fanatical sports fan (cricket, rugby, tennis, football and racing), Roy carefully budgets his meagre earnings so that he can travel around England and watch the cream of British sporting events. As a result he now has the sort of overwhelmingly detailed knowledge of all sporting minutiae that Jim Rosenthal would envy and John Motson shares.

He first developed an interest in sport at the age of twelve when he was on an outing with his parents in Bournemouth. Out of the blue, Roy announced that he wasn't going to the beach, but to a cricket match he had seen advertised on a sign. Off he went, completely on his own, saw the match and found his way back to the coach for the trip home to Swindon. That was thirty-eight years ago. Since then, Roy has notched up attendances at several hundred major sporting events, ranging from the 1966 World Cup final and Viv Richards's double

century to Arkle winning the Gold Cup at Cheltenham. In fact, he barely knows the meaning of the words 'action replay'.

Roy says he never made a conscious decision to devote his life to seeing live sport, it was just a natural progression. Even so, his limited financial resources mean that every spare penny is used to pay for this. Roy doesn't go drinking, or to the cinema or even have girlfriends, but he says he still doesn't see this as a sacrifice. 'This is what I want to do most with my life and I'm quite happy to lead a very quiet life in between the events I attend. It's all a case really of getting priorities, what you want most in life, and you get these priorities, and that's what it's all about.'

A recent day out for Roy, to Cheltenham races, set him back £19.24. His cheap-day-return train ticket cost £6.70, entry to the racecourse was £12 and a race card cost £1. While he was there he bought two sausage rolls at a cost of 54p each. Every penny is painstakingly accounted for. And betting on the races, a prerequisite for most track visitors, is very much a no-no for Roy. Usually, to save money on food at the grounds, which always charge exorbitant prices, he takes a pork pie with him. Roy, who considers himself a bit of a pork-pie connoisseur, always patronizes the same pie shop in Broadhidden, where he catches the bus for the train station in Swindon. Wouldn't it be

▶ Roy with one of his proudest sporting trophies. Answers on a postcard.

To every sporting event he attends, Roy takes a pork pie. Here is evidence of it.

Roy Diaper's Top Ten Sporting Events

1 ENGLAND v. WEST GERMANY
World Cup Final, Wembley, 1966

2 BARBARIANS v. NEW ZEALAND
Cardiff,1973

3 CHELTENHAM GOLD CUP
Arkle and Mill House, 1964

4 BARBARIANS v. NEW ZEALAND
Twickenham, 1967

5 WEST HAM v. MUNICH
European Cup Winner's Cup, Wembley, 1965

6 KING GEORGE VI AND
QUEEN ELIZABETH STAKES
Ascot, 1975

7 BRITISH GRAND PRIX
Silverstone, 1969

8 MANCHESTER UNITED v. BENFICA
European Cup Final, Wembley, 1968

9 SOBERS'S CENTURY
Rest of World v. England, Lord's, 1970

10 RED RUM
Epsom Derby, Eclipse Stakes, King George VI
and Queen Elizabeth Stakes, 1971

easier to stay at home and watch it on the telly, in the comfort of David Coleman? 'Maybe when I'm older,' says Roy. 'At the moment, it's something I look forward to in life, and as long as I want to be at these events, I hope to continue.'

According to the sociologists, psychologists, pollsters, statisticians and other self-appointed experts, Roy's happiness derives from having set himself attainable targets which he then duly achieves. On the other hand, maybe he's just very interested in sport. Either way, there's something special for him in attending these occasions in the flesh. 'It's given me tremendous pleasure. I think looking back on my life I couldn't really have done anything better with the resources that I've got available. It's no good just sitting back and saying I wish I'd have done this and I wish I'd have done that when it was just too late. So I started from a young age and I made the effort, and I can look back on my life with a great deal of pleasure.' And if ever Des Lynam decides to pack it in . . .

Roy at Lord's – one of the larger crowds of the season.

AN EMBARRASSMENT OF RICHES: DONNA BEARD

I'm tired of Love: I'm still more tired of Rhyme.
But Money gives me pleasure all the Time.
Hilaire Belloc

No one would have remembered the good Samaritan if he'd only had good intentions. He had money as well.
Margaret Thatcher

'When I was about fifteen I started acting like I owned the world, and you'd be amazed, pretty soon I did.'
Donna Beard, owner of the world.

I wake up jet-lagged, slightly confused and seeing double. My room, curiously, seems to have two of everything: two TVs, two beds, two complimentary boxes of chocolates. I'm about to take some aspirin when I spot the hotel's slogan: 'Embassy Suites – twice the hotel.' My visual aberration turns out to be merely a marketing ploy. I'm in Atlanta, Georgia, USA, capital of the rebel states, home of the Atlanta Braves, Scarlett O'Hara, Coca-Cola, Ted Turner, the Ku Klux Klan, the rich and the super-rich. I've come here to meet Donna Beard, a self-made multimillionaire and proud of it. Can money make you happy? Donna Beard says it can. And I have the enviable task of letting her show me how.

Donna lives in a suburb known as Buckhead, the Beverly Hills of Atlanta. Huge antebellum-style mansions, built well after the Civil War (and, for that matter, the First and Second World Wars), nestle in acres of carefully manicured lawn and artfully wild parkland, surrounded by high walls and state-of-the-art security gates. The rich folk of Atlanta haven't allowed town planning or good taste to get in the way of their dreams. Here you can see mock-Plantation houses sitting side by side with mock-Tudor and mock-Colonial mansions, all of them worth genuine big bucks. Just down the road from Donna's home are the mansion of the Governor of Georgia and a large pink monstrosity built by Al Capone to house one of his mistresses while he was serving his time in the Atlanta State Penitentiary. Aesthetically, I think the prison probably just shaves it.

I arrive at Donna's comparatively modest house to find that Donna herself is missing presumed shopping, so I sink into

a well-padded chair in a plush living room to await her return. As one might expect from a woman who made her fortune importing chinoiserie, the house is full of what can only be described as oriental knick-knacks – painted screens, giant vases, bits of carved ivory, large gold statues – but all in the best possible taste. I get a message saying she has been called away to speak to the principal of her son's school, as apparently there has been some trouble. This being the USA, I immediately suspect drugs. But when Donna finally pulls up the drive in her gold Rolls-Royce convertible and tumbles into the room, breathless and apologetic, she confides to me that her son is experiencing difficulties with his algebra.

Donna is originally from Tulsa, Oklahoma. This is something I've always noticed about Americans – they never refer to a city without adding its state as well. Rather like an Englishman describing his home town as 'Brighton, Sussex' or 'Warwick, Warwickshire'. Anyway, Donna hails from the Tulsa that is situated in Oklahoma. Nevertheless her years in Atlanta have

▲ 'What other people might consider extravagances, I consider just run-of-the-mill living. Whether it's going wherever I want, buying fur coats, new cars and pieces of jewellery, if I see something I want then I'll buy it. Only if you can afford to buy whatever you want do you really have money.'
Donna Beard, pictured with something she wanted.

▶ 'Honey, I have enough sequins to cover a whole town hall.'

▼ 'I bought about seven furs in one go last year. I had this one dyed red to match my hair.'

given her the bearing and mannerisms of a Southern Belle. And, despite being of a certain age and of a certain waistline, Donna is obviously no stranger to the art of flirting: 'Angus, honey, do you like my mink?' she drawls. Long red nails flail dangerously. 'It's Christian Dior. I had it dyed red to match my hair.'

It soon transpires that the red Dior mink is just one of a stable (well, several closets) full of expensive pelts to which I am soon given a guided tour. The Animal Rights movement could keep a paint manufacturer in business for a year trying to keep up with Donna's collection of dead animals. Lynx, mink, silver fox, Persian lamb and even coyote jostle for space in what Donna informs me is one of her smaller coat closets. 'If I see something I want I just go in and get it. I bought about seven furs in one go last year. Hee-hee.' Every sentence is punctuated by at least one of these high-pitched giggles. I wait for her to sneeze to see if she actually says 'Atchoo' – although since she's wearing the fur coat and I'm standing jacketless in the freezing air conditioning, it's more likely to be me who sneezes first.

Donna displays a delight in her own wealth, and an enthusiasm for the purchasing power that this gives her, which seems to be reserved for those who have experienced the reverse side of the coin or, indeed, no coin at all. Sure enough, Donna's description of her childhood is a cross between a Tammy Wynette song and something out of *Gone with the Wind.* 'As a child it wasn't just a question of whether we had enough money to be happy, it was whether we had enough to eat. But although we were poor, there was a lot of love in our home.' Donna says she made a conscious decision to be rich. I have visions of Vivien Leigh, clutching a handful of dirt and declaring to the painted backdrop of a sunset behind her, 'I, Scarlett O'Hara, swear that I'll never be poor or hungry again.' In fact, what Donna actually says is, 'When I was about fifteen I started acting like I owned the world, and you'd be amazed, pretty soon I did.'

Although Donna describes her teenage self as 'a real over-achiever – Beauty Queen, Basketball Queen, straight-A student and voted "Miss Personality" by her classmates', she decided that her best chance of being rich was to marry a wealthy man. In retrospect, she says that was a big mistake. Husband No. 1 was super-rich, part of the Exxon Oil family, and Husband No. 2 was a successful advertising man, but although this gave her all the outward trappings of wealth – a big house, fancy holidays, a fast car – it didn't make her happy. Donna says, 'Wealthy men use their money to control their women. A middle-class woman is much more blessed and happier and financially independent than a rich man's wife. It's better to be a rich man's mistress than a rich man's wife.'

▶ 'The Scarletts'.
Donna's advice to other women: 'It's better to be a rich man's mistress than a rich man's wife.' Or best of all, perhaps, a rich man's ex-wife.

Both of Donna's husbands made her give up her career when she married them, and kept her on a small allowance – '$1,500 a month, when now I might spend $30,000'. As a further example of her first husband's cautious attitude to spending, she relates, 'Our first Christmas, I gave him a present of a Rolex, he gave me a twelve-pound box of chocolates. Isn't that tragic?'

Two children, two divorces and no alimony later, Donna decided to give up rich husbands and make bucket-loads of money herself. (She has, however, no inclination to give up men, and has since been officially engaged seven times.) Left to her own devices, Donna proved to be as good at business as she had been at basketball. Several successful ventures and several million dollars later, she decided that 'all the money in the world meant nothing if I had no life'. Four years ago she sold off her latest company (importing oriental art and furniture) to enjoy

what she had earned. So does she miss running a company? 'No, I hated it. But it made me rich.'

Now that she isn't breaking her neck to work all hours running her business, Donna has the time to throw herself whole-heartedly into favourite pursuits like travelling, shopping and giving parties, but not necessarily in that order.

A feast is made for laughter, and wine maketh merry: but money answereth all things.
Ecclesiastes

Donna always travels first class ('You can't wear a $25,000 mink and travel steerage') and will only stay in the most luxurious hotels. I asked her if she thought it was worth the money. 'Oh absolutely, honey. For instance, when I took my son to Europe recently there was always chilled champagne waiting for us in the rooms when we checked in. In Venice, they arranged a private tour of the glassworking factory, fired up their kilns for us, everything. That's not the kind of treatment you get if you're just middle-class. And when we were in Monte Carlo last year, we decided to go to the Grand Prix at the last minute and, although there was no room in the harbour, the harbour master actually arranged for other yachts to be moved to make space for us in the prime area. That's the type of treatment you get when you're rich. More respect. More snap-to.'

If shopping were an Olympic sport Donna would win gold medals in most categories. Rumour has it that Neiman Marcus are thinking of naming a wing after her. So what does she consider her greatest extravagances? 'What other people might consider extravagances, I consider just run-of-the-mill living. Whether it's going wherever I want, buying fur coats, new cars and pieces of jewellery, if I see something I want then I'll buy it. Only if you can afford to buy whatever you want do you really have money.'

I ask Donna if she considers herself one of the Atlanta in-crowd. 'Come on, Angus honey, I'm the *leader* of the in-crowd.' As far as parties go, Donna is definitely still an over-achiever. 'My social life is fabulous,' she declares. 'I probably live one of the most glamorous social lives in the United States.' Here in Atlanta, a 'glamorous social life' seems to consist predominantly of the species of party known as the charity ball. In other words, it's not enough to be invited, you have to pay for the privilege as well. Not surprisingly, this means that only the wealthy can fully participate. 'It takes a great deal of money to afford the expense of parties. A ticket for a charity fund-raiser is going to cost anywhere from $250 to $2,500 per person.' And it's not just the designated charity that benefits: caterers, florists, limo companies and, of course, department stores like Saks, Neiman Marcus and other purveyors of party clothes all flourish from their symbiotic relationship with the party-givers and goers.

As well as being invited to the parties of everyone on the Atlanta social register, Donna is not averse to throwing a bash or sixty herself, often at the last minute. She is also founder and chairperson of a group of 'eligible' (that is, rich, white and single) Atlanta women, known collectively as 'the Scarletts' (after O'Hara not their morals), who organize many of their own charity balls. As luck and careful planning would have it, Donna is throwing one of these enormous shindigs tomorrow

evening – this one a charity fund-raising singles party for about three hundred eligible Atlanta socialites aged between thirty-five and fifty-five – and I am invited. And just in case I am thinking of turning up in something unsuitable, like a wet-suit and flippers, Donna confides, 'Atlanta is an unusual city because in the day and age where many people are getting away from black tie and formal events, that is not true in this city. A tuxedo is mandatory here if you're going to have a social life.' Hint taken.

But what does a modern-day Scarlett wear? Donna invites me to stay and talk to her while her dress-maker, Debbie, deftly jabs long pearl-headed pins into one of her latest creations. Since Donna is wearing it at the time this is a dangerous task, especially since Debbie's fingernails are even longer than the pins.The gown in question is a floor-length purple affair, with a bodice and sleeves encrusted with gold brocade, shoulder pads like a vulture's wings and two matching cut-out scallops baring flesh at the back and at the front, displaying shoulder-blades and cleavage respectively. If you put this dress on backwards in the dark it wouldn't matter, although since the skirt is embroidered with thousands of sparkling purple sequins I very much doubt whether you could find anywhere dark enough to try this experiment.

Even so, Donna isn't sure that this particular dress is going to get to go to tomorrow's ball. 'Angus, honey, you choose' are the ominous words, as Donna slides open the closet doors. When my seared retinas have adjusted to the glare, I am treated to the sight of an acre of silk, satin, chiffon and taffeta in a range of technicolour shades guaranteed to get even John Major noticed.

'It's very pretty, don't you think?' Donna holds up a turquoise sequinned number for inspection. 'Actually I like it so much that I ordered a red one and a black one as well,' she says, dumping it over a chair and pulling out a shocking pink frock, covered, you'll be astonished to hear, with gold brocade and sequins. 'This is a classic, very simple dress.'

'Nice colour,' I venture.

'Hot pink, honey,' Donna replies. 'It's my second favourite colour after turquoise.'

'How much would one of these cost?' I enquire.

'Oh, anything from $2,000 to $7,000. I got this one in Thailand – when I go there I buy several dresses – in fact, whenever I like something I have a lot of them made. This one is just a basic sequin dress. I usually get a new dress for every party . . . and this one, too, is a great dress. The best thing about me are my spectacular legs and this shows them all the way up to the point where they're incredibly indecent.'

'So you're quite keen on sequins?' I ask, rather redundantly.

'Honey, I have enough sequins to cover a whole town hall.' At least, if she ever loses her money, Donna can always sell her wardrobe to Dame Edna.

It is a kind of spiritual snobbery that makes people think that they can be happy without money.
Albert Camus, existentialist and goalkeeper

Sure enough, the party is a glittering affair. As the courtesy stretch limo drops off guest after guest at the Palladian entrance to the house, I realize that Donna (who has gone for a bright green dress I have never seen before) isn't the only woman in Atlanta with a penchant for tinsel. The men are dutifully kitted out in their tuxedos, the champagne flows, the nibbles are nibbled and the only black faces in sight seem to belong to the waiters. And as the evening wears on I realize a couple of small but potent truths: the first is that wherever you go in the world, the men are generally much uglier than the women; and the second is that no matter how much money you've got, it's still impossible to make polite conversation, balance your glass and eat off a paper plate while standing up.

So, in the end, does wealth automatically bring happiness? Donna believes that it can, but only so long as it is you that controls the purse strings, and as long as you aren't working too hard to enjoy the folding green fruits of your labour. In fact, what she actually says is, 'Money does not make you happy. The thing money is good for, to me, is freedom.' And how does she define freedom? 'Freedom from worry. Freedom from worrying whether my sons are going to have shirts on their backs and whether they're going to be made fun of if those shirts aren't Ralph Lauren polo shirts.' The sort of worry most people could probably just about live with.

'I probably live one of the most glamorous social lives in the United States.'
Donna Beard, pictured here with one of the waiters.

WHO WANTS TO BE A MILLIONAIRE? – I DON'T: CHARLES GRAY

It's the same the whole world over
It's the poor wot gets the blame
It's the rich wot gets the gravy,
Ain't it all a bleedin' shame?
Anon.

I don't care too much for money.
Paul McCartney, multimillionaire

Charles Gray puts his money where his mouth is. At least, he did when he still had money to put anywhere. Sixteen years ago, Charles was an affluent college professor with a huge six-bedroom house in downtown Eugene, in Oregon. Today he lives in a one-room trailer in the backyard of someone else's house. He grows his own vegetables, scours the neighbourhood for fallen fruit and scavenges in skips for his clothes and other bits and pieces.

But this downward mobility is no sob story. There are no tales of stock-market crashes or gambling debts or sudden crippling illnesses. Charles Gray is poor on purpose. Tired of being a 'have' in a world full of 'have-nots' and deciding that political action was not enough to assuage the guilt he felt or rectify the inequities he beheld, Charles Gray made the deliberate choice to divest himself of his wealth. And this, he says, has brought him happiness or, as Blur might have it, 'an enormous sense of well-being'.

Now, at almost seventy, Charles Gray looks fit, relaxed and pleased as Punch with his lifestyle. He lives on a small monthly stipend of $160. This is not a figure plucked from the air, or the amount of his social security cheque, but the correct income stipulated by an economic system known as the 'World Equity Budget' This is not the newest idea of a United Nations think-tank or the hare-brained scheme of a Russian President, but the brainchild of the man himself.

Charles devised the WEB as a means of finding what he describes as 'a kind of non-violent economics': 'I feel that

'I'm immensely happier now – I wouldn't go back to being rich for anything – no way.'
Ex-millionaire Charles Gray, outside his former home.

the system we live in now is very violent. I mean we've got incredibly wealthy people at the top and starving people at the bottom, and this does not seem to me to be a morally justifiable economic system.'

The WEB is an effort to live on 'an equal share of sustainable world income'. The basic idea is to divide the world's wealth by its total population, and then to work out a world economy that is sustainable so that future generations will have their share too. In order to work out how much each person is entitled to, Charles must also calculate the purchasing power of money in different countries. $100 will go further in Mexico than in the USA than in Switzerland, and further almost anywhere than in Harrods' Food Hall (see p.156).

Charles recalculates the WEB every quarter, taking into consideration changes in population, exchange rates, cost of living, etc. When he started living on the WEB in 1978, his monthly budget was $60. As if all this altruism wasn't enough, since 1980 Charles has contributed 20 per cent of his budget (now $32) to social causes he believes are important: environmental action, anything to do with homelessness and many projects in Central America. 'I call this reparations for past damage – damage that this rich culture has imposed on the world.' If there's anything left at the end of the month after his personal expenses and his reparations, Charles saves it for a rainy day. 'It rains a lot here in Eugene.'

To make his WEB easier to understand, Charles has drawn many graphs and charts illustrating the unfair distribution of the world's wealth. His most spectacular and eye-catching demonstration involves him unfurling a roll of paper on which are marked the proportional incomes of the poor, middle-class, rich and super-rich. We trail the paper across the yard from trailer to tree to see how much more a US congressman earns than a Kalahari bushman. It's all very impressive, although I can't help feeling like I'm in the middle of an Andrex commercial. 'Where's Oprah Winfrey on this?' I ask Charles.

'Oh, we don't have enough paper for her,' replies Charles. 'She'd be somewhere in Montana.'

▲ Charles explains his economic theory using seven and a half rolls of Andrex.

◀ Charles has just reached the Duchess of York.

▼ 'I declare this field open.'

That state of life is most happy where superfluities are not required and necessaries are not wanting.
Plutarch

It is raining – not much of a surprise in Eugene, Oregon. If there were trophies for rainfall, Eugene would have a mantelpiece full. Luckily Charles Gray has an umbrella, in reasonably good condition, which he discovered in a dumpster only last week. We are in one of the more upmarket neighbourhoods in the city, standing outside a white mansion easily as large and far more tasteful than most of those in Buckhead, Atlanta, or, for that matter, Henley-on-Thames. 'That's where I used to live,' gestures Charles nonchalantly. 'It's a fine old house, very fancy, very lovely inside.' Unfortunately we can't go inside to check it out and dry our feet, since what was once home just to Charles and his wife now houses the offices of about a dozen doctors.

Although Charles Gray was born into a poor family where he picked up, as he puts it, 'a kind of working-class antagonism to the rich', he climbed the rungs of society, in traditional American Dream fashion, to upper-middle-classhood. Charles passed his exams, got his car and his credit cards and a good middle-class job as a university professor. He married for love but, as in the best traditions of Hollywood, he inherited both a large mansion and a small fortune – a little over $2 million. Most people would have been quite happy to see things turn out this way; Charles Gray was different. 'I went on with the whole middle-class thing. But none the less it bothered me that I lived this way when I knew that people all over the world were starving and couldn't have a fair chance.'

Charles Gray was obviously one of those rare children who took his mother seriously when she pointed accusingly at his left-over tapioca pudding and said, 'Think of all the starving children in Africa.' In his teens, when most boys of his age were gazing at the breasts of Amazonian tribeswomen in *National Geographic* magazine, Charles was reading Mahatma Gandhi's autobiography, something which he claims has had a lasting influence on his life. Not something that can be said about many of the Amazonian tribeswomen. Charles continued to be politically active, and became what he describes as a 'liberal philanthropist' making sizeable donations to political causes. Even so, Charles still felt guilty and uncomfortable. 'It didn't seem to me that I had the right to have that kind of power just because I was born in a rich country, or came into a rich social class one way or another – I mean what made *me* so wise? So the idea of equal rights always affected my thinking and was a kind of pressure on my spirit.' If ever the Queen decides to start handing out sainthoods along with the MBEs, OBEs and knighthoods, Charles must surely be in with more than a shout.

It was during the Vietnam War that Charles said he first started making connections between war and the economic system of the USA and other rich countries. 'I felt that we had to move in the direction of simplifying our lives and divesting ourselves of this unequal privilege, this silver spoon.'

The silver spoon dropped with a clang when his wife Leslie announced over breakfast one morning that she thought they should give away half their money, at that time a little over a million dollars. Yet instead of spluttering into his cornflakes, Charles's reaction was, 'My God, what an excellent idea!' So before you could say Mercedes 30 SL coupé, the Grays had set up a small foundation and dispersed half their money to fund their favourite causes, 'environmental peace, social justice, women's struggle and so forth'. Soon afterwards, they moved out of their big house, which they considered too luxurious, into a modest apartment. All in all, an act of charity that puts buying your Christmas presents from the Oxfam catalogue into its true perspective.

But despite having given away more money than most people make in their lifetime, Charles still wasn't happy. Although he was a lot poorer than he had been the year before, he simply wasn't poor enough. Enter the World Equity Budget, and sadly, albeit amicably, exit Leslie.

Charles was now living simply on the budget he had worked out for himself, but he still had quite a bit of money and property left. 'I still had these resources and it wasn't consistent with living on my share. I had to decide what to do with it.' Charles embarked on a final spending spree, writing cheques to various good causes. When he was down to his last couple of thousand dollars he decided 'to have fun and do something a little more random and a little more personal'. Having withdrawn all his money from the bank in $5 bills, Charles decided simply to leave it in the street in a poor inner-city neighbourhood. Unfortunately this idea seemed to have one major drawback: due to the aforementioned rain, the money would probably end up a soggy mess at the bottom of some Oregon drain. Plan B involved individually wrapping the $5 bills around little blocks of wood on which Charles had written slogans like 'Share the Wealth' and 'Robin Hood was Right'.

These he loaded into shopping bags and, having identified the Skid Row districts in Portland, Seattle and Eugene, spent a happy few weeks strewing them on the ground and then watching around the corner to see who would pick them up – presumably hoping that it wouldn't be some city businessman or a wealthy estate agent. Did he feel like Father Christmas? 'It was a lot of fun,' says Charles. Not the sort of fun I can see catching on in a big way.

Now, sixteen years later, Charles Gray is no longer living high on the hog. In fact, the price of meat soon made him turn vegetarian. 'Before I never had to worry about paying the bills. I have to pay attention to what I spend now,' says Charles cheerily. We are sitting in his kitchen, although for that matter we are also sitting in his bedroom, his office and his living room. Home for Charles is now a small, rickety caravan, which sits

'I'm not into being a saint or being austere. I live as richly as I can within what I think is my share.' Charles Gray, who chooses to live on £16 per week.

in the backyard of a house in what seems like a modest but pleasant enough neighbourhood of Eugene. In exchange for a small rent, Charles gets to use part of the yard, the bathroom and the telephone. A far cry from the mansion at 1056 Hillyard Street. The trailer isn't the first of his WEB homes. For several years he lived in a bamboo house he built in Nicaragua. The trailer itself would have been junked but he restored it: 'It's small, it's comfortable, it doesn't take much to heat and I've got everything I need in it. It's less wasteful than a big house. I've got a nice view over the garden – so I'm as happy as a clam.'

One of the side effects of all this is that Charles has now perfected the rather mysterious art of negotiating fees downwards. When he dropped out of academia, he went from a comfortable salary as a professor to relying on carpentry work and gardening to support himself. Charles claims that this was easy. 'As well as having a World Equity Budget, I have a World Equity Wage. It's not hard to convince employers to pay you less than they expected.' Recently Charles has come into a small pension – about $128 a month – so he only has to do a few odd jobs to bring it up to his $160. 'Even when I was working to support the WEB I only had to work a third of the time,' enthuses Charles. 'What's valuable in life? It's time. And I had two-thirds of my time to do anything I wanted to do – which in this case was working for social causes to save this planet.' As you can see, Charles is the sort of person who makes Mother Teresa look selfish.

'I used to be embarrassed about climbing into a dumpster – because being a scavenger has a low place in the social-status system. But then I realized that I was reducing the waste by taking advantage of things that were perfectly good.' One of those things being an umbrella.

In fact, Charles Gray believes that working too hard is a major cause of unhappiness, a claim not many people would disagree with. 'The whole culture has lost some of our traditional values as we have got richer, because the consumer goods that are put before us are tantalizing. And we're told that you can't be a full person unless you have the latest this, the latest that, the right fashion and the right kind of car. And in order to make the payments on the bigger house, the fancier car and all that kind of stuff everyone has to put in an enormous amount of work. It doesn't contribute to their happiness – in fact many people are more miserable. They can't figure out how they're going to make the payments even though they're living vastly richer than their parents did.'

So, forget the fancy consumer durables, what about the bare essentials? Charles reckons that he only spends about $20 a month on food. Even in a country where you can get a KFC family-size 'bucket o' wings' for a couple of bucks, how is that possible? 'I've become a vegetarian and I get most of my produce

from the garden. There's a lot of fruit that people no longer harvest because they're too busy working. I take advantage of the food they have right on their own property – these days it's easier for people to pick it off the supermarket shelf than off the trees. One month out of the summer I spend all my time gathering fruit and drying it.' Last summer Charles picked and dried forty quarts of fruit. That gives him enough dried pears, apples, apricots, plums, etc., to last a whole year, and presumably justify whatever rent he's paying for the use of next door's toilet.

As well as the food he scrumps from neighbouring gardens, Charles buys day-old bread, which, apparently, is perfectly delicious. 'I'm not into being a saint or being austere,' he says. 'I live as richly as I can within what I think is my share. That's kind of the idea. I'll spend a lot of time looking after my own comfort so long as my brother and sister have an equal chance.' If someone treats Charles to a meal, he logs it into his expenses book, so that he can't kid himself about how much he's living on. 'I take what it costs me to make a meal for myself and put that into my expenditures, I don't take the value of the food that people give me because when I'm a guest I eat what I'm served. If they serve me fancy food, that's what I eat. Because I don't like to put people out, or make them feel uncomfortable about their own lifestyle.' That's all very well, but isn't there anything he secretly hankers after? 'Oh, I'm very corruptible – I love chocolate and I love beer.'

During his years on the WEB, Charles has become an expert at foraging. 'This high-consumption lifestyle produces enormous waste and one of the ways of living simply is to take advantage of this, recycle the waste.' Charles finds that the best places to practise this recycling are skips, or 'dumpsters' as they are known in the US. Charles's dishes, his pots and pans, his radio and at least half his clothes have been retrieved from the dumpsters at the university where students chuck things out at the end of the year. Isn't it a bit dismal to be wearing clothes that have even been rejected by *students*? 'I used to be embarrassed about climbing into a dumpster – because being a scavenger has a low place in the social-status system, and here I had been a university professor and all that. It was a matter of dignity. But then I realized that I was reducing the waste by taking advantage of things that were perfectly good.' But . . . *students*? The upshot of his dumpster digging is that in the past sixteen years he has spent only $19 on shoes and virtually nothing on clothes, except for socks and underwear. Charles's tips for would-be foragers:

wear covered shoes and old clothes. Well, it would make the exercise slightly pointless if you went out and bought new clothes specially for it.

After a nice bit of scavenging it's back off home on his bicycle. 'I love my bicycle. I think if anything would symbolize my lifestyle for me it would be this: it's so efficient, it's such a wonderful way of transport, it's non-polluting, it's good exercise and it's cheap to repair.' If Charles has to go on a long journey he either hitch-hikes or get rides with other friends. 'I realize that in a country built round the automobile there are problems in trying to live without one – but then there are problems and contradictions and compromises in my lifestyle just trying to survive in this high-consumption society.' The biggest compromise is not being able to visit his children, who live in New Zealand. 'I'm not that good at swimming, you know.' They do come and visit him, from time to time, but on average he only gets to see them about every five years.

And what about his social life? Thanks to the WEB he lost his wife, and, to a certain extent, the rest of his family. What about his old friends? 'I've found that I have not had trouble having a rich social life. People react in a lot of different ways. Some feel that I'm making a judgement on them by choosing to live very simply, that somehow I'm feeling that they're not doing the right thing. Other people have a kind of grudging respect for what I'm doing.' Sometimes friends feel guilty when they see him, and try to give him gifts. One friend gave him a jar of peanut butter that was so gigantic he couldn't fit it in the trailer. Charles says if anyone keeps giving him things he takes them aside and explains that he doesn't want to be subsidized.

'I don't go to paid entertainments or eat out in restaurants, which carried some costs because I used to enjoy eating out, the sociability of it. The most common place where people meet is over a cup of coffee or in a restaurant – I kind of miss that.' Nowadays many evenings are spent at home, reading, mending clothes, listening to the radio or on Charles's new-found hobbies: knitting, crocheting and embroidering.

Recently he wrote a book about his life and the WEB. Isn't he worried that it will sell a million and make him another fortune? 'I don't believe in owning copyright. Anyway, this is not likely to become the most popular movement in history – thousands and thousands delighted to reduce their lifestyle and live more simply.' He has no doubt, however, that his way of life has brought him happiness. 'I've chosen this life for what seem to me good reasons, and because I'm living this way I have a kind of peace of mind. I developed a philosophy and then I tried to live it, and I think that a very important ingredient in happiness is living according to what you believe.' He agrees that the fact that he has actively chosen to live this way is important. 'There are homeless people in Eugene living in similar circumstances, but because they're trying to get back into the usual establishment they feel deprived and are miserable.'

And, according to Charles, being rich can make you just as unhappy. 'Rich people worry that someone will try to take it away – they worry about con artists, about bad investment counsellors and whether people are relating to them just because they're rich. If I'm developing a friendship with someone now, obviously it's not because of my money.' Charles believes that most people hope to escape from the rat-race by earning so much money that they become free from everyday worries. Most never make it. He has found an easier way of dropping out of the rat-race and in doing so discovered that choosing to be poor makes you free. Furthermore he has rid himself of the terrible guilt he felt at his 'undeserved' wealth. 'I'm immensely happier now – I wouldn't go back to being rich for anything – no way.'

Charles Gray's equivalent of a welcome mat.

Welcome Friend I hope you enjoy being in my cozy little home
I would like to introduce myself a little. I believe in equality and
sharing. I live on about $100 a month. If you have less income
than This and you need something that is here, please consider
it a gift. [illegible]. There is food in
The cupboard [illegible] if you are hungry.
Drinking water is in The bottle on The counter.
Peace and good wishes
Charles Gray
Message phone 344-7196
P.S. If you make your living or support a habit by theft, don't bother
to search for money because I don't have any here. If you are in
a Financial emergency, leave a note or phone message for me. I can't
promise anything, but who knows, we might think of something Together —

... the *Homo erectus*
humans?

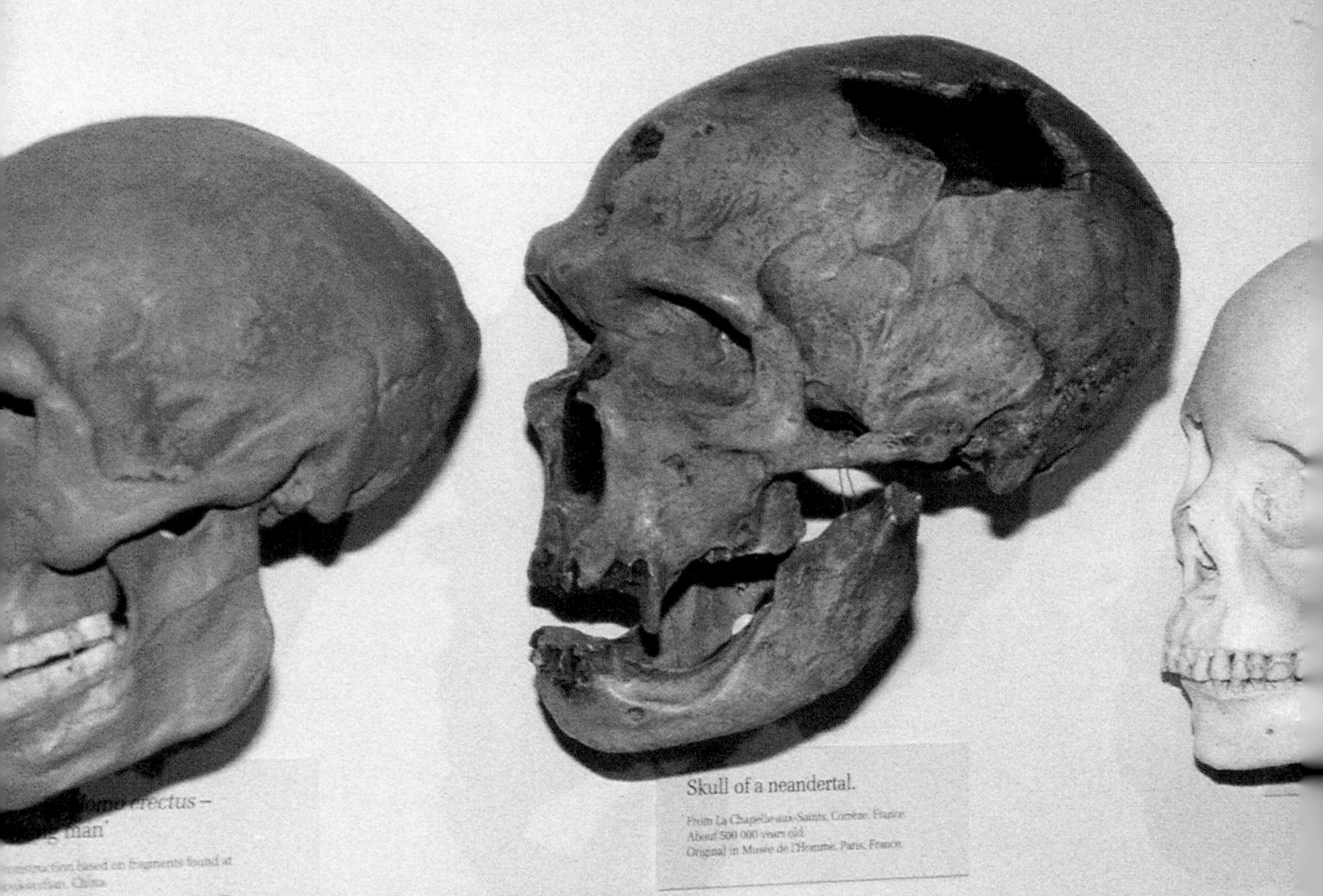

CHANGE

The Magic Wand Theory

have large brow
Homo erectus people.

more closely related
ctus people than to

But, like modern humans, the neandertals had larger brains than the Homo erectus people. (The neandertals had an average brain size of about 1400ml.)
And, like modern humans, the neandertals buried their dead.

So we think that the neandertals are more closely related to modern humans than to the *Homo erectus*

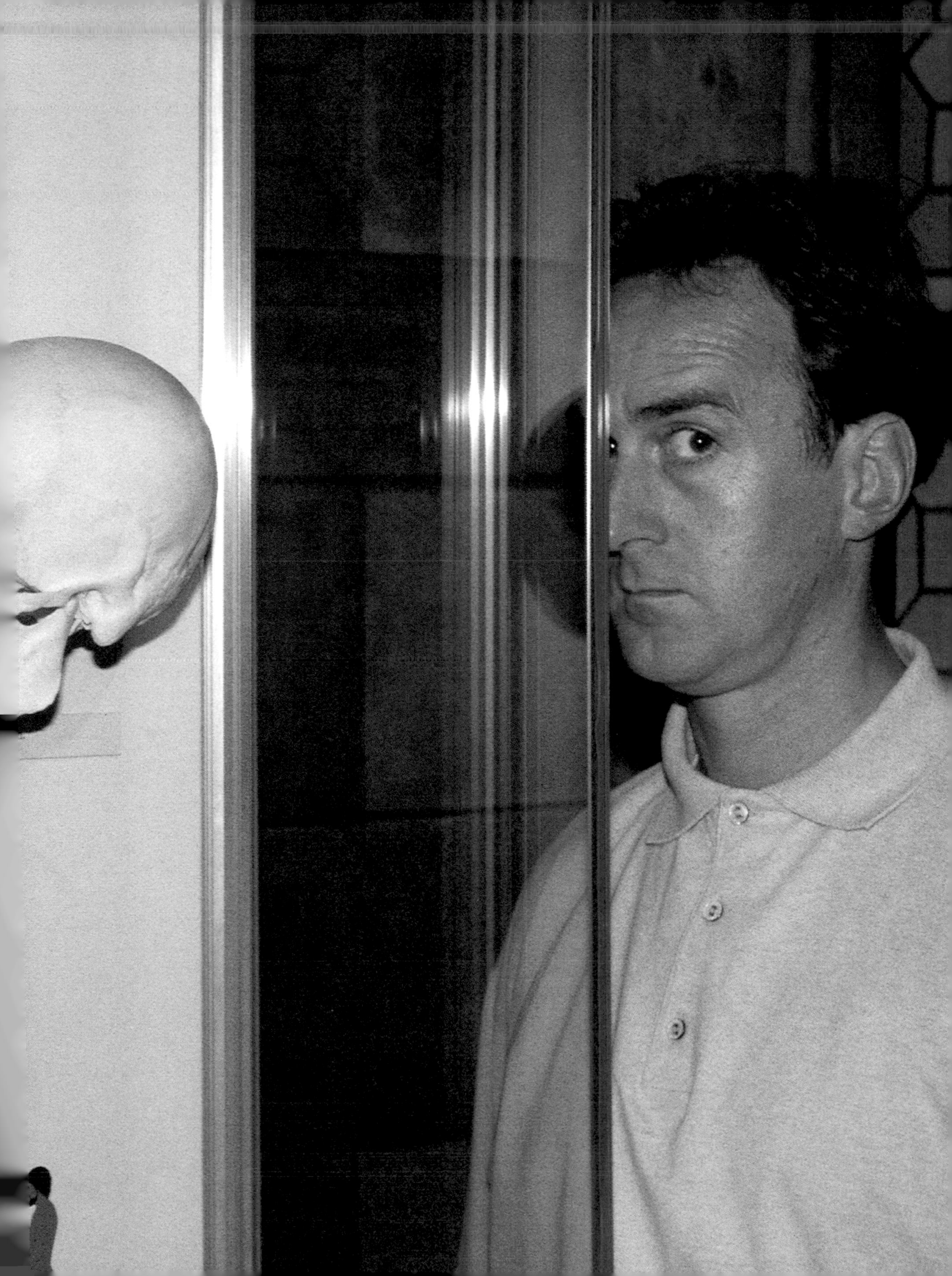

If we want things to stay as they are, things will have to change.
Giuseppe di Lampedusa, novelist

Change is not made without inconvenience, even from worse to better.
Richard Hooker, theologian

Every self-help book and women's magazine extols the unfailing benefits of change:

'Just split up with your boyfriend? Paint your bedroom a different colour. Change your hairstyle. Buy a new pair of shoes. If he ever comes back – he won't recognize the new you!'

'Are you getting unsightly wrinkles? Are your thighs fat and dimpled? Have you got a nose like a turnip? Why not pay a lot of money to a Harley Street specialist who will promise you'll end up looking like Michelle Pfeiffer? But remember – beauty is only skin deep. It's the *inner* you that counts. So, while you're at it, why not book an appointment with one of our psychotherapists?'

'Financial worries getting you down? Why not slip off your luxury yacht in the middle of the night and meet up with a friendly plastic surgeon? Then you and your numbered Swiss bank account can start afresh without those niggly Inland Revenue chaps to fret about.'

There are some changes that happen to you whether you like it or not. We all know about advancing age and retreating hair. We've all started to notice that the policemen are getting younger, and that the Rolling Stones are looking more and more like the Rolling Stones' dads. But sometimes change is a choice. We came across people who, in their search for happiness, had changed themselves in many different ways – mentally, physically, spiritually, nominally, geographically and, in one rather disturbing case, cranially.

The most extreme example we came across was a man called Umberto Gallini who runs a company in Rome called The Happy Expatriate, which specializes in helping people to completely change their identity. We made an appointment to see him, but by the time I got there he had become Mrs Dorothy Simpson of Adelaide. This is not his story . . .

Anthony Robbins – still able to see the lighter side of life despite being a six-foot-seven-inch sun-tanned multimillionaire.

DATE WITH DESTINY: ANTHONY ROBBINS

The world is undergoing a paradigm shift and unless you not only get used to change but get excited about it, you have nothing but pain in your future.
Anthony Robbins

I took my blind date with Destiny, saw my future and now it is mine!
Simone Myers, card-shop owner and Robbins convert

It's easy to be cynical about Anthony Robbins. But just because something's easy doesn't mean it's not worth doing. In many ways, Anthony Robbins is exactly the sort of man you'd love to hate. He's too rich, too confident, has too much hair and too many gleaming white teeth. He measures six foot seven in his Calvin Klein socks and bandies about phrases like 'kinaesthetic sub-modalities' and 'empowering neuro-associations' without even blushing. For some reason, the word 'Californian' springs to mind.

Anthony Robbins is the Guru of Positive Thinking. Or as he prefers to term it: Optimum Performance Technology, Neuro-linguistic Planning and Ultimate Success Formulae. Ten years ago, so the story goes, Tony Robbins was broke and overweight. He lived in an apartment measuring forty square yards and washed his dirty dishes in the bath. It often meant he got bits of baked beans in his hair, but in those days, he didn't care. Now Robbins is a multimillionaire, the founder of nine companies, he lives, overlooking the Pacific, in a mock-Spanish castle near San Diego and has one perfectly formed wife, four bouncy wholesome children and incredibly clean hair. He flies his own private jet helicopter and owns a resort hotel in Fiji, where he likes to relax with his family and twenty of his closest friends. But is he happy? Irritatingly, the answer seems to be yes. Tony Robbins radiates happiness and bonhomie. And yet, despite this, you can't help liking him.

Robbins was born in Los Angeles. His mother was a waitress, his father a parking attendant. When Tony was five years old, they divorced. Even as a child, Robbins had aspirations to greatness. He decided 'to make books my friends', and claims to have

read seven hundred in five years, mainly on the subject of psychology. He also says he decided have model himself on great men like Churchill, Roosevelt and Martin Luther King, and imitated their diction, habits and posture (although he doesn't smoke cigars or do 'V' signs, so I think he was making up the Churchill bit). At the age of eleven his mother and stepfather were so poor they couldn't afford a Thanksgiving turkey. Out of the blue, a stranger appeared on their doorstep and presented them with a magnificent turkey and all the trimmings. It may sound like one of those embarrassing Bernard Matthews commercials, but the boy Robbins thought that, as magnanimous gestures went, it was second only to the feeding of the five thousand. So, while still a teenager, Tony started distributing food to poor families on Thanksgiving Day. (Last year the Anthony Robbins Foundation provided turkey dinners for seventy-five thousand people, and not a Golden Drummer in sight.) But, despite his success on the charity front, he still had a long way to go before he was to crack it as a businessman. At the age of seventeen, Robbins attended a sales seminar given by a man named Jim Rohn and was so impressed that he went to work for him. However, five years later Robbins had blown everything. There he was – depressed, fat, broke, dishes in the bath and probably clothes too.

Handsome, wholesome, all-American, the sort of man who cleans his teeth between each word.

'I think what changes most people is pain. You get to a point of enough pain that either you just give up, or you get mad as hell and you decide to do something about it. I decided to do something.'

The 'something' which he decided to do was to market himself as a 'one-stop therapist'. Anthony Robbins is the Cambridge Diet of psychology. After all, why bother with years on the analyst's couch when you can do it instantly? Why take two bottles into the shower when for a mere £529 plus VAT you can just change your life 'n' go?

Now Robbins's empire embraces a dozen different companies. His books *Unlimited Power* and *Awaken the Giant Within* have sold over a million copies each and been translated into eleven languages. Robbins has sold over thirteen million videotapes and provides a thousand top US companies with management training packages. About two thousand business and sales people pay top dollar to attend his seminars every week and he has been known to hold meetings attended by upwards of ten thousand people. (He played to fifteen thousand in Madison Square Gardens – so just slightly more popular than Barbra Streisand.) So far, more than a million Americans have paid to see Robbins (and with no support band). But for those who want the more personal touch, Robbins stages intimate little weekend courses for a mere five hundred paying guests. One of his trademarks is 'The Firewalk' in which Robbins gets his audience to walk barefoot over burning coals. Or he'll get them to stand on a tiny platform at the top of a fifty-foot flagpole. Amazingly, almost none of them come to any harm. In his spare time, which must amount to all of one weekend a year, Anthony Robbins acts as an adviser to government, the military, top athletes and celebrities. Apparently Demi Moore never goes anywhere without one of his books. Even Bill Clinton recently consulted him – not that it seems to have done much good.

All this would seem to imply that Robbins has something new and special to tell the world, some profound insight on the human psyche, some revolutionary technique for obtaining spiritual well-being. But what exactly is Anthony Robbins's message? Is his philosophy of CAN-I (Constant And Never-ending Improvement) in reality a philosophy of CAN-T-I (Constant Additions to Notch-up Tony's Income)? Has Anthony Robbins got the secret of happiness? Well, the brochures for his seminars in Birmingham certainly sounded promising . . . Watch out for the abbreviated first name – nice touch.

DATE WITH DESTINY is Anthony Robbins's most personal and intimate seminar, limited to only 450 people. It's three and a half days spent with Tony, dedicated to establishing your goals, values, core beliefs and rules to create lifelong success. Experience physically, emotionally, mentally and spiritually those decisions that will carry you effortlessly into the direction of your dreams. You will have hands-on opportunities to alter whatever doesn't work for you, so that you can become the person who will accomplish what you truly desire.

What I truly desire is to understand what Anthony Robbins is talking about. I make a decision that I hope will carry me effortlessly in the direction of my dreams. I decide to make an appointment to see the man himself, my very own date with Destiny. His assistant informs me that 'Tony' will be happy to meet me at his home on Tuesday the 15th at 3.15 sharp.

'His home in San Diego?'

'That is correct.'

Well, I suppose if instant and lifelong contentment is at stake, southern California isn't such a long way to go. And who knows? Demi might pop round while I'm there.

Anthony Robbins often flies his own private jet helicopter from his mock-Spanish castle home in San Diego to his private resort hotel in Fiji, where he likes to relax with his family and twenty close friends.

The following Tuesday, at 3.15 sharp, I am sitting on a sun lounger on the beautiful sweeping lawns outside Anthony Robbins's huge, turreted castle overlooking the Pacific Ocean. It bears a remarkable resemblance to the billboard picture of a theme park called Frontierland which I passed on the drive from the airport. I keep imagining that there are Apache braves creeping round the palm trees, waiting to shoot an arrow into the white canvas sunhat I bought that morning in a last-minute skin-cancer panic, and which makes me look like I am off on a fishing trip or have just stepped off the set of *Skippy, The Bush Kangaroo*. After a while I realize that the Apache warriors are actually a platoon of gardeners, who seem to be hoovering up fallen leaves with a giant outdoor vacuum cleaner. There is, as yet, no sign of the great man himself. His assistant pops out – four times – to say that he'll be with us shortly.

Anthony Robbins arrives at 4.45 sharp, so profusely and charmingly apologetic for his tardiness that I begin to feel ashamed for having been so punctual. I ask him if he thinks anyone could make themselves happier. (That's after the weather and the journey from the airport have been covered.) 'Happiness has to become a must instead of a should and I think for most people there are all kinds of shoulds. I should spend more time with my kids, I should work harder at my work, I should do whatever . . . but they don't actually change, they just should all over themselves.' After a brief but embarrassing interchange based on a mishearing, he continues: 'So I turned my shoulds into musts.'

I begin to be fascinated by a small piece of spittle poised precariously on his lower lip. Will it fall? Or will it be sucked back into the sun-tanned chasm that is his perfectly formed mouth? 'Are you saying that before you can achieve happiness, you have to decide that you must be happy?' I ask.

'You have to decide you're going to be happy, you have to decide you're not going to settle for anything less and you have to decide that happiness is a natural state.'

I think of asking Tony, as I have been encouraged to call him, if that isn't just a little over-simplistic. But there is no need.

'You may think that sounds just a little over-simplistic,' he continues, 'but our beliefs control all of our actions. It's like the Roger Bannister four-minute-mile story. Most people know that for thousands of years man wanted to do that and nobody could do it, but what most people don't know is that within a year of his running that four-minute mile, thirty-seven other people did it. It's like he broke the barrier not just for himself but for everybody else.' By this time, the bead of spittle has transmogrified into a row of tiny glistening pearls.

'You have to realize that it is a choice, and as corny as it sounds Abraham Lincoln said that everyone's about as happy as they really want to be. And that's an over-simplification of it because there are certain strategies to make you feel happy consistently even during tough times.'

'So you have to have a strategy, Mhthmph?' (I can't decide whether to call him 'Mr Robbins', 'Anthony', 'Tony' or 'Tone' and end up making a sound like a smothered gerbil. Not, I hasten to add, that I have ever, personally, smothered a gerbil.)

'Definitely. You can believe you're gonna see a sunset but if you start running east looking for it, you've got a problem.'

'So what is the strategy?' At last I am going to find out the secret.

'I'll give you happiness in one word. It's gratitude. I go to Fiji a lot, I have a resort there and I go there about four times a year, and I take twenty of my friends, and I go there because it's one of the happiest cultures on the face of the earth that I know of. I mean, you drive down the street and people jump up and go, "Bula Bula Bula!" which means, "Welcome, be happy, we love you!", and you're a total stranger. I try to every day spend time just feeling incredibly grateful for what I have and when you're grateful you have no fear and when you're grateful, you're happy . . . What you focus on will determine how you feel, so if right now we can look out here and see the ocean, we can look around the trees, we can hear the birds, I mean, as simplistic as

'Bula Bula Bula!'

it sounds we can sit here and just be in ecstasy if we want and feel so grateful for being alive.'

I try to focus on the beauty of my surroundings, but the afternoon sun is full in our eyes. I squint at Tony's earnest face and see there are now little meringuey peaks of saliva in both corners of his mouth. 'Or,' he continues, 'we can focus on the sun is in our eyes, you know, simplistic as it is.'

I am obviously dealing with a mindreader of some talent. Feeling like the character in *The Midwich Cuckoos* who has to concentrate on a brick wall to conceal the bomb in his briefcase from the telepathic alien children, I decide to change tack, and ask him about his scheduled visit to England. After all, it's all too easy to get Americans to whoop and holler and tell complete strangers intimate details about their private lives, but would the British really go for that sort of thing? Isn't there something a bit un-British about being too happy?

Robbins considers. 'I do think your culture puts a great deal of value on things being, quote, "natural", and that if something's too perfect, it's not natural . . . Toasters, for example, is an area where I noticed this. I just noticed that . . . that technology is not always embraced as thoroughly there . . . there's almost something suspect about something that could be too good and too fast. I think that the British toasters are fascinating. I love hearing people complain about them. I say, "Why don't you get a new one?" and they say, "No, no, I love this toaster."'

I return to the hotel via the Del Mar beach, where I walk up and down shouting, 'Bula Bula Bula!' It doesn't quite do the trick for me, I'm afraid, but I think a couple of the seagulls are quietly grateful. I can't help thinking what a strange language Fijian must be, that you can use the same word to mean 'Welcome', 'Be happy' and 'We love you'. Must all be in the inflection, I suppose.

Our brain is the ultimate computer but most of us have never been given an owner's manual on how to use it.
Anthony Robbins

My initial feeling is one of severe geographical displacement. Was this Birmingham, England, or Birmingham, Alabama? Here are all these British people. You remember the British? The ones with upper lips so stiff you could balance a sherry glass on them, the sort of people who can sit next to each other at work for six months before they introduce themselves, the kind who shake hands with their own parents. Here they are, all two thousand of them, behaving in a way you might normally associate with the audience of *The Oprah Winfrey Show.*

It is the last day of Anthony Robbins's 'Unleash the Power Within Weekend' at the NEC, and he's certainly succeeded in unleashing something. The audience whoop and holler like home-grown Yankees fans at the finals of the World Series as Tony strides up and down the stage, somewhat comically sporting a pair of khaki shorts and a short-sleeved shirt, with a microphone strapped to his head like some gigantic demented telephonist with no dress sense, or Madonna in concert.

I slip into a seat only to find myself in the middle of a 'group back-rub' – everyone massaging the shoulders of the person in front of them. I never managed to see what the people in the front row did. The whole experience was not in itself unpleasant, but in Birmingham?

'Sit the way you would be sitting if you were in ecstasy!' booms Robbins. 'Breathe the way you would be breathing if you were in ecstasy. Picture what you would be picturing if you were in ecstasy. Step into the picture so you begin to feel it. Breathe it. Feel it. Experience it. That's it!'

The room is getting decidedly warm. I wonder whether to take off my overcoat. Someone in the audience gives a loud, low moan. Everybody laughs.

'Add the sounds. That's good, sir, very good. Go on – make the sounds of being in ecstasy. Come on, go for it. Oh, keep making the sounds and make it feel even better. Go for it!'

The whole room is panting and heaving now. I definitely should have taken my coat off.

'Now I want you to double the intensity of ecstasy. Go on – double it.'

I'm seated next to a prim-looking woman in her late thirties. She looks like a PR consultant or an estate agent. Suddenly she begins to groan.

'Now I want you to triple the level of ecstasy. Really go for it.'

The estate agent actually sounds like she's in pain, but somehow I can't bring myself to ask her if she's OK.

'Now, as soon as you think you have hit your peak, break through and make it four times more pleasurable. Come on!'

Now she's clutching her chest and moaning loudly. I begin to wonder if she's having a heart attack . . .

Unleash the Power Within Weekend

17 OCTOBER. N.E.C. BIRMINGHAM
TICKETS (on the door) £529 plus VAT

STEP 1: Friday Evening. *Fear Into Power: The Firewalk Experience.* You will learn: To eliminate the fears that block you from realizing your goals. To begin to master the breakthrough technology of Neuro-Associative Conditioning. To develop the consistent ability to develop yourself mentally, emotionally and physically for lifelong success. To transcend your limitations to achieve whatever you want.

STEP 2: Saturday and Sunday. *The Psychology of Success Conditioning.* You will learn: To define your goals so they are specific and more easily accomplished. To inspire yourself and others for performance that is consistently at the highest levels. Love and relationship strategies. To instantly transform unresourceful emotions into resourceful ones.

STEP 3: Monday. *Breakthrough to Vital Life.* You will learn: To dramatically increase your energy level. A stress-free exercise programme for endurance. A nutritional approach to the control and prevention of degenerative diseases. To combine foods in the proper sequence for greater nutritional value.

STEP 4: Tuesday. *Back to the paper round.*

'And when you know it's all you can take, make it five times more pleasurable. Now!'

I decide there's definitely something amiss. Her face is flushed and sweaty and . . .

'And six times more pleasurable. Come on, come on, come on, come on, come on, come on. Even more! Even more! Even more!'

She flings herself out of her seat and raised her arms aloft, eyes shut, lips parted. 'Oh yes, oh yes, oh yes!'

Robbins grins at us.

'Feeling good? Now, how many of you were actually able to experience ecstasy just now? Raise your hand if you actually felt it, and say "Aye".'

The air of the NEC is filled with waving hands and cries of 'Aye!'

'Now, raise your hand if you don't allow yourself to feel ecstasy, because, after all, it's a public place, and you are British and you certainly wouldn't feel ecstasy in a public place. Let's see a show of hands there.'

It's absurd, but I feel like Tony's gaze is aimed directly at me. I shift uncomfortably in my seat, but I can't even bring myself to raise my hand. After all, I am British, and it is a public place.

I can't recommend Mr Robbins's book highly enough.

A ROSE BY ANY OTHER NAME: LAURENCE Y. DAVID G. ADAMS

A person with a bad name is already half hanged.
Anon.

No, Groucho is not my real name. I'm breaking it in for a friend.
Groucho Marx

'What's in a name? That which we call a rose by any other name would smell as sweet.' Or would it? Not according to Laurence Y. David G. Adams, who believes that a name can mean the difference between happiness, success and health, and unhappiness, failure and, in certain cases, death. Is life treating you badly? Do you want romance, or financial gain, or perhaps just to lose a bit of weight? Then don't waste your time finding a partner, earning more or eating less. According to Mr Adams, it's your name that's the problem. If you want to change your life, it could be that filling out a deed-poll form will bring about the results you are hoping for. And it's even quicker and cheaper than a Date With Destiny.

'When you boil it down, when you analyse what makes people different you're left with two things only. A date of birth and a name. That's been known by every police force in the world – because if you're ever stopped by the police what do they ask you but full name and date of birth? They know that identifies you.'

Laurence Y. David G. Adams explains the principles of Name Analysis to me as we sit together in his office, a converted garage at his home in Stockport, Manchester. Laurence Adams, as I call him for short, is well qualified to discuss the subject, since he is a professional Name Analyst, with a thriving business. 'What about fingerprints and dental records?' I wonder. 'Aren't they unique?' Or perhaps I've just been watching too many episodes of *Quincey*.

Laurence Adams continues: 'The only thing you can change about a person that is long term is their name.'

I suppose one of the great things about names is that every-

Laurence Y. David G. Adams attempts to persuade me to change my name to Gordyn.

body has one. Just as well, for it might prove impractical to say, 'How's that tall man with the sticking-out ears who threw up in your bushes last New Year's Eve?' or 'Tonight's news is read by that man with the huge bulbous nose and the notorious drink problem.' Names can tell us a great deal about each other, or at least about each other's parents. You're unlikely to meet an American called Torquil, an Englishman called Buddy or an Australian not called Bruce or Shane. You would rarely meet a cleaner named Eugenie, a duchess called Mavis, a girl named John or a boy named Sue. And you would never, ever find a baby being christened Eric Ryan Lee Mark Gary Paul Steve Andrei Peter Dennis Roy whose parents did not live somewhere in the vicinity of Old Trafford.

What most of us can't tell from a name, however, is someone's personality, their characteristics, their vices and virtues. Laurence Y. David G. Adams believes that he can, and will either help you to maximize on the positive elements of your name or, if your name bodes ill for the future, he'll help you to change your name legally to a better one. Over the past fifteen years Laurence Adams has helped to change the names of about a thousand people. The results, he says, are often spectacular.

'If you want a funny story read the Bible. The Church has known about name changes for centuries. Sarah and Abraham were visited by an angel and told they would have a baby, a boy, and they would call the baby boy Isaac and he would found a new religion and be father to thousands. He would father the Jewish religion. Nothing happened – not surprising : if you read the Bible, Sarah was ninety and Abraham was ninety-nine years old. Then the Lord appeared and changed both their names, they gave birth to a baby boy, they called him Isaac and he founded the Jewish religion.'

So there you have it – in one fell swoop both a solution to infertility and a means to create an enduring worldwide faith. Although I can't help wondering whether if God had told them to name the baby Muhammad it might have solved a lot of problems later on.

The basic premise of Name Analysis is entirely simple – that is 'simple' in the extremely complicated and tortuous sense of the word. Each of the letters which make up your name indicates a different personal characteristic. Furthermore various combinations of the letters are significant. Depending on your age, different letters of your name are 'active'. In order to calculate where you are in your name, you give each letter in the alphabet a numerical value, counting up to 9 and then starting again at 1 – i.e., A=1, B=2, C=3, D=4, E=5, F=6, G=7, H=8, I=9, J=1, K=2, etc. Next you add up the letter values in each name, and work out from your age which letters you are 'in' at any particular time. For example, if your name is John Brown, not only are your parents hugely unimaginative, but your numbers are: J= 1, O=6, H=8, N=5 (total 20) B=2, R=9, O=6, W=5, N=5 (total 27). If you are ten years old, you are in the H of John, and the R of Brown. If you give yourself a middle initial, you are always in that letter, and constantly enjoy its beneficial or detrimental effects. As you may notice, the letters 'G', 'N', and 'Y' seem to be particularly sought after. Which is good news if your name is Gyngell, Gaynor or Gynaecologist.

A Name is a Kind of Face Whereby One is Known

A lot of famous people have changed their names. And you can see why. Would John Wayne have been considered such a tough guy if he'd kept the name Marion Morrison? Would Reg Dwight and David Jones and Harry Webb have given us 'Candle In the Wind', 'Space Oddity' or 'Summer Holiday'? Would Boris Karloff have made us hide behind the sofa as Bill Pratt? Would Diana Dors have been a sex siren with a name like Doris Fluck? (Actually she might have been even more of a sex siren with that name.) Laurence Adams has analysed the names of several famous people who came to a somewhat sticky end, and has worked out where they went wrong:

Marilyn Monroe

The problem with this name is the excess of nervous energy which comes from the name Marilyn, which would promote insecurity, anxiety, worries, plus a great need for attention.

Monroe is too nice a name for the world of entertainment and, in addition, the combination of the M from Marilyn and M from Monroe is especially dangerous.

A similar but greatly improved name would be: **Mary G. Munroy**.

The name Mary is very loving, very giving and gives a great love of music, singing and acting. This name also remains young. Munroy gives strength of character, executive ability and determination, the Y at the end giving success from age twenty-seven to thirty-four. The middle initial G. would bring permanent gains – both financial and emotional. With this name the two Ms cannot come together.

Mary G. Munroy would be very attractive, but also intelligent and capable – sorry, but she would never be a dumb blonde.

Elvis Aaron Presley

Presley is the same number – 37 – as Liberace, Glitter and Elton Hercules John, so this name has to be retained as it gives showmanship, style, love of clothes and jewellery.

The names Elvis and Aaron both total 22 and these names are extrovert, selfish and bad tempered. They can also indicate weakness of character and too great a love of social life.

This name would be more well balanced and happier if changed to: **Jon G. Presley**

Jon is bright, lively, impulsive and very loving, and balances Presley. The middle initial G. brings permanent gains – both emotionally (missing from the original name) and financially.

James Dean

Dean is almost the exact opposite of James. The name James is bright, lively, impulsive and gives a great love of music and acting. It is very caring and giving.

Dean, on the other hand, is a name which can be moody, likes being alone and can have difficulty in relationships. In health matters it indicates the liver, and care is often needed with alcohol.

The name to change is Dean and the original name would be greatly improved by legally changing to: **James Deyn.**

Deyn is bright, lively, impulsive and blends well with James. The Y indicates seven years of success from age nine to sixteen and this is repeated at age thirty to thirty-seven. The sudden death of James Dean could have been avoided, and his personality would be changed for the better.

Anxious to avoiding crashing my Porsche into a Ford Sedan next time I'm speeding along Route 466, I confess to Laurence that my full name is actually Gordon Angus Deayton. It was all my father's fault. My mother wanted to call me Angus, but my father insisted that it was an address, not a name. Hence the compromise: they put the Gordon first and called me Angus, thus ensuring that for the rest of my life I would have to explain to receptionists and tax officials why G. stands for Angus.

Luckily the science of names is all about the letters which make up your name, not how badly you are going to get teased at school or whether your brothers are going to call you 'Gussie' and 'Aberdeen Steak House'. I turn out to be in the N of Gordon, the G of Angus and the E of Deayton, which luckily doesn't seem to signify any imminent car crash. In fact, Laurence is positively glowing about my name, although he does eventually suggest that I either change the Gordon to Gordyn, or lose it altogether. If only he had had a word with my father thirty-eight years ago.

Not wife-swapping in Esher, but name-swapping in Stockport.

If ever I was to have a girl, if ever I was to have a dozen girls, I'd name 'em all Jane.
H. G. Wells, *Kipps*

Laurence David Adams (34, 23, 11) was once a regional sales manager for a company selling vitamins and minerals. He was happy in his work, and rarely suffered from colds. One day, by chance, he was browsing through a friend's bookshelf when he came across a book called *Name Analysis* by Violetta Park Boyile (32, 19, 32) and Elvira Park Boyile (31, 19, 32) at a friend's house. Laurence was fascinated and offered to buy the book. For the next two and a half years it was just a private hobby, but one Christmas Eve it all changed.

'We had a party. One couple arrived very, very late. The wife was upset and wanted a cup of tea. While we were in the kitchen waiting for the kettle to boil, she burst into tears. She said her son had totally ruined his life, there was no future for him. So I said to her without even thinking, "Well, what's his name?" She gave me her son's name and I said, "Well, I'm very sorry, he got involved with the wrong crowd, they're into drugs, he's been arrested, he's got a short sentence and then in eighteen months there's a new job for him with travel abroad."'

The woman was astonished at the accuracy of Laurence's analysis, and cheered up by his predictions for the future. By the end of the evening everyone at the party was clamouring to have their names analysed.

'I said, "It's my party, I'm not here to work. Come back in the new year, phone up, make an appointment and have it done properly." I thought, By then, they'll forget. But no – in the first week of the new year they all rang and made appointments with me. Next they told their friends and before long I'd come home from work and there'd be a long list of people for me to see in the evening. I was often busier than I'd been at work. So I thought, I'll stop it – if I make a charge they won't come. So I made a charge and they still kept ringing, and I put up the charge and they still kept ringing.'

When Laurence was made redundant a few years later, his

wife Hazel (25) suggested that he start doing the name analysis full time. The first thing he did was to change his own name. 'I knew when I went into the 'U' of Laurence there would be three years of losses, so before I went full time into Name Analysis I added a 'Y' into my name. Within three weeks of doing that I was on three radio stations.' Maybe Simon Bates (25, 11) should give it a go. A few years later Laurence Y. David Adams (34, 7, 23, 11) became Laurence Y. David G. Adams (34, 7, 23, 7, 11) after a palmist told him that your palm-print changes within a year of changing your name. (A useful tip for jewel thieves.)

If the sign of a successful businessman is the number of satisfied customers he can get to come forward and testify, then Laurence Y. David G. Adams is the Donald Trump of Stockport. I got glowing reports from Marc N. G. Thompson (previously Mark Stephen Thompson), Clare G. Glynn Payge (previously Grace Clare Elvington Fletcher Lord Armitage), Stanley G. N. Watt (previously Robert Stanley Stuart) and Richard David G. N. Vardey (previously Richard David Vardey Thompson), Michael G. N. Dicks (previously Michael Mills-Hayward Dicks), Barry G. N. Crowther (previously Barry Crowther) and Uncle Tom G. N. Cobbley and all.

One of the most glowing testimonies to name analysis comes from Alan G. Kyng, who, in his former incarnation as Alan Craig Dirkin was a nightclub owner with thirty-seven convictions for drunk and disorderly behaviour, who boasts that he regularly drank fifteen pints a day (of what he doesn't say), and has scars all over his body, including one from a knife wound and one from a bullet. 'You can even see my knuckles are bent a bit backwards, from constantly using them. Every time you hit something, your knuckle goes back an inch.' By which token, Chris Eubank's fists should be up around his neck by now.

'Laurence told me everything about myself and what were wrong. When you look at the name of Dirkin it led into the social-animal side and he wasn't surprised that I drank fifteen pints a day – it didn't surprise him one little bit. The name analysis side of people isn't a magical trick, it's very, very accurate – 99.9 per cent accurate.'

Now Alan G. Kyng is married (to Gillian G. Kyng) and they have three children named Ryan, Jayd and Leeanne, and a dog called Amy. Alan says he is deeply into 'personal growth' and runs his own company, which, from what Alan says, I gather is something to do with people. 'It's all about people – we teach people and we develop people. It's about people.' He is a great admirer of Anthony Robbins, who he refers to as 'his American Guru' and says *Awaken the Giant Within* is 'the finest book ever written'.

Alan G. Kyng has no doubts that as Alan Craig Dirkin he would never have achieved anything, except perhaps a prison sentence.

'The name change was the start of what I am now – I don't drink any longer, I don't go in public houses. I have had a total change in life. I got married, I'm happy – 100 per cent – 150 per cent, in fact. I have a beautiful family, I feel better, I feel healthier, I have changed my career and I have a lot of greater love of what I do. I'm a lot happier in general.'

Laurence Adams* glows with avuncular pride at the sight of his happy band of name changelings. He is so positive that a name is the single most important factor for attaining personal happiness that he offers a money-back guarantee. 'I make an offer when I change someone's name. I charge £10 for a name change and I say to all my clients that if, after twelve months, you're not totally happy then come back and I'll change your name back to what it was free of charge.' As for the sceptics who continue to cast doubt on the scientific basis of his work, Laurence is philosophical: 'Name analysis is six thousand years old. Name changes are known in marriage, religion, entertainment. And yet people will not accept it. I don't mind – it's your life. You can walk away from here and say what an absolute load of rubbish and you can carry on in the same way. But I know your life will change. Whether *you* believe it or not.'

* Since this interview, Laurence Y. David G. Adams has now legally changed his name to Laurence Y. David G. Page.

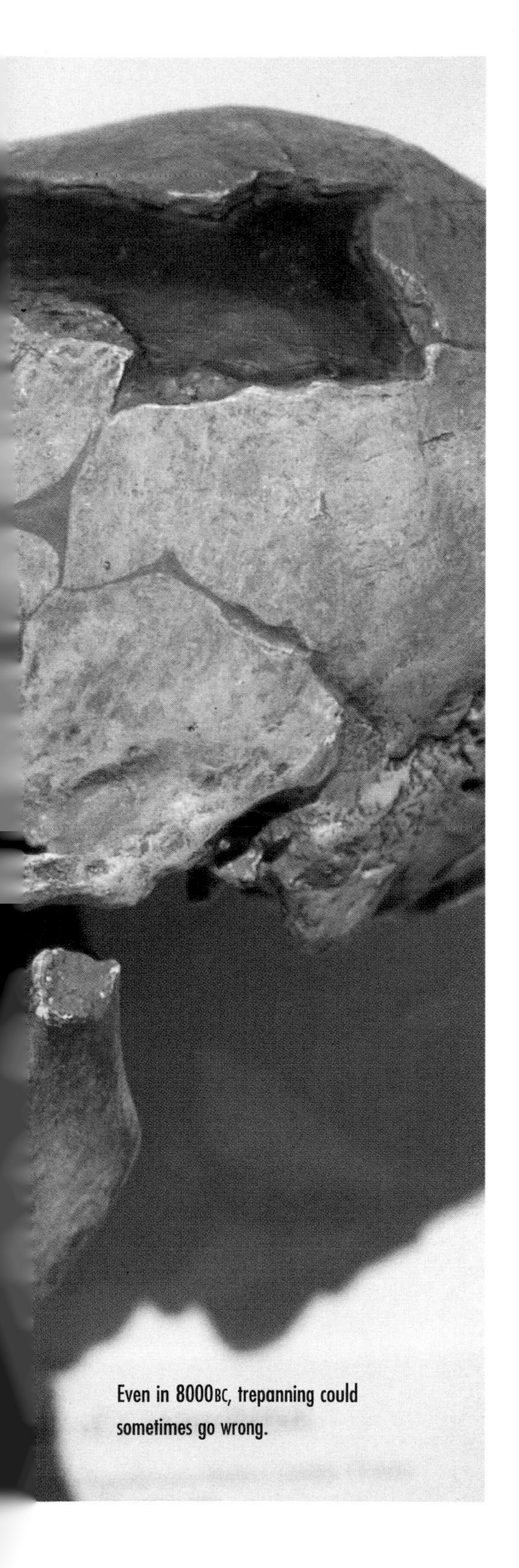
Even in 8000BC, trepanning could sometimes go wrong.

A HOLE IN THE HEAD

In Search of More Oxidation of Glucose with Joey Mellon and Amanda Feilding

People say it's bonkers, but the nineties will be all about bonkers people.
A trepanning enthusiast as quoted by the *Sunday Sport*

Joey Mellon will tell you that things started to go badly wrong for the human race about forty million years ago when man first decided to walk on two legs. The upright stance meant that while certain parts of the brain became more highly developed, the flow of blood in the head was limited by gravity, and this in turn caused other parts of our brains to dwindle or cease to function altogether (cf. day-time television presenters). Although there were certain obvious and undeniable benefits to mankind of being vertical, like the ability to develop speech, use tools and wear trousers without getting the knees grubby, the range of human consciousness, and therefore our levels of happiness, decreased. *Homo erectus* might have been vertical and bright, but Neanderthal man was horizontal and happy.

This revolutionary evolutionary theory was first put forward by a Dutch doctor, Bart Huges, in the 1960s, a decade in which, by complete coincidence, there was widespread exploration into higher states of consciousness using marijuana, mescaline, LSD and Moody Blues records. Bart Huges believed that to increase your level of vision, you must also increase the volume of blood in the brain. While it was possible to achieve this state by using methods like standing on your head, jumping from a hot bath into a cold bath or, indeed, by taking lots of hallucinogenic drugs, these practices could prove difficult, expensive or, indeed, fatal. Worst of all, the effects were, unless fatal, only temporary.

Dr Huges (pronounced 'Huggers', incidentally) noted that small children, whose skulls have not yet fully sealed, are often intensely imaginative, perceptive and free of the neuroses of adulthood. The facts that small children are also by and large incontinent, enjoy throwing mashed banana on the kitchen floor and are inordinately fond of yellow plastic ducks didn't deter the Dutchman. In order to liberate his brain from its bony prison, and once more to enjoy the conditions of infancy, he decided to remove a small disc of bone from his cranium. Or to put it another way, he drilled a hole in his head. When he emerged from the psychiatric hospital in which the narrow-minded Dutch authorities had thought fit to incarcerate him, Bart Huges set out to convert the world to the beneficial effects of head-holes.

Trepanation, as knocking a hole in your skull is known, does in fact pre-date the 1960s by many thousands of years, as do many members of the Moody Blues. A Stone Age skull with nine trepanations was exhibited for many years in the Natural History Museum, until it was removed from display on the grounds that it was too frightening for children (no doubt the same timid children who had spent the previous night watching *Nightmare On Elm Street 17*). In the Middle Ages, a hole in the head was believed to allow devils to escape from those possessed by them, and until the twentieth century trepanning was sometimes used to treat epilepsy sufferers and the insane. The most famous practitioners of trepanation were the Incas of Peru, but whether they used it as a cure, as a punishment or merely as a fashion accessory for all those colourful knitted jumpers you find in Kensington Market is unclear. Of course, before choosing the Incas as your role models, it might be worth noting that they are equally famous for practising human sacrifice.

Joey: 'There are different degrees of "high". Say the adult is zero and LSD is one hundred, and say some hash is fifty or sixty, then trepanation is probably thirty.' I wonder where he'd put a pint of cream sherry – minus forty?

Joey Mellon was born during the Second World War, and was educated at Eton and Oxford, where he was captain of the boxing team – another way of increasing the volume of blood in the brain. When he graduated he moved to London and embarked upon a career as a chartered accountant. Then one day, the sixties happened. One minute it was pin-striped suits and deferred taxation schemes, the next it was Carnaby Street and cannabis. Soon Joey had left his job and was living at the heart of Bohemian society, which, curiously enough, had chosen Torremolinos as its European headquarters. For a while, life was sweet and Joey had simple ambitions. 'I'd taken mescaline and I thought: Well, the only thing I really want now is more mescaline.' However, although it was still many years before Club 18–30 had decided to lure the nation's youth to the Costa Brava with the promise of naughty beach games involving an orange, an empty beer bottle and a 50-peseta piece, Joey and his friends soon found that Torremolinos was getting too crowded for their taste. In 1965 Joey went to Ibiza. His very first evening there was to prove momentous.

'LSD had just become available, and I'd heard of it, but no

one in my beatnik circle had actually taken it. It took me about a year to find it. I first took it in 1965, in Ibiza, and the person who gave it to me had trepanned himself.' It was, of course, none other than Bart Huges. 'I'd heard that someone had drilled a hole in his head to get high, and I thought: Come on, this is really carrying things too far; but when I met him, and he gave me my first trip on LSD and he described to me what was happening physiologically, it all made sense.' But then, after fifteen pints of lager, getting 'I Love Mother' tattooed on your left buttock makes sense. As most other British visitors to Torremolinos will testify.

Amanda: 'People say, "Aren't you frightened that when you walk through the jungle, a thorn might pierce you?" But I think there are a lot of other more frightening things, like snakes.'

Joey was deeply impressed with many of Huges' ideas and became a convert to the idea of trepanation as a means of expanding one's consciousness. 'It's about increasing the volume of blood in the brain capillaries. The oxidation of glucose is the brain metabolism. You burn wood on the fire, you get heat and light; you burn glucose in the brain, you get consciousness.'

Joey returned to London to spread the word. Headquarters was the World Psychedelic Centre in Chelsea, something which could only have existed in London in the sixties, or in California any time, and which was run by an acid guru calling himself Mike 'Holingshead' after the symbolic hole in the head or 'Third Eye' of Eastern mysticism. (Presumably Mike Thirdeye just didn't have the same ring to it.) Joey tried to convince him to get a real hole in the head but, despite the amount of LSD he was taking, he chose to remain Mike Holingshead by name but not by nature. Joey decided to seek wider publicity for his and Bart's theories. One of their converts was the American folk singer Julie Felix, and although she didn't go so far as to trepan herself, she did record some propaganda songs composed by Joey, which bore catchy titles like 'The Great Brain Robbery' and 'Brainbloodvolume'. Sadly, they never made it on to *Ready Steady Go*. Joey and Bart agreed to do an in-depth interview with the *Sunday People* and spent an entire night expounding their theories to two tabloid journalists from that paper. Astonishingly enough, none of their thesis on membrane pulsation or glucose oxidation appeared. Instead, the paper published a picture of Bart Huges under the headline 'This Dangerous Idiot Should Be Thrown Out'. Nice to know some things haven't changed in the last thirty years.

In 1970 Joey decided that he had finally better put his money where his mouth was, or rather, put a hole where his skull was. He purchased a manual drill from a surgical store, bought some local anaesthetic, needles and a scalpel and set about the task. He wasn't overly worried about damaging his brain: 'The brain itself is like a blancmange – it's a very soft organ,' but even so, drilling a hole in your own head is not as easy as it doesn't sound.

Warning: those of a nervous disposition should not read the next four paragraphs.

Joey's first attempt to trepan himself failed when the needles broke off in his head, but on the second attempt he actually managed to expose the bone of his skull, just above the hairline. The drill, which was 'rather like a corkscrew, only with a circular ring of teeth at the end of a column', proved difficult to operate by himself. 'It is difficult to do it yourself with a hand trepan because it's rather like trying to uncork a bottle from the inside.' I'm sure this analogy does make sense – it's just a little gruesome trying to work it out. Joey's partner, the artist Amanda Feilding, returned from a visit to Amsterdam in the middle of the night to find Joey attempting the operation. Immediately she leapt to his aid, by forcing the drill spike into his skull until the circular teeth bit and he was able to crank the handle himself. But unfortunately, although not that surprisingly, at this point Joey fainted. They still hadn't managed to drill all the way through the bone, and were forced to abandon the attempt. All this was still not enough to deter Joey, and the next time the operation was more successful:

'After some time there was an ominous sounding *schlurp* and the sound of bubbling. I drew the trepan out and the gurgling continued. It sounded like air bubbles running under the skull as they were pressed out. I looked at the trepan and there was a bit of bone on it. At last! On closer inspection I saw that the disc of bone was much deeper on one side than on the other. Obviously the trepan had not been straight and had gone through at one point only, then the piece of bone had snapped off and come out. I was reluctant to start drilling again for fear of damaging the brain membranes with the deeper part while I was drilling through the rest or of breaking off a splinter . . . Amanda was sure I was through. There was no other explanation for the schlurping noises. I decided to call it a day. At that time I thought that any hole would do, no matter what size. I bandaged up my head and cleared away the mess.'

But Joey, despite what Amanda said, was still worried that size really does matter. He decided to make one last attempt. It had become clear to him that he needed a more powerful tool, so this time he used an electric drill that he could operate with a foot pedal. Again his initial attempt was doomed to failure. Half an hour into the operation the electric cable burnt out. Could he get an electrician round to fix it straightaway? Of course not. It's difficult enough trying to get one when it's a case of 'All the lights in the house have gone and I think I smell burning' let alone 'I'm in the middle of boring a 3mm hole into my cranium and the drill-flex has fused.'

For Joey Mellon it was a case of fifth time lucky. 'This time I was not in any doubt. The drill head went in at least an inch deep through the hole. A great gush of blood followed my withdrawal of the drill. In the mirror I could see the blood in the hole

'The drill was rather like a corkscrew, only with a circular ring of teeth at the end of a column.'

rising and falling with the pulsation of the brain.' Joey had at last struck brain-blood.

OK, it's safe to start reading again.

By now it was the start of the seventies. The Age of Aquarius was busy dawning and Amanda was also keen to be trepanned, but not at all keen to do the job herself. 'I was very against going through with the operation – I mean, who wants to drill a hole in their head? It wasn't something one looks forward to doing one Sunday afternoon.' But then neither was watching *Poldark*, and yet millions of us did it every week.

She embarked upon a long and fruitless search for a doctor who would perform the operation for her. Some were horrified, others, although they were not against it in principle, were afraid of losing their jobs if they bored into a healthy person's skull. One Hindu brain surgeon agreed to do the operation in India, but Amanda couldn't raise the necessary cash for the journey. Eventually she realized that if she wanted a hole in her head, she'd have to put it there herself. 'I thought: Well, I'm a sculptress, I drill holes in bone all the time, I'll just get my chisel and do it myself – auto-sculpture.'

As it turned out, you'll be relieved to learn, Amanda's operation went a lot more smoothly than Joey's. 'Joey's trepanation was a lot of examples of how not to trepan yourself, and mine was one perfect attempt.'

Stop reading.

Amanda describes her operation. 'You pick your spot. You can do it anywhere, any hole in the cranial cavity will have the same effect, but there's less blood on the median line. Infection is the biggest danger, so you shave it, and then anaesthetize so there's no sensation.'

You can read the next bit.

'You cut the skin, hold it back and then insert the drill. I used a flat-bottom drill so it wouldn't slip in any way and puncture the membrane. And then you just drill away, for an amazingly long time. The drill did break down, but I knew it would break down, so I had a spare.'

Sorry about that, it really is safe from now on.

D.I.Y. TREPANNING FOR BEGINNERS

Step One: trim the hairline.
Step Two: frame bald patch.
Step Three: check apparatus.
Step Four: there may be a small amount of blood.
Step Five: and here's one I did earlier.

1

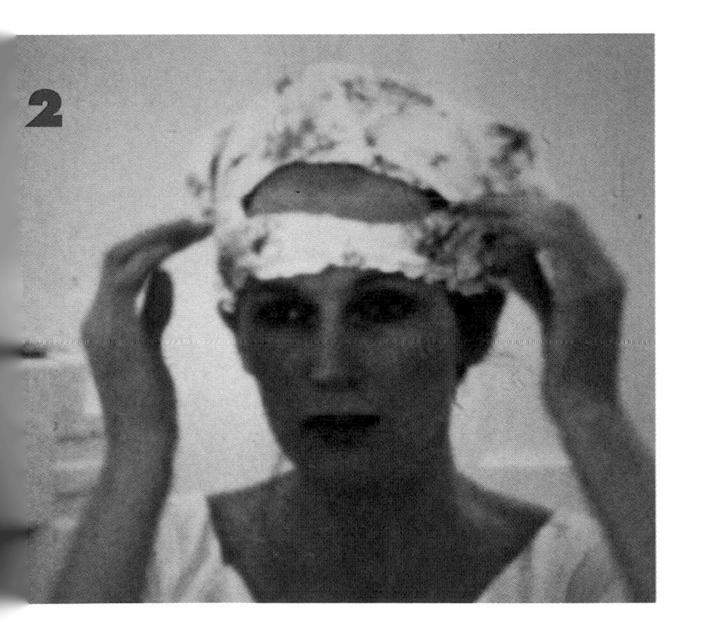

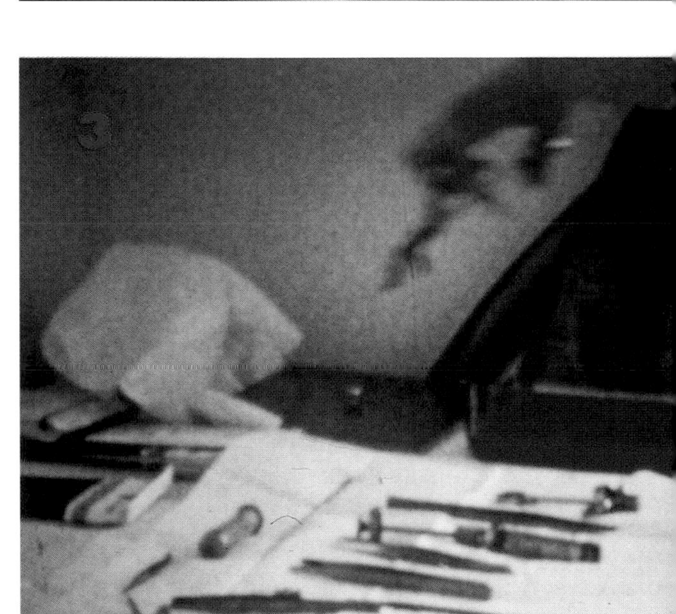

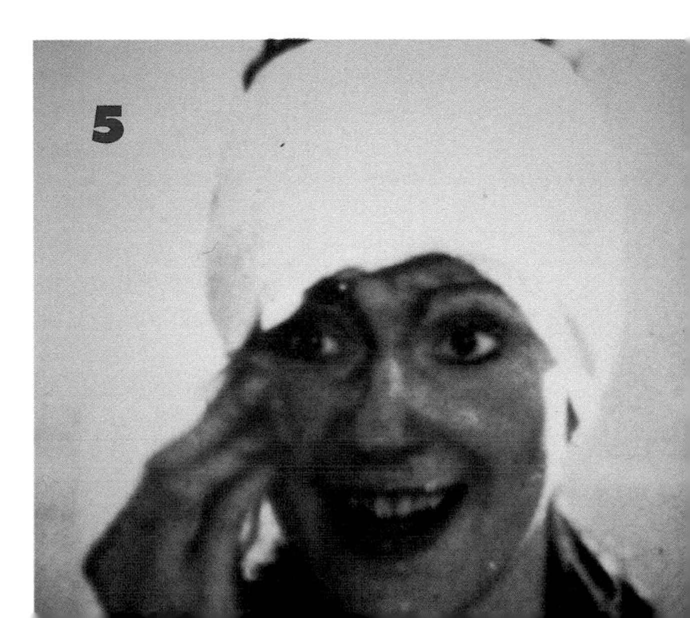

Amanda had also decided to record her entire operation on Super 8 and titled the film *Heartbeat in the Brain.* It has been shown to small, invited audiences around the world. Once, after it was shown in London, a critic reported that 'the air was filled with rich thuds as the audience began dropping off their seats one by one like ripe plums'. Martin Scorsese is currently rumoured to be planning a remake.

So – was it all worth it? Both Joey and Amanda say they started to feel the benefits about four hours after the operation: 'Gradually you feel yourself rising a little bit and then you just stay there. And that's awfully nice,' says Joey.

Amanda thought it was 'nice' too. 'I noticed a kind of silence in the head. It was like waves of a tide coming in, this lovely peaceful silence, and it was very nice.' Personally, I think if I'd just shaved my head, bored a hole through the skullbone and spattered the room with blood I'd want it to be a bit more than just 'nice', but both Joey and Amanda insist that that's not the point.

'It doesn't change your personality, you know, it's not big, you're not suddenly someone else or anything like that,' says Joey.

Amanda adds, 'It's not auroras and bright lights or whatever, it's the same old ball game, with just a little bit more energy. It's a healthier, happier level from which to have your problems.'

With some trepidation, I asked Joey and Amanda to show me their head-holes, and found, to my relief, that there was nothing there to disturb even the most squeamish individual – which, coincidentally, I happen to be. In fact, there was nothing to see at all. The skin grows over the hole almost immediately after the operation, and now, twenty odd years later, all you can feel is a small indentation. Joey insists that is an extremely minor surgical procedure. 'It would be no more difficult than going in for a blood donor thing. You'd go into a caravan or something in the car park, a nurse would trepan you, you'd come out with a bandage round your head and you're up there for the rest of your life.' 'Up there' meaning a higher level of consciousness, if the operation goes right, or heaven, if it doesn't.

Both Joey and Amanda maintain their belief in the benefits of trepanning. Both have lectured extensively on the subject and Amanda has even stood as a parliamentary candidate for trepanation on the National Health, arguing for greater research to be carried out by the medical authorities. Joey has also written and published a book about his experiences called *Bore Hole.* So are Joey and Amanda hole bores?

'Le Manoir aux Trous dans la Tête.' – Joey and Amanda's home near Oxford.

If you were hoping to encounter a couple of sixties acid casualties, sitting cross-legged on bean-bags in a haze of joss-sticks, you would be sorely disappointed. Joey and Amanda are both articulate and disarmingly normal people. They live in a large, beautiful and exquisitely furnished manor house in Oxfordshire. Joey runs a thriving fine-art publishing business and Amanda continues to paint and sculpt. They have two children who are still at the age when their brains pulsate and the glucose simmers away happily in the brain pan. If they grow up and rebel against their parents, the worst that can happen to them is that they'll become insurance salesmen, live in a semi-detached in Ruislip and shop at MFI.

Joey and Amanda don't make extravagant claims for trepanation, neither do they advocate that we all rush off and get holes drilled in our heads. They both say that they believe that trepanning has made them each a little less neurotic, a little more childlike, a little happier. I believe them, but as far as doing it myself goes, I think I'd rather move to Bolton. . .

WHEREVER I LAY MY HAT: MARSHALL HOLT

Wherever I lay my hat, that's my hat-stand.
R. Curtis

Globetrotter, Marshall Holt, who moved in search of happiness from . . .

Marshall Holt was born at 45 Legendre Street, in Bolton, Lancashire. Not in itself a remarkable feat. As a child his greatest pleasure was walking in the nearby hills, known locally as the Jolly Brows for reasons too Lancastrian to go into. After he married, Marshall and his wife Joyce made the gargantuan move of some two and a half miles to 47 Harden Drive, Bolton, where they lived and raised their family. Marshall worked as a boilerman with a local firm, and three times a year he and his family would take holidays in the Lake District. Perfectly reasonable behaviour. The years passed, the way only years can, the children grew up and started families of their own and gradually Marshall began to become dissatisfied with his life.

'I used to look round and I thought to myself: No, no, I'm in a rut. Like I said I got this feeling, as I was in a rut. And it gradually got worse and worse and worse. Now, what we'd been doing, we'd been going up to Lakes for holidays and we really enjoyed it up there. And I thought, I'd love to live up there. So one day I said to the wife, I said, "How would you fancy packing everything up and going and living in the country miles from nowhere? Away from all this?" And she said, "Yeah, it'd be quite nice." So I thought: Well, that's it then; and then, before we knew it, we'd got this little house up there, we'd sold up down in Bolton and we buzzed off to Lakes.'

And so Marshall and Joyce moved to Westrigg in the village of Long Marten in the Lake District. For a while everything seemed perfect . . . Not that long a while, as things turned out.

'Oh, yeah, it were gorgeous – I mean, out of this world. The people were nice, the view were out of this world.'

But the holiday feeling started to wear off . . .

'After about four or five months, I got this sneaking feeling, something weren't quite right. Then it gradually dawned. Boredom were setting in. There was absolutely nothing to do. In Bolton, I'd say to Joyce, "Where shall we go?" and I could think of a dozen places we could buzz off to. But up there, there was

. . . this house at 45 Legendre Street, in Bolton, to . . .

. . . 47 Harden Drive, Bolton, to . . .

. . . this house, in Long Marten in the Lake District, to . . .

absolutely nothing. All we had were Dufton Dance once a month, and the pubs, and that's all there was. The peace and quiet which had attracted us in the first place were gradually destroying us. We finished up more or less bored to death.'

And so Marshall began to contemplate the unthinkable – to look for a life beyond Long Marten and the delights of the Dufton Dance.

'I was looking for something but I didn't know what. The complexity of it, you wouldn't believe it. Sometimes I've sat down and I've said, "What do you want? What are you looking for?" I used to sit there and argue with myself. "Look, make up your mind. What do you want?"'

The answer he came up with was about as far away from Long Marten as you can get . . .

'And then one day I thought: Yeah – Australia's definitely it. Let's get out of this country altogether and make an absolute fresh life right from the word go.'

Now it was just a question of running the idea of moving again past Joyce.

'Well, Joyce and I were having a chat one night and I said to her, "It's not quite right. I love the place, everything's smashing, but it's not quite right, you know, it's too dead." And I said to her, "How do you fancy going to Australia? Let's buzz off to Australia, we'll emigrate, start a new life there. It's an up and coming place, how do you fancy it?"

And so before you could say 'Jack Robinson', or before Joyce could say, 'Actually I quite like it here,' Marshall had packed up their belongings, sold their furniture and found a buyer for their house in the Lake District.

The day of the move dawned. 'It was a January morning, there were about six inches of snow on the ground. And I said to Joyce, "Don't worry about this," I said. "When we get over to Australia, beautiful sunshine, everything'll be absolutely perfect."'

And for a while everything was perfect . . . Only this time the 'while' was slightly shorter . . .

'My family, who lived over there, had sorted everything out. I had a job, no worries, they met us at Sydney Airport. That was the beginning of it. Lovely weather – it was champion – and I thought: Yeah, this is definitely it, I'm going to be happy here.'

However . . .

'After about six weeks, you know, I got these niggling doubts, creeping into my mind. And I thought, Er, no, forget it, shrug

. . . one of these flats in Sydney, Australia, and finally . . .

them off, forget it, this is home now, this is where we're staying. But unfortunately it doesn't work like that.'

Apparently Australia isn't the paradise it's cracked up to be. Unless you're an entomologist.

'Australia has got its drawbacks. Mainly, the thing that's never mentioned is the insects. There's millions of them, absolute millions. I mean, you see on telly, don't you, they're having these barbecues and what-have-you, in the garden, because the weather's lovely, and you can always plan in advance, but what they don't show you is the insects. The gnats – the mozzies, they call them – come from nowhere. They bite you, honestly, they're biting you all over. You're stood there constantly spraying your arms, spraying your legs, spraying all parts of your body to keep these things away. In the end I used to say to Joyce, "Ooh, forget it, let's go inside." It's the same with the Australian people – once mozzies are attacking they don't stand there, like it shows on telly, they're all in the house out of it. I mean, here in Britain you've got your mozzies, especially up in Scotland, but not like Australia. I mean they're like damned birds there, mosquitoes.'

Something to bear in mind when you next watch a barbecue scene in *Neighbours*. But there's more than just *Neighbours* and the mozzies to put paid to any plans you might have had of emigrating . . .

'There's insects over there that we've never seen – stick insects, praying mantis . . . One night we were watching television and I said, "Oh, I fancy an apple." So I went into the kitchen, switched the light on, you know, to get an apple, and there were this black thing in the middle of the floor. I'm not kidding, it was like something out of a horror film. It were about an inch and a half long, and it had three-inch antennas, and it were motionless, it just stood there staring at us. What it were, I've no idea at all, but it was the ugliest damned thing I've ever seen, and it were massive. I thought: There's only room in here for one of us, and it's going to be me. So I went for the spray. I thought: I'll give it a good do. But honestly, it took twenty minutes to kill it. Now, over here you see an insect in the house, you give it a quick spray and in about two seconds it's dead. But not over there – that's what they're like over there.'

After the monster insect incident, Marshall began to get more and more homesick.

'I started finding myself looking for excuses. I started looking for all the things in Australia that I didn't like. Where we lived must have been in the flight path from Sydney Airport, because the aircraft used to go flying over the top, pretty high, you know, but they'd be flying across. And I found myself thinking, I wonder if he's going to England? There's a song that goes, "A ship stands rigged and waiting in the harbour, to take me back once more to England's shores", and I were singing it constantly, I just couldn't get it out of my head. And I had all these photographs I'd taken of the Jolly Brows, a pile about half an inch thick of all the different parts of the Jollys. And I thought about these photos, and I thought, let me just have another look at the Jollys. And so I got them out. It were fatal, absolutely fatal, worst thing I could have done. I went through 'em, I went through 'em again and I went through 'em again. That was it. I had to come home. I'd had enough, it wasn't right. There was no happiness.'

It was time to broach the subject of moving again to Joyce. After all, she'd only been uprooted from two homes in the last two and a half years, moved to the other side of the world and spent less than six months there. How could she possibly object?

'I loved the place, so I said to Marshall, "Well, *you* go back. Stay with your brother for six months to see how you feel, and if you still feel the same, well, all right, I'll come back." But, no, I couldn't do that, could I? Because the next day he went down to the booking office and booked our tickets home. Without telling me, drew all our money out of the bank, booked our tickets and said, "That's it." I had no money – I had to go home. But I was very disappointed because I didn't think we had given it long enough.'

So, once again, Marshall and Joyce Holt packed up their belongings and headed for the airport.

Marshall was delighted. 'When I were on the plane and we'd left Australia, that's when my happiness started coming back. All I wanted to do was get back to Bolton and carry on where we'd left off a couple of years before. I'd missed it all you know, all the little things. So when I got back there, I thought, Yeah, Manchester Airport, and then we got back into Bolton and I knew I were back in my own surroundings. This is where I'm happy. I didn't realize it at the time, but this is the place.'

And how does Joyce feel about being back in Bolton?

'I'm happy here now. We're both happier. I realize that now. Because Marshall wouldn't have been happy in Australia, would he? So if he weren't happy, I wouldn't have been happy. So we're back.'

Back to Stay?

'It's like the old adage, isn't it? You know, the grass is always greener on the other side. It's not. You just take it for granted while you're here, when you've been here for ages. You think, We'll buzz off somewhere, and you find out that it's not there – you've left it at home. All of a sudden you're back and you know that, Yeah, this is where I should have been all the time.'

So, in other words, you had to change in order to find out that you didn't need to change?

'I had to make a move, before I really appreciated what I'd got here. You know what I mean – you take the little things for granted, don't you? Then you make the move and it comes back to you that you left what you really wanted at home.'

. . . back to this house – in Bolton. (Roughly three minutes' walk from 45 Legendre Street.)

DEVOTION

Hopefully Devoted to You

HIGHWAYS
TO HEALTH
AND
HAPPINESS

Joy is the serious business of heaven.
C. S. Lewis

If Jesus Christ were to come today people would not even crucify him. They would ask him to dinner, and hear what he had to say, and make fun of it.
Thomas Carlyle

In both Europe and North America, researchers have discovered that religiously active people score above average marks in the happiness stakes. Religious people are apparently much less likely to become delinquent, to abuse drugs or alcohol, to divorce or commit suicide. Statistics show that they're even physically healthier than non-religious people, although perhaps that's because of the lack of drugs, alcohol and indeed suicide.

Although religion can't prevent suffering it can provide support during a crisis, and lend meaning and purpose to life. Members of Churches or religious organizations cite the benefits of having a network of social support and a feeling of 'belonging to a group of trusted friends', although admittedly Joan of Arc might possibly disagree.

Religion may be the opiate of the masses, as Karl Marx said, but then, perhaps, so is Marxism. There is no evidence to show that one particular brand of faith washes your soul whiter than any other brand. Rather, it is the devotion to that faith and the sense of purpose that it brings which is responsible for the increased levels of happiness. Sacrilegious as it may sound, there is no evidence that worshipping God brings greater happiness than worshipping Michelle Pfeiffer, although on balance you probably stand a better chance of going out with God. On the surface, dedicated socialist Ian Saville, whose magic act is permeated by Marxist rhetoric, has little in common with Kent housewife Mavis Righini, who devotes her life to nursing sick hedgehogs. Yet experts argue that devotion to a cause, a job, a hobby and any political party (with the obvious exception of the Liberal Democrats) can bring the same benefits, at least in this world, as conventional religion.

To see if there was any truth in this theory, I went in search of six devoted people: a Christian, a rock fan, a workaholic, a Buddhist monk, a lone yachtsman and, perhaps most dedicated of all, a supporter of Northampton Town Football Club.

Claire: devoted to the Wildhearts.
(Readers under the age of eighteen should refrain from reading the wall-posters.)

THE WILDHEARTS, THE COBBLERS AND GOD: CLAIRE, JACKIE AND EMMA

You are never dedicated to something you have complete confidence in. No one is fanatically shouting that the sun is going to rise tomorrow. They know it's going to rise tomorrow. When people are fanatically dedicated to political or religious faiths or any other kinds of dogmas or goals, it's always because these dogmas or goals are in doubt.
Robert T. Pirsig, *Zen and the Art of Motorcycle Maintenance*

'Shut Your Fucking Mouth And Use Your Fucking Brains' is the title of one of The Wildhearts' most popular ditties. I would be tempted to describe The Wildhearts as a heavy metal band but, according to Claire Templeman, they don't like people putting labels on their work. (One imagines this must make life extremely difficult for the staff in Our Price.) Claire Templeman is The Wildhearts' No. 1 fan. When Claire heard their first EP three years ago, she was an instant convert. Now she has devoted her life to following the group; she buys all their records in every format (even though she doesn't own a CD player), collects every magazine that mentions them, buys all their merchandise, writes frequently to the band members and their record company and, whenever possible, goes to see them play. She's the sort of person for whom the word 'fanatic' was invented.

Claire is twenty years old, unemployed and lives in Yeovil with her parents and younger brother. Her bedroom walls are papered with Wildhearts posters, photocopied pictures of band members, magazine cuttings and a letter she received from the band's bass player, Danny, in reply to a card she sent him when she heard he was sick. Claire even spent £8 on placing an advertisement in *Kerrang!* to check with other fans whether her collection was missing anything. (It wasn't.) In fact, Claire spends all of what little money she has on her Wildhearts obsession, but she says she doesn't see it as a hardship because it's what she wants to do. It's probably more of a hardship for her parents and brother, who have to put up with Claire endlessly playing songs like 'Shitsville' and 'Caffeine Bomb' at top volume.

The Wildhearts have yet to achieve the massive following of bands like Aerosmith or Take That. As far as Claire knows, there are only two other Wildhearts fans in Yeovil: her next-door neighbour, James, whom she converted by playing their records so loud that he had no other option but to listen to them through the party wall, and some other bloke she has seen in the street wearing a Wildhearts T-shirt – although admittedly it may just have been given to him by his Auntie Vera last Christmas.

Before she discovered The Wildhearts, Claire listened to all kinds of bands- Love-Hate, the Sex Pistols, the Clash, but in the years AW (After Wildhearts) all other bands have paled into insignificance. The Wildhearts make Claire happy. Their philosophy, 'Just do what you want it doesn't matter what everyone says', is now her philosophy. Although Ginger, their lead singer, said, 'We are not gods, we're just ordinary blokes,' Claire says that to her they are gods: 'I don't think they realize the effect they have on people like me – although they should know by now – I tell them all the time in letters and stuff . . . It's almost like a spiritual thing – it's someone you can follow, and because I have been with them almost from the start of their career, I feel like I have grown with them like a family. They're so welcoming to their fans and when you're there at a concert, you feel like it's your place. If they ever split up I would just be so upset.'

▲ Emma and Hannah: devoted to God.
'My relationship with God is better than with my best friend Hannah. God is perfect whereas me and Hannah aren't.' (Emma)

Three years ago, Emma Mortimer was saved. A friend invited her to a birthday party and when she turned up at the address she'd been given, she discovered that it was the Rainbow Church, located in the old Rainbow Theatre in Finsbury Park. 'It's not the sort of church you see on *Songs of Praise*. We meet in a theatre and we have a full worship band – bass guitars, drums, keyboards, acoustic guitars, all things like that. We have very jazzy songs, we have dancers who dance with massive colourful flags. We do dramas, we do live art and stuff like that.'

Emma thinks her church is more relevant to young people than many traditional places of Christian worship. No tea parties on the vicarage lawn and 'We will now sing hymn 87: "He Who Would Valiant Be . . ." for this lot.' 'In some churches God is this amazing great big being that you can't touch, you can't speak to and you've got to take your shoes off and all that. But here God is really real, and you can see God in people's lives, and he's a mate.'

Emma started to visit the church every week, but it was six months before she became a Christian. 'I was like: Yeah, I like this, but I'm not into the commitment.' One night Emma went to a prayer meeting to hear her friend Vanessa sing, and afterwards stayed at her house because she'd missed the last bus home. That night her friend gave her a prophecy. 'God says you have got to get your bum in gear and stop ignoring him,' she said, and that really hit me. The next morning I woke up and I was really scared and I felt sick and I said to her, 'Look, this Christian thing, I don't want to do it.' And she laughed at me and said, 'But you've already done it.'

Emma was seventeen when she found God. Since then she has devoted herself passionately to the church, slavishly adhering to that Eleventh Commandment: 'Thou shalt get thy bum in gear.' She attends services every Thursday and Saturday, and often has several extra meetings during the week. The Rainbow is an evangelistic Church and it is Emma's duty to spread the word. So far she has chalked up at least two souls: her friend Hannah, and Blair, who is now her husband – so something of a double whammy there. 'Two days after I started going out with him he was saved. He's much better than me. He's only been saved a year and a half and he's already at my level.' Emma says Christianity has changed her life. 'Before I became a Christian I thought I was fine. I was going along great, I was going out with the girls, getting drunk, I was out clubbing and partying, and it was funny, because I was the biggest atheist ever. And then I became a Christian and it just opens your eyes and gives you a totally different outlook on life. Now I'm a lot more fulfilled within myself. Fulfilment obviously produces happiness, and so I'm happy.'

Emma says joining the church has made her much more confident. 'God's given me a real sense of security. I might still think: Oh, gosh, I feel really self-conscious in this top, but God says, 'No, you look great,' and I think: All right, fine, OK. I know that God's in control, whatever happens to me good or bad, God's in control. I couldn't live without God now – I'd curl up in a ball and dry up.'

▼ Jackie: devoted to the Cobblers.
Jackie Wiseman has been a supporter of Northampton Town since 1988, hence her expression.

Jackie Wiseman was converted in 1988. She first got into football after the World Cup in 1986 but it was two years before she went to a home game of her local team, Northampton Town FC. By the end of the first game (which they lost 1-0 to Darlington in a dull wind-swept slug-out) she was completely hooked – she loved the atmosphere, she loved being part of a surging crowd, she loved the team. Jackie, a twenty-two-year-old teacher-training student, says it's not so much an act of devotion as an addiction. You can see her point. Northampton Town, a.k.a. 'the Cobblers', have the peculiar distinction of being the only team ever to have gone from the fourth to the third to the second to the first division and then straight back down again in consecutive seasons. That was back in the sixties, and they have languished at the bottom of the bottom division ever since. (Some might say it's not so much an addiction as a form of mild insanity.) The Cobblers are certainly no glamour team either – no Georgie Bests or Kevin Keegans, no Plattys or Giggsys or Cantona-ys, not even the occasional Vinnie Jones. No cup finals at Wembley, no forays into Europe, not even, to be honest, many wins. If the Cobblers do well this season they get to stay in league football. If they fail, they face the ultimate ignominy of being relegated to the Vauxhall Conference – football's amateur league.

Jackie Wiseman says she wouldn't ever try to convert anyone else to supporting the Cobblers, which has probably saved her several years of her life in wasted effort, but neither would she ever consider abandoning her team. Since 1988 she has never missed more than a couple of games per season, including away matches, and can't imagine life without football (well, without Northampton Town, anyway). 'I'd be lost without them. I don't know what I'd do with myself on a Saturday.'

Claire is going to see a Wildhearts gig at the Bierkeller in Bristol. For the last six months she has been trying to save about £10 a week to pay for tickets, transport and all the Wildhearts merchandise she is hoping to buy at the concert. That is to say any she doesn't already have – a Wildhearts fridge magnet, maybe. The night before the longed for event she is too excited to sleep and she gets up at 6 a.m. to sort out her outfit for the concert. This time she has chosen a skimpy black dress, black tights, black suede thigh-high Puss-in-Boots boots ('Ten miles to London Town and still no sign of Dick!') and a Wildhearts T-shirt, which is carefully draped and tied around her waist. Claire wears her long, wavy hair loose and lots of make-up: pale skin, red lips, black eye-liner. Around her neck she hangs a black ribbon and a large silver cross. Claire is tiny and looks very young (at least to anyone old enough to remember using a threepenny bit or sewing inserts into their jeans) and by the time she has finished she looks like a cross between Morticia Adams and a contestant on *Mini-Pops* (another reference for the over-thirties).

'I get really possessive and jealous when other people fancy them and are mad over them. I don't know why I should get like that, like I'm going to kill them or something.' Fortunately for Claire not many other people do fancy them.

Claire likes to keep abreast of the band's movements and, to this end, phones their record company and fan club almost every day. The tour was meant to start a few months back, but was postponed when Ginger broke his arm hitting a kitchen cupboard while under the influence of alcohol. (Y'know, the way you do.) As soon as she found out the new dates, Claire immediately started phoning the Bristol box office, and continued to phone every day until the tickets finally came on sale. She travels to Wildhearts gigs with her faithful convert, her next-door neighbour, James. Last time they went to see the band, at Poole Arts Centre, she insisted on getting there by 11 a.m. in order to see the band arrive for their sound check at 4 p.m. As soon as she catches sight of the group Claire starts to shake with nervous excitement and often starts crying.

You'd think that this would be just about as much fun as a person could take in one day, but Claire's next priority is to stake out a place at the front of the queue so that as soon as the doors open she can get a spot by the foot of the stage. It astonishes Claire that people call themselves fans when they don't even have all the band's records. She knows all the words to all their songs and sings along to them during the concert. 'Whaddo I do to get close to you,/Whaddo I do to get close to you – ah fuck it!' – one of Bacharach's finest.

Claire has met all the Wildhearts and has all their autographs. She even had her picture taken with Ginger, and Rich the drummer, and got them published in a fanzine. 'One person wrote back and said I was a slag and a bimbo and then someone else wrote back and said they didn't think I was a tart – they thought I was fat and ugly and the Wildhearts would be blind to spend a night with me. But, you know, it was only his opinion.' Actually Claire would be quite happy to sleep with any of the band, but she doesn't think it's very likely to happen. 'They're not interested in money or fame or women or anything like that. Anyway, they're not a band that got where they are because of their looks because, to be honest, most people don't fancy them, really.'

After the high of the concert and the thrill of meeting her heroes, Claire comes down to earth with a resounding thud. 'When the concert's finished you're still on a real buzz for about an hour or so afterwards, but when I get home it's a real anti-climax. Last time I was depressed for about a week afterwards. I just couldn't do anything. I kept thinking: This time yesterday I was with them, this time yesterday I was seeing them in concert. I just wanted to go off with them in their tour bus and never come back again.'

▼ 'They're really genuine and down to earth – they're not like: "Oh, I'm a rock star and I haven't got time for you." They'll sit there and talk to you and they're just really nice.'
Claire chatting away to the band.

▲ 'I don't have a religion, I've got a relationship with God. Just like I could be your friend, I'm God's friend. I chat to him in the mornings, in the bath, on the toilet, wherever I am.'
That's a closer relationship than most friends would ever wish to have.

Emma's worst times are on Saturday nights or Sunday mornings before she goes to church. 'You can feel really crap because Satan knows you are going to worship God and something's going to happen – "Let's give this girl a headache, let's make her have a row with her husband." Someone at the church has done a survey on it and found that most couples row before church or before a meeting. Because it's in Satan's best interest to destroy you.'

This Sunday Emma wears jeans and a jacket and carefully applied but understated make-up. The congregation at the Rainbow Church dresses in casual clothes. Just as well, really, because the Rainbow – formerly the largest rock venue in London, is now an unheated, semi-derelict shell. (Actually they've done a pretty good job of preserving it. The last time I was there was for a Yes concert in 1972, and as far as I remember the place was exactly the same.) About fifty or sixty people mill about the room before the service gets under way. There are spontaneous group hugathons, and a lot of spontaneous outbursts of dancing and flag waving (in so far as you can be spontaneous when presumably you must have had to make the flag and lug it all the way there on the bus). The congregation ranges in age from the very young indeed (some of whom are deposited under a painted sign saying 'Baby Hang-Out') to the church elders, who might be as aged as thirty-five. It's like a sixties Happening, only with Jesus and lemonade instead of Lindisfarne and dope.

Emma explains their philosophy: 'The Rainbow is very much not a religious church, 'cos we're constantly doing things in new ways, and trying to stay up to the minute, 'cos God is up to the minute, and he will always be up to the minute, he will always be in 1995 and then next year he'll be in 1996.' In this regard he can be considered as not a million miles away from the rest of us. This year they seem to be into standing with their arms in the air, singing jolly-sounding hymns and calling out things like 'Let's focus our eyes on Jesus!' or 'I want something supernatural to happen.' Sometimes something supernatural does happen: someone might suddenly keel over (it's called 'Going Over in the Spirit'), or be given a prophecy, and sometimes someone will even start to 'talk in tongues', i.e., gabble in an unintelligible language. 'It's basically a language between you and God. Very powerful stuff. It's something Satan can't understand, which is a key point, because it pisses him off.' No doubt a sentiment that many customers in French restaurants can share.

◄ One of the congregation at the Rainbow Church, of which Emma Mortimer is now a member. She was converted after being given this prophecy: 'God says you have got to get your bum in gear and stop ignoring him.'

Emma loves the atmosphere. 'We all share a love and you can tell everyone is so happy. I just close my eyes and get into worshipping God. Sometimes I can feel the Holy Spirit go into my body and I get butterflies in my stomach and start to shake because I am full of God.' I wondered whether the freezing temperature of the Rainbow might have something to do with the shaking – but what do I know? After all, according to their beliefs, I'm going straight to hell. Still, at least it might be a bit warmer.

► Supporting the Cobblers: the triumph of hope over experience?
'I'd be lost without them. I don't know what I'd do with myself on a Saturday.'

The Cobblers are away to Shrewsbury Town in a crunch game. If they win the last two games of the season and get the six vital points, they can ward off relegation. If they lose or draw, their only hope is that Darlington, the other team at the bottom of the division, will also do badly in their games. But unlike any other sport, 'in football anything can happen'. At 9 a.m. Jackie dons her Northampton strip – white with claret sleeves – wraps her claret and white Northampton scarf around her neck and goes to James End, Northampton, to board the double-decker supporters' coach. Considering their team has lost the last four matches, they're in high spirits. There are several loud renditions (to the tune of 'Land of Hope and Glory') of 'We'll follow you Cobblers – Over land and sea – and water! We'll follow the Cobblers – on to Vi-ic-toreee' and, to the tune of 'She'll Be Coming Round the Mountain', the rather more unusual football chant (which I'm sure had nothing to do with my presence) of 'You can stick it up your arse, BBC.'

Jackie sits quietly, gazing out of the window at the gorgeous scenery flanking the M6. 'I'm a bit nervous the morning of a game,' she confides, 'and if they were ever relegated, which they

8 611
MPTON
N F.C.

◀ 'If they were ever relegated, which they won't be probably, I should be gutted.'
Jackie Wiseman, one week before Northampton Town faced certain relegation.

won't be probably, I should be gutted.' After being sick as a parrot, presumably. It's nerve-racking enough for supporters of big, successful teams like Manchester United (to pluck an example from thin air), and it's a time-consuming and expensive pastime to attend matches in any division. But it takes a particular kind of devotion to give your allegiance to a team whose greatest hope is not to come bottom of the third division. Perhaps there were other factors at work. I asked Jackie if her enjoyment of the team was purely to do with football, or whether she found any of the players quite attractive. 'You haven't seen the team, obviously,' was the swift retort. (Not that that seemed to matter to Claire.)

The Northampton fans were ecstatic when, twenty-five minutes into the first half, their striker Kevin Wilkins chipped one into the corner of the net. 'We shall not be moved . . . we are staying up,' rose from the terraces. But lo – disaster struck when Shrewsbury's Wayne Clarke equalized at the start of the second, and fifteen minutes from the end they went ahead with a goal by Ray Woods. Even the news that Darlington had also lost was not enough to raise the spirits of the fans as they trooped back to the car park for the long journey home. It was going to take one of Emma's miracles to save the Cobblers now. Devotion indeed, but how can Jackie claim that this brings her genuine happiness? 'It's just belonging to a club, really, everyone's supporting the team. I suppose it's the camaraderie, really. Even after we've lost and I go home thinking: Oh, I'm never going again, by the next Saturday I'm all raring to go for the game.'

▼ Northampton Town score a goal, as an airborne pig is sighted over the ground.

TOM McNALLY

Proud Holder of the World Record for Crossing the Atlantic Ocean Solo in the Smallest Sailing Yacht Ever

All men dream: but not equally. Those who dream by night in the dusty recesses of their minds wake in the day to find that it was vanity: but the dreamers of the day are dangerous men, for they may act their dream with open eyes, to make it possible.
T. E. Lawrence, *The Seven Pillars of Wisdom*

Dream,
Dream, dream, dream,
Dream,
Dream, dream, dream
The Everley Brothers

After several unsuccessful attempts, Tom McNally succeeded in his lifelong ambition of crossing the Atlantic single-handed in a five-foot-four-inch boat made out of an old wardrobe. But Tom McNally is not the sort of man to rest on his laurels. Next year Tom McNally hopes to cross the Atlantic single-handed in a four-foot-one-inch boat made out of an old wardrobe. Tom describes himself as 'an individual who dares to live his dreams'. The only time I had that sort of dream was at the age of thirteen after my friend Ken and I consumed an entire bottle of his father's malt whisky.

Broaching the subject with all the necessary diplomacy, I ask Tom if he is a nutter. 'What's a nutter?' he replies. 'People tell me I'm crazy. I ask them, "What do you do?" and they say, "I count ball-bearings all day in a factory and my father did it before me." Who's the nutter? In society today you have to conform, you have to stand in the right queue, and do the right thing and have two point four children. I like to be different. I mean, if everyone started crossing the Atlantic in four-foot boats, I'd stay ashore and take out a mortgage.' And no doubt drive to work in a car made out of a Welsh dresser.

When he's not off on one of his voyages or scouring junk shops for old cupboards from which to construct his ocean-

going vessels, Tom paints. His studio is a cell in an old police station in his native Liverpool, rumoured to be haunted with the ghosts of the unfortunates who died there. At the moment he is putting the finishing touches to a rather robust reclining nude. Tom says it's no one he knows. Models are too expensive so he tends to paint from his imagination. At least you hope it's his imagination when you see the next work of art: a large portrait of Margaret Thatcher in stockings and suspenders, standing next to an upturned German helmet full of blood. It was, apparently, commissioned by a right-wing friend, although it's hardly the most flattering image of Her Iron Ladyship. If he wanted, Tom could earn a much better living from his painting than from his nautical expeditions. But he doesn't want. According to Tom McNally, happiness is navigating a thirty-foot swell in an MFI hanging unit.

'I like the element of risk involved. I like the element of challenge, and there's probably some ego involved, of course. There's a satisfaction in seeing how far you can push yourself,

Now that he's got the transatlantic small vessel record, even Mrs Thatcher will pose for him. (She's the one on the right.)

because people don't push themselves as far as they really can. I'm quite good at survival, I'm good at sailing, I'm lucky, I have confidence, I think positive, I think I have the right qualities to do the job – so why not exploit it, you know? I feel what I do is very positive. It inspires people. They say, "Hey, that old feller, he's no spring chicken. If he can do that, well . . ." I mean, I don't think everyone should be out in little five-foot boats, but there's other things, isn't there?'

If Tom McNally was from California he'd probably say that his love of water stemmed from pre-natal memories of his mother's womb, or that he had traced it back to a previous incarnation as Spencer Tracy in *The Old Man and the Sea.* But Tom McNally is from Liverpool, thankfully, and he claims his love of the water began as a child when he and his father went fishing in the docks. 'Don't worry, we never ate the fish,' he says, as a couple of condoms and an old shoe float past us on the murky waters of the Mersey. Later he got a job fishing Icelandic waters and the Barents Sea but, at the time of his first attempted Atlantic crossing, his only experience of sailing was from reading books. And they didn't include *The Old Man and the Sea.*

Tom's first serious record attempt was made from Newfoundland in 1983. 'It was a badly organized, low-budget affair,' he says, distinguishing it from a series of slightly better organized, low-budget affairs which were to follow. After fifty-two days at sea his boat (in those days a massive six foot ten inches) ended up wrapped around the propeller of a Russian super-trawler four hundred and seventy miles south-west of Ireland. At the time of the collision, Tom had already been drifting helplessly for weeks after losing his sails in a hurricane. Shipping in the area had been warned to look out for 'a man in a battered six-foot yacht', but unfortunately the Russian radio officer had interpreted the message as 'Look out for six battered men in a yacht.' When they finally spotted Tom's craft crumpled under their stern, they assumed he was a survivor in some kind of life raft and tried to haul him on board. Not surprisingly, they couldn't understand why every time they threw him a line, Tom would lash it to his boat instead of to himself. The reason was, of course, that, despite his craft's crumpled mast, totally demolished port side and a split keel, not to mention his own cracked ribs, broken collar-bone, fractured knee-cap, crushed vertebrae and a number of deep lacerations, Tom still wasn't ready to call it a day. So he beat off the would-be rescuers with a paddle until they hoisted both him and his boat, or what was left of it anyway, on to the trawler.

When Tom emerged from the ship's hospital a few weeks later, covered from head to foot in heavy casts and bandages, he was still insistent that he and his boat be put back in the sea as soon as he had finished the necessary repairs. The horrified captain attempted to dissuade the 'crazy English' by offering him a free holiday in the Canary Islands, courtesy of the Soviet government, if only he would abandon this plan. To no avail. The distressed Russian might have guessed that anyone who was determined to cross the ocean in a boat half the size of a Reliant Robin was not susceptible to bribery. Neither was he about to let a slight hitch like being mangled in the propellers of a super-trawler stand in his way.

Five weeks later the Russians lowered Tom and his boat *Big C* (which, by this time, was looking rather more like a little 'w') back into the ocean. Although they had patched it up as well as they could with the materials at hand (chicken wire, rubber bed sheets and parcelling tape, to be precise), the keel plank was split and the boat immediately started sinking. Even Tom finally had to agree that it was time to abandon the Atlantic record attempt. But not for long. He says, 'It's about putting yourself in a position where you have to win. The thought of conceding defeat is just out of the question so you have to push yourself and go on

'You're supposed to start off with a dinghy, and aspire to one day owning a yacht. I started with a big yacht and I'll probably end up with a pedal boat or something.'
Tom McNally in his ocean-going wardrobe.

pushing yourself. I can't actually imagine a situation where I'd say, "OK, I'm beaten," unless the boat actually disappeared from underneath me. While you're afloat and while there's some way of surviving you just push yourself onwards and onwards.' And, as if by way of illustration, this is how Tom spent the next ten years:

August 1983: 1st Atlantic attempt abandoned after Russian tanker collision.
September 1983: Boat shipped to Canada for repairs.
October 1983: Tom refused entry into Canada because he only holds a one-way ticket.
October 1983: Canadian customs authorities agree to store boat.
November 1983: Canadian customs authorities sell boat at auction as 'unclaimed cargo'.
January 1984: Tom starts building a new boat in a room above a friend's second-hand bookshop in Liverpool.
February 1986: Boat almost completed.
March 1986: Second-hand book shop (and boat) burnt down by vandals.
January 1987: Tom starts building another boat.
January 1992: Hull almost complete, but Tom out of funds.
February 1992: A Yorkshire businessman and fellow dreamer, Ian Wallace, steps in as a sponsor.
May 1992: Boat launched in Liverpool and shipped to Canada.
June 1992: Tom's first attempt to get underway fails because of freak south-easterly winds.
July 1992: The current small-boat record-holder Hugo Vihlen turns up with a boat only one and half inches longer. They agree to share record, if successful.
August 1992: Tom's second attempt to clear land fails due to unfavourable winds.
August 1992: Hugo Vihlen abandons record attempt until following year. Tom decides to persevere.
August 1992: Tom sets out, but is soon becalmed in pack ice and has to return.
September 1992: Tom sets out, but has hardly cleared the harbour when he has to get a fishing boat to tow him back to port.
September 1992: West–east attempt abandoned. Boat shipped back to England for modifications.
September 1993: Boat shipped to Lisbon for east–west attempt. Portuguese customs refuse to release boat.

September 1993: Ten days later Tom is run down by a truck, while looking the wrong way.
October: Tom gets out of hospital. Twenty-seven stitches and other minor injuries. Waits for north-easterly winds.
October: Sightseers ask to look at boat and accidentally sink it. One of them nearly drowns.
October: Hires crane and pulls boat up. Equipment and provisions a write-off.
November: Tom gets new sponsorship from a sports-watch company. They replace equipment. Boat moved to fishing port of Sagres.
25 December: Portuguese authorities refuse Tom permission to sail. Tom living in fish shed on harbour. Celebrates Christmas with stray cats and pet snail 'Ernie Shackleton'.
27 December: Tom illegally sets sail, helped by British family on yacht.
28 December: Winds take boat across a shipping separation zone.Very dangerous. Essential to stay in radio contact with other vessels.
29 December: Radio transmitter breaks.
30 December: Hit by a ferry. Boat full of water. Spends night bailing out water. Everything drenched. Ernie missing. Split in hull.
31 December: Shock sets in. No lights, no radio, no power, no dry clothing, diarrhoea. Only 150 more days to go. And it's New Year's Eve.
1–8 January 1994: Sets about repairs. Split hull plugged with T-shirts and porridge. Makes splint for mast with two hacksaw blades and parcelling tape. Sets course for Canary Islands.
14–24 January: Freak south-westerly storm. Boat blown 240 miles off course.
30 January: Lands at Madeira.
31 January – 7 February: Repairs boat, fixes radio, replaces supplies.
8 February: After a couple false starts, sets course for Canaries.
9 February: Battery on the blink again, radio and navigation lights stop working.
24 February: Two days of gales push boat wildly off course.
7 March: Lymph gland under left ear swollen to size of small orange. Antibiotics having no effect. Performs DIY surgery with blade from disposable razor.
9–24 March: More gale-force winds. Too far south. Boat almost totally submerged. Has to stay inside with hatch shut to stop water pouring in. Listens for wave patterns and tries to snatch occasional breath of fresh air.

'I feel what I do is very positive. It inspires people, especially children. They say, "Hey, that old feller, he's no spring chicken, if he can do that, well . . . " I mean I don't think everyone should be out in little five-foot boats, but there's other things, isn't there?'
Tom McNally (sponsored by MFI)

THE
SHOP
Tom McNally
PRIDE OF
MAGELLAN

25 March: Favourable winds. But food running low.
1 April: Badly scalds stomach and 'other bits and pieces' while trying to make tea. Too painful to wear proper clothes. Devises 'nappies'.
7 April: Determined to land at designated port, San Juan in Puerto Rico. Sceptics had said it was impossible to navigate such a small craft so precisely.
9 April: Food supplies exhausted. Living off dorado fish caught with home-made spear, and eaten raw. Only problem, lots of sharks following boat and sometimes crashing into it. Has to hit them on the head with a paddle.
26–29 April: Becalmed. Desperately short of water, and desalinator's filter split in three places. Urine the colour of Guinness – indicating renal failure.
4 May: Sight land; Tortola in the British Virgin Isles.
4–7 May: Atlantic gales left behind, but even more danger from off-shore currents and huge volume of shipping. Has to stay awake, so sits on deck with a life-line tied round foot. Falling asleep would mean falling into the sea.
8 May: San Juan harbour! Has to paddle the last few hundred yards. Arrival covered by international press. Has lost three stone but gained world record for the smallest craft ever to have crossed any of the world's oceans.

So, having finally got the world record, having dreamed his impossible dream, what do you suppose Tom McNally did next? That's right, he got back in his boat and sailed on to South America. Now he is planning his next world record attempt in an even smaller boat.

Tom says he realizes that devoting himself so wholeheartedly to his dreams also means making certain sacrifices. 'I like comforts, but when I commit myself to these things I know you've got to make some sacrifices, you've got to be able to put up with some discomforts. The biggest sacrifice of all is being away from Edna – she's the light at the end of the tunnel.'

I point out to Tom that he could be with his darling Edna if he didn't choose to spend five months bobbing around the open seas in a five-foot craft. 'That's right. You've got to compromise in this life, haven't you? I mean, she won't sail. But if you've got a dream and the dream can be a practical reality – well, chase after it. Do whatever it takes and be optimistic and never think negative. Just don't let them take your dreams away from you.' Even if your dreams are the stuff of other people's worst nightmares.

MONKS, SAPPHIRES AND TETANUS JABS: KATE McLAUCHLAN AND THE VENERABLE BODHI

▲ Kate McLauchlan – devoted to work.

▼ A couple of trishaws – devoted to each other.

I have recently been all around the world and have formed a very poor opinion of it.
Thomas Beecham, conductor

Whenever I prepare for a journey I prepare as though for death.
Katherine Mansfield, writer

The more I travel abroad, the more I thank God I live in Esher.
David Tate, actor

England in April is, unsurprisingly, cold and wet, with the added attractions of gale-force winds and hailstones the size of guinea-pig droppings, so it suddenly seems like an incredibly good idea to continue our search for happy devotees in Sri Lanka.

The BBC doctors kindly provide us with a long list of the various fatal tropical diseases we are likely to contract and pack the whole crew off to the airport with arms and bottoms full of jabs and suitcases full of malaria tablets, Diocalm and, inexplicably, about three hundred yards of gauze bandages. They also warn us that Sri Lanka is the snake capital of the world, with over eighty-three species, five of them deadly, including the country's national emblem, the cobra, which can kill an average-sized TV presenter in less time than it takes to say: 'Security has never been so interesting.' The expert advice on to how to avoid this fate is 'don't annoy them', which is just as well because otherwise my first instinct would almost invariably be to run up to one and start prodding it with a stick.

Perhaps if anyone had thought to warn us that we'd be working in 100° heat and monsoonal rain, would have leeches crawling up our legs or that our hotel would be bombed by Tamil guerrillas, we would have decided to film in Leicester. But, then, it has to be said that as far as golden sandy beaches, coconut palms, densely forested hills, exotic wildlife and spectacular sunsets go, Sri Lanka has a slight edge on most parts of Leicestershire, excluding Rutland. Besides, there probably aren't quite so many sapphire dealers or Buddhist monks in Leicester.

Sri Lanka (formerly Ceylon, Taprobane, Ceilao, Ceylan and 'that island full of big poisonous snakes') is an Ireland-sized teardrop off the southern tip of India. Ancient travellers named the island Serendib, and it's from this that the word 'serendipity' – the gift of finding valuable things in unexpected places by sheer luck, like say, a decent piece of jewellery at Ratner's – derives. It certainly seems applicable to the country's rich seam of precious and semi-precious gemstones, which are washed down from the mountains in the rainy season to lie in the dark, alluvial soil of the paddy-fields below. If you walk around the countryside staring at your feet, it's not impossible to find a rock worth upwards of US$100,000 (more than the value of the entire contents of a Ratner's store put together). For natives and foreigners alike, the dream of hard-cash dollars gives Sri Lanka the same pull that the Klondike held for the prospectors of the 1840s, or that British Telecom shares held for the yuppies of the 1980s.

'It's your choice in life, you can't have everything. So I can't sit at home and cry when I'm by myself in Tai Pei for my birthday.'
Kate McLauchlan

So if it's gem dealers you're looking for, Sri Lanka's not a bad place to start. The particular dealer we had set out to find is a young woman named Kate McLauchlan. She is, we have been told, one of those rare people who are only truly happy when they are working – a rare form of devotion, often mistaken for madness. Kate is completely devoted to her job, travelling all over the world and working impossible hours to the benefit of her bank balance but to the detriment of social life, holidays and the occasional lie-in on Sunday mornings.

As if to confirm our expectations Kate agrees to meet us at our hotel in Colombo at 5.30 a.m. She turns up promptly in a large blue Mercedes, looking, as far as I can tell through bleary eyes, like she's had her Weetabix hours ago. She is accompanied by two of her partners – Mark, a tall, burly Australian sporting a huge chunk of sapphire on a gold chain round his neck, and Rizwan, a Sri Lankan Muslim from an old gem-dealing family. Kate and Mark had met Rizwan ten years ago, when he accosted them in the street, saying that Allah had sent him to work with them. After an initial, and somewhat understandable, moment or two of scepticism, they agreed, and have found in him an invaluable and trusted partner.

Kate herself presents an immediately striking picture – tall and glamorous with big green eyes and big black hair, and on her

The Sri Lankan Highway Code

Do Not Overtake

(1) If the road ahead is clear.

(2) If you can see more than twenty yards ahead of you.

(3) If there are no pedestrians/cows/dogs/ox carts/elephants on the road.

(4) Unless another vehicle is trying to overtake yours at the same time.

You May Overtake

(1) Anywhere you like, especially on level crossings, blind corners or hump-back bridges.

Use of the Horn

Use the horn at all times. It signals to other drivers and pedestrians that your horn is working.

On-coming Traffic

Aim for all forms of on-coming traffic, veering to the side only at the last minute, or after your passengers' screams become unbearable.

Convoys

Only drive in convoy, particularly if the car in front, e.g. a Mercedes, is much faster than your car, and is driven by the only person in your group who knows the way. (See overleaf.)

middle finger a big gold knuckle-duster of a ring, set with a pink sapphire the size of Essex. Half French, half Scottish (the Auld Alliance), she was born in Saudi Arabia and educated in an English convent school. At the age of twenty she went to Australia and found herself a job in a sapphire mine – no mean feat in an industry dominated not just by men, but by big, tough, gun-toting Queensland men. Eleven years later she runs an international business and owns homes in Sydney, London, Colombo and Singapore. She takes about twenty-two long-haul flights every year, spending a few weeks at a time visiting mines and dealers, buying and then cutting hundreds of thousands of dollars' worth of gemstones and the next few weeks selling them to other dealers, manufacturers, designers and a few select individual collectors, including a smattering of maharajahs and sheiks.

One of the sapphire mines is about two hours' drive south-east of Colombo. Mark warns us to keep our windows wound up when passing through the forest. My fears that it is a precaution against poisonous snakes are, thankfully, completely unfounded. It is, in fact, only a precaution against leopards, one of which had apparently jumped on their car during one of their last trips up there. What he fails to warn us about is the crazed Sri Lankan driving, which, on balance, probably poses a slightly greater risk to the traveller than the leopards and snakes put together. (See Highway Code, left.)

We set off in convoy after Kate and Mark's Mercedes. After one or two brushes with certain death and a great deal of getting lost, we finally reach the sapphire mine. This turns out to be a shallow, water-logged hole, about twelve feet in diameter, in the middle of some paddy-fields. No mineshafts, no slag heaps, no men in hard hats singing about the Rhondda in close harmony. The edge of the hole is a bank of mud about four feet high where a dog is happily sleeping in the sun, which at 8 a.m. is already absurdly hot. Inside the hole about half a dozen men and a couple of children stand thigh high in muddy water panning for stones in large, flat, wicker baskets. The mine manager, dressed in a shirt and long white sarong, stands to one side, watching carefully. The gem business is run completely on trust, and consequently no one seems to trust anyone else. In theory everyone who works in a particular mine gets a profit share (worked out in advance) on every gem found, the owner and manager usually getting the lion's share. The manager is also responsible for looking after his employees and their families in times of sickness or when they aren't finding any valuable stones. In practice, everyone seems to watch everyone else like a hawk, and you have only to stop and stare at the ground for a few seconds to have a small crowd rush over to see what you're looking at. (This can be very useful if you lose a contact lens, or very embarrassing if you're simply having a pee.) A hundred yards away from the mine a farmer is ploughing his rice fields with a water buffalo and a wooden plough.

▲ On a good day, these men can dig up half a dozen valuable sapphires. On a bad day, they can dig up over one and a half tons of mud.

Kate walks across a wooden plank to the edge of the mine and crouches down on her haunches to look inside the basket. The soil here is dark grey – a good sign, apparently, as it indicates volcanic soil – and the pans are bringing up lots of little spherical pieces of ironstone, another good sign as it means that the stones have been washed down from the mountains and are therefore likely to be accompanied by sapphires. Dollar signs begin to ring up on the mental till. Kate sifts through identical-looking muddy pebbles in the basket, identifying them and then chucking them back. Sapphire . . . ruby . . . garnet . . . yellow sapphire . . . quartz . . . star sapphire . . .' And these are just the ones she's throwing back!

Today Kate's only interested in big stones, and is hoping in particular for padparadscha – a rare type of reddish sapphire which is currently popular in Japan because Prince Naruhito chose one for his fiancée's engagement ring. The blue sapphire enjoyed a similar vogue in England after Charles gave Diana one (engagement ring), but the British and European market is now considered so poor as to be almost not worth the bother. According to Kate, Europeans don't like to wear big stones, whereas in the Middle and Far East size is still what counts. Tiaras are out; kimono pins are in.

The farmer wanders over and stands on the edge of the mine, chewing betel and staring blankly at the grown men and women who are peering in fascination at these dull grey pebbles which he has probably been trampling underfoot all his life. Mark gestures to the growing crowd of villagers who have turned out to watch the camera crew and the lady in the blue Mercedes. 'You see the ones with bikes and cars? They're miners. The ones on foot – they're farmers.' Perhaps yet another reason why, statistically, farmers are the least happy profession in the world.

Kate finds a stone she likes and starts bargaining furiously with the mine manager. They agree a price of 55,000 rupees (£785), and she shakes hands with the manager and the man who found the stone. No money changes hands. It's too dangerous to carry large sums of cash around; the transaction will take place later in Colombo.

We get in the cars and set off on the return journey to Colombo. Kate is glowing with excitement and vigour even though she must have made this trip hundreds of times. I'm glowing, too. The air conditioner in the Merc has died and I feel like I'm on the

▶ Fifty-five thousand and how much?

verge of following suit. About a mile down the road the mine manager is mysteriously waiting to meet us. He has a couple of large stones to show Kate which he didn't want to produce in front of everyone at the mine. So much for trust.

Kate's house is palatial in size, but in atmosphere and décor it's more like a bus station with bedrooms. When we arrive there are about thirty other people in the house. (You can tell such things instantly in Sri Lanka because etiquette dictates that you leave your shoes on the doorstep, so unless someone's entertaining a lot of one-legged people or a caterpillar you just have to count the shoes and divide by two.) A row of gem dealers sit waiting in one room while sari-clad women appear with huge bowls of rice and mutton and string hoppas (a type of shredded noodle dish) and quickly lay the table. An assortment of small children run shrieking after a cat that has wandered in, and another burly Australian, who turns out to be Kate's younger brother Duncan, appears from the lapidary upstairs, where he has been busy cutting and polishing some black opals he has just brought over from Queensland.

After a quick meal, washed down with lime juice and soda, everyone repairs to the lapidary to examine and start cutting the rough stones they have bought. Kate picks up a large sapphire crystal and holds it up to the light to show me an opaque thread running through it. I scrabble around for something faintly intelligent and complimentary to say about it and come up with, 'Oh, very nice.' Naturally, this turns out to be completely the wrong thing to say. The value of a stone is based on size, colour and clarity, and an inclusion such as this reduces its value considerably. Experts can sometimes get rid of these impurities by 'cooking' the sapphires, but they also risk losing everything if the stone blows up in the furnace. Double or quits. Kate decides to go for it, but she won't start the process (a carefully guarded secret) until late at night. There are dealers to see and sapphires to be bought. Or perhaps the other way around.

Next stop? A gem market. This takes place in Beruwela, a small coastal town about an hour and a half south of Colombo. Beruwela is predominantly Muslim, and was the site of the first recorded Muslim settlement of the island in 1024. It seems like a prosperous place – large houses with raised terraces set back from the road and a fair smattering of newish-looking (i.e. post-1960) cars. A bit like Surbiton with palm trees and without the Tupperware parties.

The market isn't at all how I'd envisaged it (assorted stalls selling fruit, veg, dish-mops, emeralds) but turns out to be about

Exercising my chameleon-like powers, I don't think anyone even noticed I was there.

two hundred men, identically dressed in sarongs and long-sleeved white shirts, jammed together on the front porch of one of the larger houses. As soon as I appear, each man reaches into his shirt pocket, produces a piece of folded paper containing two or three gemstones and starts waving them under my nose. There is a 500-rupee note burning a hole in my pocket but, after considering the matter for a few nanoseconds, I decide it would be safer to seek out a patch of shade and wait for Kate.

Sure enough, as soon as the blue Mercedes appears, all four hundred eyes swivel and a mini-stampede begins. A table appears from nowhere, it is covered with a white cloth and Kate is more or less thrust forcibly into a chair beside it. Somehow, despite the stifling heat and the airless crush of the dealers surrounding her, Kate spends over an hour looking at every single gem at the market. She balances the stone between her index and middle fingers and holds it up to the sun, or sometimes simply dismisses it after a cursory glance. From time to time she calls out directions. 'Today we're buying yellows. Only top-quality stones . . . cat's eyes, pink sapphires, padparadscha.'

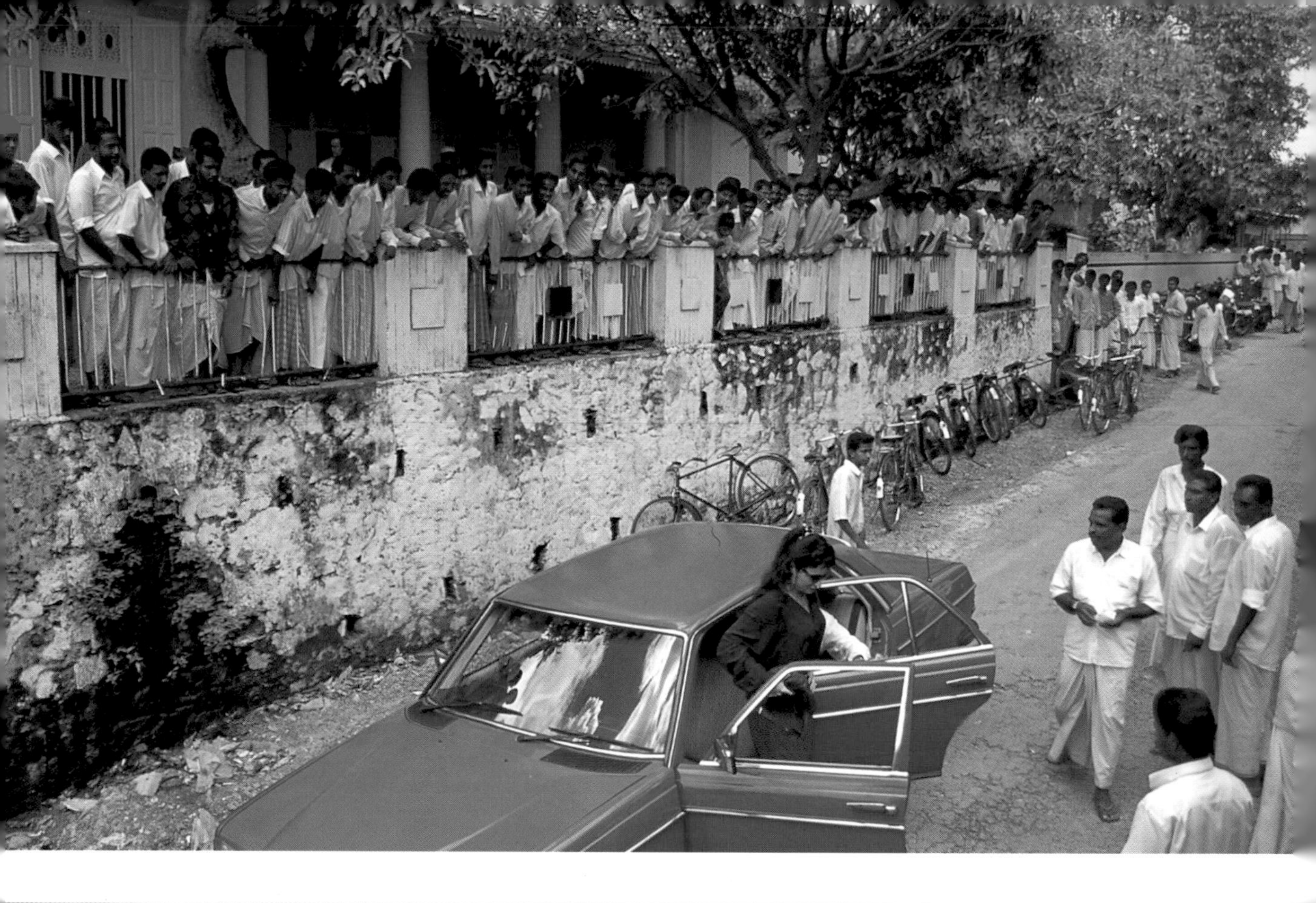

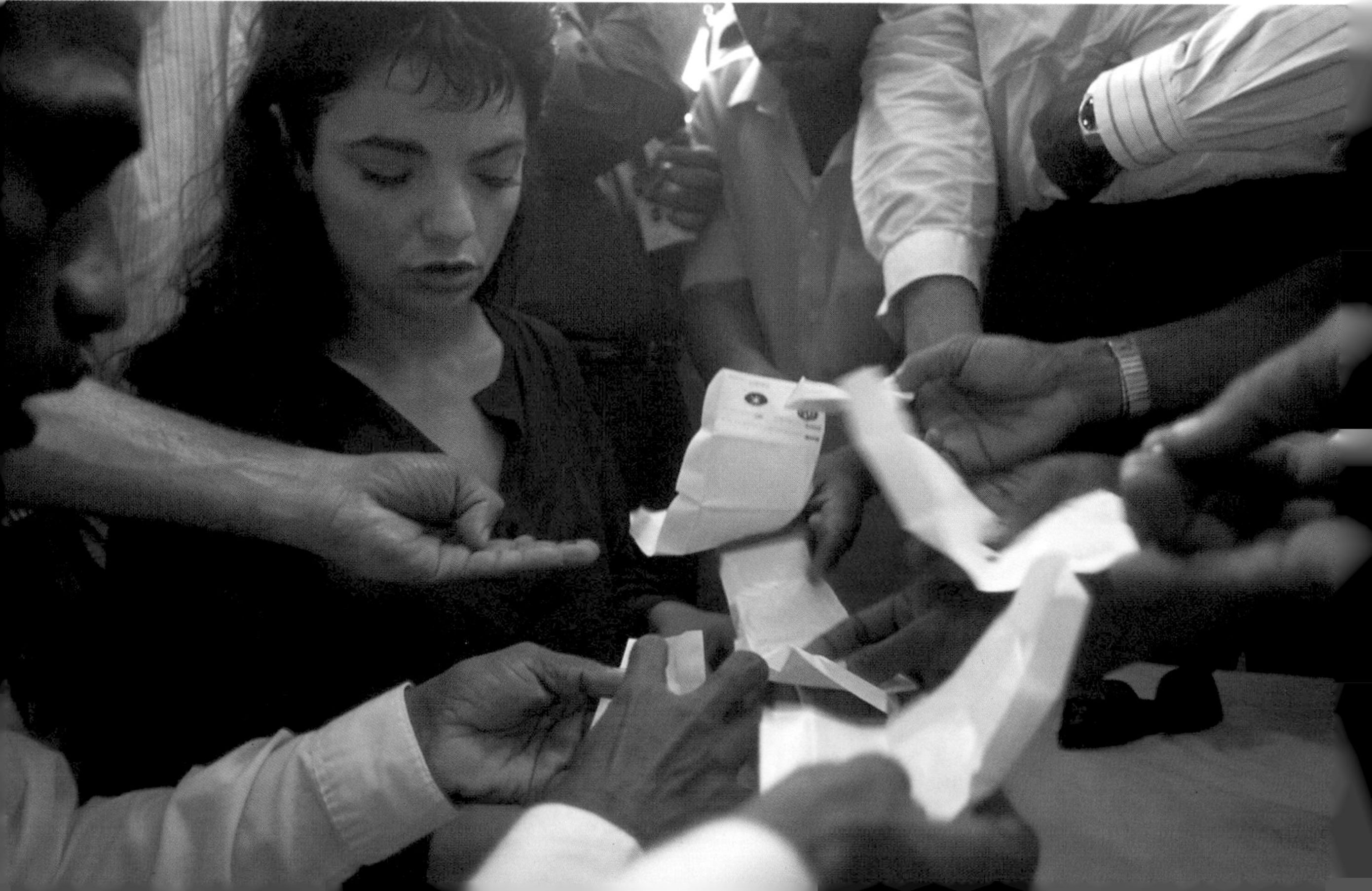

◀ The Beruwela gem market: the arrival of the Queen of Sapphires. No one could say Kate McLauchlan doesn't attract her fair share of attention.

◀ Kate McLauchlan and two hundred sellers – something of a buyer's market.

'Do you ever get fed up with looking at gems?' I ask Kate. She looks at me as though I am a Martian.

At the end of it all Kate has bought only ten stones. The blue Mercedes sets off again, this time for the airport. Kate is intending to spend the next week in London, Paris and Zurich, selling some of the gems she has recently purchased. We collapse into our mini-bus, drink several litres of water and then sleep fitfully all the way back to Colombo, where, we have just learned, bombs have gone off in four hotels, including ours.

'It's very unusual,' we are told. 'This is obviously the start of a new campaign aimed specifically at tourists. Or perhaps the terrorists heard there was a BBC crew on the island.'

How very reassuring. Always nice to know someone's thinking of you, even if it's with a view to spreading your insides across a hotel lobby.

Arise! Do not be heedless! Lead a life of good conduct. The righteous live happily both in this world and the next.
Buddha

The meek shall inherit the earth – if that's all right with everyone else.
Old joke

The next morning we leave Colombo and head east towards the interior of the island. (This has nothing to do with the terrorist attack, although I have spent the previous night discovering the delights of room service, keeping well away from the windows and writing my will.) This time my quest is to find the Venerable Sumedha, a Buddhist monk and recluse who is reputed to spend all his days in solitary meditation and study. Perhaps through his devotion and sense of purpose, and through following the teachings of the Buddha, he has managed to find the path to True Happiness. On the other hand, perhaps he just sits in his cave all day, yearning for cream cakes and the latest Ken Follett?

Like the Buddha himself, Sumedha lived a very full life before his 'enlightenment'. Born Aja Iskander Schmindlin, of Swiss and Coptic Christian parents, he grew up in Zurich and became a successful artist in the sixties and seventies, selling paintings for $50,000 a go. He was also, according to all accounts, a bit of a one for the ladies, and had a series of failed marriages and love affairs. It was after the end of one of these romances that he jumped on a plane to Ceylon. It must have been a thirsty trip, because the first thing he did upon arrival was to order a lime soda, and this lime soda was apparently so delicious, so utterly and completely gorgeous and thirst quenching, that he decided to leave the land of cuckoo clocks, Toblerone and money-laundering and stay in Ceylon. Personally, when I tasted it, I just felt it could've done with a bit more sugar.

For the next few years he lived and continued to paint in a beautiful house in a smart area of Colombo, but in 1976, the very year that Brotherhood of Man won the Eurovision Song Contest with 'Save Your Kisses For Me', he suddenly packed it in, sold all his possessions and became a mendicant monk. For a while he was a Hindu swami and learned to do things like walking across hot coals (see Anthony Robbins, Chapter 3), but he eventually plumped for Buddhism. Sri Lanka is one of the traditional homes of the Theravada school of Buddhism, which is particularly strict. To be a monk you first have to serve an apprenticeship, and then take 237 vows – rather like marrying Donald Trump, but less lucrative. Anyway, he eventually became a fully fledged monk, took the name Sumedha and moved to a cave near Kandy, a holy city just an easy three-hour drive from Colombo.

What has been described to us as an 'easy three-hour drive' is turning into five, and still no sign of Kandy. It is later explained to me by Mahil, one of our guides, that Sri Lankans consider it rude to give someone bad or disappointing news and therefore they will always underestimate the time of any journey by at least 50 per cent. Moreover, if you ask a Sri Lankan a 'yes or no' question, they will invariably answer in the affirmative, rather than risk upsetting you. You therefore have to learn how to rephrase questions: for instance, instead of 'Is this the right way to the post office?', to which the answer will always be 'Yes,' irrespective of which direction you are pointing, you say, 'Which way is the post office?; and rather than 'Is our hotel safe?' you ask, 'What are the chances that the Tamil Tigers will blow up our hotel today?'

About thirty kilometres outside Kandy we decide to take a short detour to Kegalle to visit the Pinnewala Elephant Orphanage, which was set up by the government to save abandoned or orphaned wild elephants. Sri Lanka has its own subspecies of elephant and you often see them lugging tree trunks and great bundles of branches along roads or in the fields. The sanctuary is home to about four dozen elephants, ranging from a gigantic

▲ Asking directions . . . ▶ . . . the reply.

male with huge tusks to one which has been born only that morning (although after almost two years *in utero*, it is already the size of a Fiat Cinquecento and has learnt to do a perfect impression of the soundtrack of *Jurassic Park*). The elephants are allowed to roam around freely in a few acres of coconut palms, except at feeding times, when the babies are herded into various pagoda-like structures. There the keepers give them oversized bottles of milk: seven bottles for each baby elephant five times a day. In short, a lotta bottle.

We arrive just as feeding time starts, and the rain arrives a few seconds later. It isn't your average British drizzle, or your scattered showers or even for that matter a straightforward downpour, but a torrential, soaked-to-the-skin-in-three-seconds, better-go-build-an-ark monsoon-type rain. I move closer to the elephants under the shelter and ask them a few general knowledge questions to test out the old adage, which by this showing is a complete fallacy: they have absolutely terrible memories. The nearest elephant, a mere toddler of two, grabs my bag with his trunk. I pull it away and step back into the rain. A bolt of lightning rips through the sky. I step closer to the elephant. The elephant trails his trunk through a pile of wet elephant dung and calmly wipes it across my shirt. Back into the rain. And so forth: elephant, rain, elephant, rain. Two hours later, soaking wet and covered head to foot in elephant shit, it is back to the delights of Sri Lankan traffic.

It is dark when we come upon the army roadblocks which signal that we are entering Kandy. The morning newspapers have proclaimed that security has been trebled since the Colombo bombings, and therefore three times the usual number of soldiers completely ignore us as we drive past the barriers. The present Hindu/Tamil v. Buddhist/Sinhalese conflict has the depressing distinction of dating from time immemorial, or, in fact, well before time immemorial, which according to a lawyer friend of mine is technically AD 1189.

Historically the kingdom of Kandy has always been a target of invaders, since it is the proud possessor of one of the holiest teeth in existence, to wit the Buddha's tooth. In 543 BC, this tooth was allegedly plucked from the flames of the Buddha's funeral pyre by one of his disciples, and spent the next eight hundred years being snatched back and forth by feuding Indian princes, until in the fourth century AD a Nepalese prince finally smuggled it to Sri Lanka, concealed in his wife's beehive hairdo. However, even in the Buddhist stronghold of Sri Lanka the tooth had its ups and downs. It was briefly carried off to India in 1283 and in the sixteenth century the tooth was kidnapped and burnt with huge Catholic pomp by the Portuguese. (Luckily it turned out that they had only destroyed a cunning replica.) This, unless I'm very much mistaken, formed the plot of an early *Man From U.N.C.L.E.* episode.

The tooth was moved from place to place until eventually the kings of Kandy built a special temple to house it. With great imagination they called this temple the Temple of the Tooth. The temple is a large building with crenellated walls and a moat running all the way around it, and to make it look extra-specially butch and impregnable the kings decided to paint the whole thing pink. The actual tooth is only exhibited every few years or in national emergencies. (The last outing was during the 1992 drought, and the next day it rained!) Most of the time the tooth lives in a little gold casket inside a series of slightly bigger gold caskets, rather like a Russian doll, and is annually carried in a grand parade by a specially trained elephant, the Maligawa Tusker.

To become a temple elephant you must meet with a very strict set of guidelines, namely long tusks, long trunk, long tail, long legs and long penis. (Pictured here the Errol Flynn of the elephant world.)

The most famous of these tooth-carrying tuskers was called Rajah. Rajah died in 1988 after fifty glorious years on the job, and if you are at all keen on taxidermied elephants you can view his stuffed remains in a specially built museum adjacent to the temple. Rajah was so popular that he became only the second elephant in Sri Lankan history to be declared a National Treasure. (I ask around, but nobody seems to remember the first elephant to be granted such an honour.) To become a temple elephant you must meet with a very strict set of guidelines, namely long tusks, long trunk, long tail, long legs and long penis. Contestants are sent to Kandy from all over the Buddhist world and the short-listed few embark on a training period which can last up to thirty years. History does not relate the emotional anguish suffered by the reject elephants – the clinics, the therapy, the expensive penis extensions – but the successful few live a life of luxury, and even have their own private swimming pools. A temple elephant will refuse to set foot on the bare earth, and will only walk on a white linen carpet which is unrolled in front of him in processions. He will also amass an impressive collection of photos of himself standing next to celebrities; having your photo taken next to a famous elephant is the Sri Lankan politician's equivalent of being in a Tracy Ullman video.

In Ceylon, as in virtually every other country in the world where the British have been, they've left their mark. There's a red pillar-box on every corner, you can't pass the smallest patch of grass without tripping over a cricket match and although the sun shines on Sri Lanka 365 days a year, everyone carries an umbrella. And also, as in virtually every country where the British have been, they've got themselves a bad reputation. Arriving at our hotel we were greeted by the sight of a statue of a Buddhist monk trampling a Union Jack underfoot. He did it to protest at the British take-over of Kandy, and naturally, as a suitable and befitting punishment for getting a piece of cloth dirty, the British shot him.

The city of Kandy is built around a large artificial lake and surrounded by hills. From a small village in these hills, about half an hour's drive from the city, a steep flight of a hundred steps leads up through the rainforest to the cave where the Venerable Sumedha lives. This cave has apparently been inhabited by monks for the past two thousand years, and is passed from one incumbent to another, like a vicarage. Sumedha was offered the cave when the nun who had previously lived there got too old and frail to handle the steep steps and was moved to more suitable accommodation, presumably a low-level cave with a ramp.

We arrive at the village early in the morning and puff our way up the stone stairs through a forest as well stocked as an average corner shop: tea bushes, coffee trees, pepper plants, papaya, bananas, Rothman trees, J-cloth groves . . . We find the monk sitting on a little paved terrace outside the mouth of the cave, contemplating an enormous bamboo plant festooned with wind chimes and other decorations, which on closer inspection turn out to be fashioned from an old kettle, tin-can lids and broken crockery. To the left of the cave a path, made of what can only be described as crazy paving, leads to a large stone basin for washing; to the right, more crazy paving leads to a smaller cave containing an outhouse (or in this case, I suppose, an outcave). The interior of the main cave consists of one room, furnished simply with a mattress, a small shrine, a little desk and, like all fashionable caves, a human skeleton.

My first impression of Sumedha is of a frail, emaciated man, with a shaven head and no teeth, dressed in the traditional saffron robes of a Buddhist monk and cradling on his lap a large metal begging bowl. A woman from the local village and her small daughter have just arrived to bring Sumedha some food. Monks are totally reliant on these alms: they are only allowed to eat what they are given, and furthermore they mustn't eat anything at all between noon and 6 a.m. the following day. I don't know whether it's worth marketing as a new wonder diet (the Lo-Cal Hi-Karma Weight-Loss System?) but if it's any recommendation, you almost never see a fat Buddhist monk.

When the woman and child have left, I introduce myself to Sumedha and he motions for me to sit on a small rug in front of him. You don't shake hands with monks – evidently it's bad manners to touch them – and you must keep your legs covered, but your feet and head should be bare. Apart from a soft Schweizedeutsch accent, it is impossible to see any traces of the European man-about-town he had once been, but as soon as I start talking to him I realize that he is as skilled as any Western politician in the 'how to avoid answering the direct question' stakes.

Angus: I am searching for happiness.
Sumedha: To search for happiness is futile.
Angus: So you think I'm wasting my time?
Sumedha: Why do you want to know what I think?

When I was told that he lived in a cave, I somehow wasn't expecting crazy-paving and a patio outside his dwelling.

Angus: I just thought you might be able to give me some answers.

Sumedha: Only you can give the answers.

We continue in this vein for some time, until I begin to get the distinct impression that my brain is going to explode. The Venerable Sumedha is one of Sri Lanka's scholar-monks and has reached a level of meditative thought which, apparently, would be dangerous for a layman even to attempt. (Monks are supervised by more senior monks as they learn to progress to deeper levels of meditation in order to avoid injury.)

'I still don't quite understand,' I plead. 'Are you saying that in order to find happiness I must stop seeking it?'

Sumedha goes into his cave and re-emerges with a copy of the *Dhammapada*, a collection of some of the Buddha's teachings.

▲ 'To search for happiness is futile.' The Reverend Sumedha renders the entire book redundant in one fell sentence.

He opens the book and points to the first verse. 'Mind precedes all mental states. Mind is their chief, they are all mind-wrought. If with an impure mind a person speaks or acts, suffering follows him like the wheel that follows the foot of the ox.'

I begin to wonder if I might understand him better if he started speaking in German.

Having lived an almost monk-free life for the past thirty-eight years, the very next morning I find myself driving through another forest on my way to see my second monk in two days. I hope they aren't addictive. Sumedha has suggested that we talk to one of his fellow monks, the Venerable Bodhi, and I am hoping he'll be able to shed some more light on the subject of happiness vis-à-vis devotion vis-à-vis Buddhism. Bodhi is another scholar monk, but, unlike Sumedha, lives in a seminary with a group of other monks and seems to have a little more contact with the outside world.

We arrive at the designated spot in the designated forest and pile out of our designated van. It has just been raining and the forest floor is still glistening with moisture. There is a sudden cry, and looking around I realize it is me. Next thing I know I am hopping from foot to foot, slapping my legs. At first I think

▶ 'If with an impure mind a person speaks or acts, suffering follows him like the wheel that follows the foot of the ox . . .' Discuss.

I must be in the grip of some powerful new dance craze, but when I look down I see that the ground is crawling with leeches. The scent of human skin has brought them speeding through the grass and jumping up my legs. In their unfed state they're about an inch and a half long and the width of a candle-wick. They travel quickly, with a sort of hunching movement like an inch worm. Once one has latched on to you you can't pull it off or you leave the head imbedded in your skin, which then gets infected. So, if you should ever find yourself in a rainforest covered with leeches, the best way to remove them is by either rubbing salt on them or burning them with the end of a cigarette If you don't happen to be carrying tobacco or a cruet set with you, you must try to prise off the leeches without decapitating them. Even then, because their bite contains an anti-coagulant, the wound doesn't stop bleeding for about ten minutes after the leech has let go. Yuck. These are the sorts of facts you don't read about in travel brochures for 'Sri Lanka – an Island Paradise'.

With all the sang-froid of seasoned travellers and the measured reactions of an SAS unit, we instantly panic and jump back into the van, tearing off our shoes to see if any leeches have got inside them. The driver, witnessing our exhibition of the kind of British courage which made the Empire great, appears with a huge bottle of washing-up liquid and tells us to smear it on our skin. Apparently, if there's one thing a leech can't stand, it's the smell of detergent. Suitably smeared, and smelling like Nanette Newman (but presumably for only half as long), we again tentatively venture out into the forest, picking our feet up like prancing horses. The Venerable Bodhi is sitting under a tree in a small clearing near by, calmly prising three fat leeches off his calf. If Buddhist happiness is the Super-Ability to Bear, Bodhi is positively delirious. I get straight to the point.

'I spoke to Bikkhu Sumedha but I'm still confused. How should I go about finding happiness if I'm not able to seek it?'

'Would you like me to try and put the teaching of the Buddha in a nutshell?'

'Yes, please.'

Buddhism in a Very Small Nutshell

Buddhism is not a religion, or a philosophy, but a mental discipline.

Buddha is revered as a great teacher. Followers give thanks to Buddha, but do not pray to him. Buddha's teachings or 'Dharma' define happiness as the 'super-ability to bear'. Life is suffering. Suffering comes from selfish desire or craving. If you get rid of craving you get rid of suffering and become free. You must strive to replace ignorance with understanding, hatred with loving kindness and greed with generosity. Your own actions determine your karma – and affect your reincarnation, or the rebirth of your consciousness. The ultimate reality is supreme enlightenment and the ultimate goal is Nirvana.

(Or at least a free copy of their first album.)

We say our goodbyes to Bodhi and the leeches and set off on the road back to Colombo. A few miles outside Kandy we pass a lone moped with a six-foot tuna balanced across the pillion – a delivery boy for Dial-a-Fish? – but otherwise the streets are strangely empty of the ox carts, mad bus drivers and suicidal pedestrians we have become so fond of. A series of loud explosions fill the air. Perhaps the Tamil Tigers have finally caught up with us. Then we remember: it is New Year's Eve. Both the Tamil and Sinhalese New Year fall in April when Pisces passes into Aries. Every year this happens at a slightly different time of day and the *Daily News* has printed a special schedule of events.

New Year Timetable

Time to stop work: Wednesday 10.07 p.m.
Time to start work (men): Thursday 8.30 a.m.
Time to start work (women): Thursday 6.20 a.m.
Time to take bath: Saturday 9.00 a.m.
Time to set off fireworks: Now!

Twelve hours later, our ears ringing, and our noses filled with sulphur fumes, we stagger on to flight AL404, an Air Lanka Tristar. Have we discovered the secret of happiness on the island of Serendib? We have witnessed two very different kinds of happy devotees. In Kate McLauchlan we have seen a life enriched by frenetic activity, constant excitement and the pursuit of riches, and in Sumedha a life of peace, meditation and freedom from the material world. Has either or both of them found the secret of true happiness? Personally, I can think of lifestyles I envy, but none of them involves sitting around in an orange sheet, shaving my head and listening to Nirvana albums. But nor would it involve working around the clock. And it certainly wouldn't involve crossing the ocean in a wardrobe, following a heavy metal band, chatting to Jesus on the toilet or supporting the crappest football team in the league. Still, we are bound for London, where we can at least be blown up by terrorists in our own beds.

The Reverend Sumedha – from man-about-town to monk-in-cave

PLEASURE

Sex 'n' Drugs 'n' Crème Brûlée

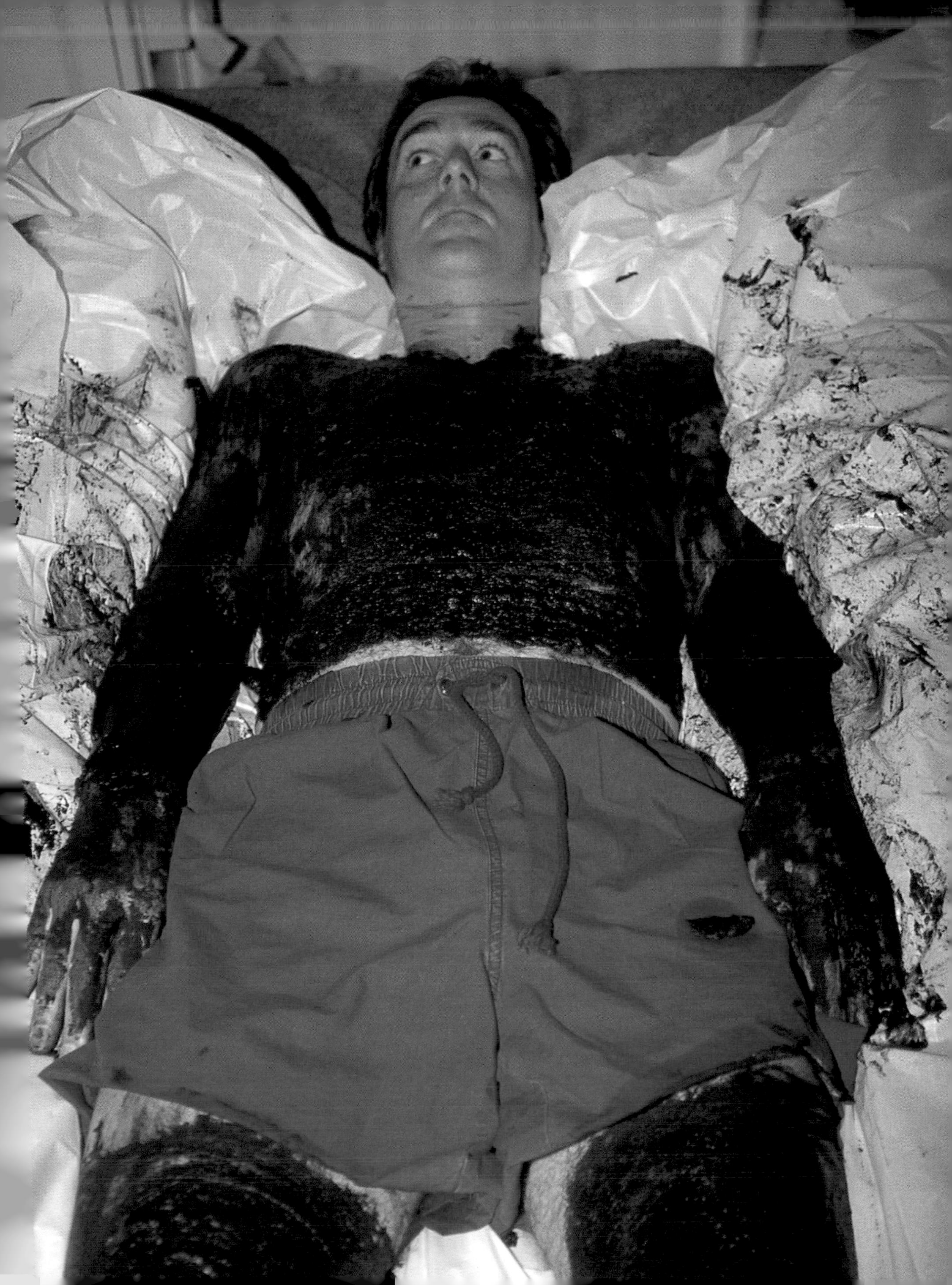

Sex and drugs and rock and roll are all my brain and body need.
Ian Dury

Love is the drug.
Bryan Ferry

I am the Walrus.
John Lennon

Part of being British is to deny yourself as many pleasures as possible. Which is probably why 'hedonism' – the belief that pleasure is the highest good – did not originate in Clacton, but in Athens. And the Greeks may have had a point. If the sole reason the gods put us on this earth is to procreate and be happy, then the hedonists are the only ones to pursue both relentlessly.

So, are our lives going to become any richer through the simple indulgence of all our fantasies and desires and the pursuit of all pleasures willy-nilly, as it were? Is someone who eats what they like, partakes of every form of narcotic and succumbs to every temptation of the flesh this side of Dewhurst's necessarily any happier than someone whose idea of a good time is discussing the weather with the vicar over a cup of caffeine-free tea? On the other hand, what's the point of a healthy diet, moderate lifestyle or devotion to a faith when eating chocolate, bathing in asses' milk and drinking malt whisky sound so much more fun? Perhaps one drawback of the hedonistic lifestyle is that everything we associate with pleasure seems to have risk attached to it. There's no gain without pain. Too much food makes you fat, too much alcohol harms your liver, too many drugs damages your mind and too much wild rampant sex tends to annoy your partner. Unless, of course, the wild rampant sex happens to be *with* your partner.

Occasionally, though, and somewhat perversely, it is the very element of danger associated with a particular pleasurable pursuit that creates the thrill. One woman, whom I shall call Miss X, in order to protect her real name, Georgina Morley, was in the news recently after continually being arrested for shoplifting. She became addicted to the habit because the fear of being caught gave her an orgasm. A bit of a giveaway in Tesco's, I'd have thought, but that's not the point. For such adrenalin junkies, the knowledge that what you're doing is bad for your health, your career or your chances of staying out of prison can be a bit of a turn-on. So presumably if you were eating a brandy-

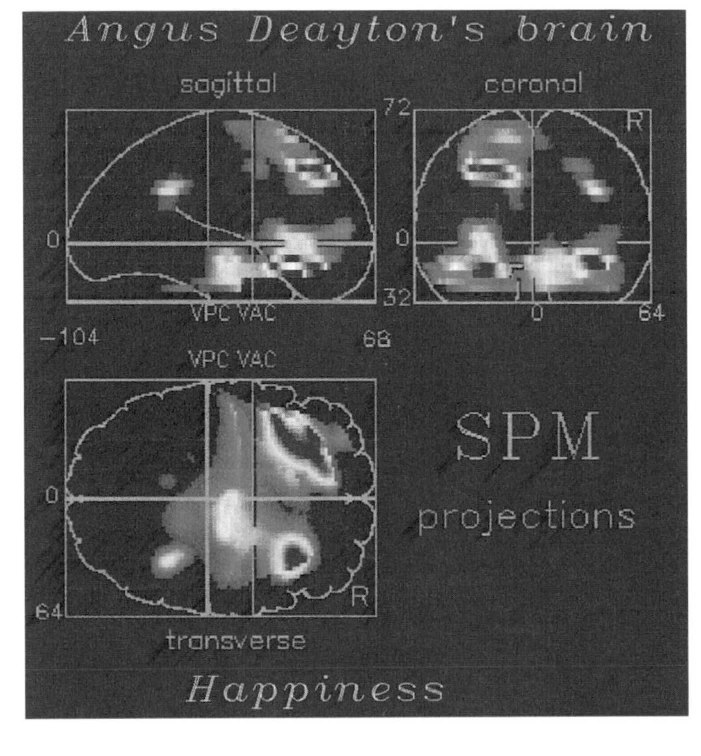

Scientists have been able to pinpoint the areas where pleasurable feelings originate. Unfortunately, the most important ones aren't anywhere near the brain.

soaked trifle while being whipped by a woman whose husband is your boss and due home any minute, you'd be having a whale of a time. Alternatively, if you're a bit of a wimp, you can just stick to paragliding, snowboarding and bungy-jumping off the Forth Bridge.

Individual pleasure-seekers may make for interesting gossip, but it's when they band together in hedonistic communities that things really get intriguing. Such as the people of Oneida Creek, a community created in the United States in 1848 on the principle that anyone could do anything anywhere with anyone they wanted to do it to. The town rather swiftly and bizarrely metamorphosed into a successful spoon-manufacturing company. But you should see what they do with the spoons.

Then there's the Trobriand Islanders, who in their South Pacific paradise have a uniquely open attitude to love and sex. Their society is one in which free love takes place at will between complete strangers. Gangs of women also have total freedom to capture and ravish men – although only at harvest time, during the Yamfest. So in Britain we have maypoles and corn-dollies, in the Trobriands they shag each other senseless twenty-four hours a day. Same idea, slightly different interpretation. (It was suggested – by me I think – that this was such a fascinating story that it merited an entire chapter to itself with several months' location research. But, sadly, their Yamfest didn't quite coincide with publishing deadlines or, indeed, budgets, given that being on the International Dateline, the islands were about as far away from Heathrow as it was possible to get while remaining within the earth's atmosphere.

Clearly hedonism is the way to happiness for some: the creed of just living for yourself, now, and never mind the future. (Although if that is the case, why was James Dean always so miserable?) But whether one's particular penchant is for sex, drugs or crème brûlée, the ultimate goal is the same – pleasure. And through pleasure, happiness.

So what exactly is pleasure? Is there a chemical formula for it? And if someone derives pleasure from great sex and someone else from a hot fudge sundae, is the core experience in the brain the same?

Surprisingly, given the inordinate length of that last question, the answer is a short 'yes'. That's according to Professor Ray Dolan, consultant neuropsychiatrist and Reader in Psychiatry at the University of London.

Pleasure has not been on the agenda for neuroscientific work until recently, but now, thanks to a few plucky volunteers, whose brains were monitored while they were alternately told they were 'absolutely wonderful' and that they were 'a piece of shit', scientists have been able to pinpoint an area in the brain where both pleasurable and unpleasurable feelings originate. 'In about ten years,' says Dr Dolan, 'we should be able to stimulate this area and people should be able to experience intense pleasure without any external trigger object.' No doubt if we can create a helmet with in-built stimulators that can feed us pleasure at the touch of a button, the hedonists of the future won't be indulging so much in wild partying as in an extensive range of designer headgear. The orgasmatron has arrived.

Not that this would be out of keeping with the modern trend. If we are to believe what we are told, the sex, drugs and rock 'n' roll generation is largely a thing of the past. When it comes to drugs we've learned to say no, indiscriminate sex is now a definite no-no and as we near the millennium, good old rock 'n' roll is getting older and older and less and less good.

So should we be looking for a more 1990s, more PC, more environmentally sound form of hedonism, with all the traditional highs and less of the traditional hangovers? Perhaps the answer lies in safe sex and legal drugs. Or maybe just a gallon of crème brûlée . . .

'The quality remains long after the price is forgotten.'
The Reverend Dr Michael Campbell Tinney, enjoying a glass of free champagne.

A LOT OF WHAT YOU FANCY DOES YOU GOOD: MICHAEL CAMPBELL TINNEY

Animals feed: man eats: only the man of intellect knows how to dine.
Jean-Anthelme Brillat-Savarin, author of
The Philosopher of the Kitchen

The discovery of a new dish does more for the happiness of mankind than the discovery of a star.
Jean-Anthelme Brillat-Savarin

Dessert without cheese is like a pretty woman with only one eye.
Jean-Anthelme Brillat-Savarin

If you're not back in ten minutes, the dog's getting your dinner.
Madame Jean-Anthelme Brillat-Savarin

'Heaven come to earth!' exclaims the Reverend Dr Michael Campbell Tinney. He is talking, not about the Second Coming, but about Harrods' Food Hall, where we are standing next to a towering display of crabs, lobster and other edible, if extremely costly, crustacea.

Michael Campbell Tinney is a gastronomic aesthete and, as such, sets pretty high store by a good bit of nosh. 'Food gives you a high like nothing else,' he declaims, 'first of all, because it excites your imagination, which generally is a pleasurable force. And secondly, the anticipation of the waiting until it is done, seeing it prepared and then, of course, finishing the product, completes it all. It is both spiritual and sensual.'

Perhaps as a legacy of his days as a deacon in South Africa, Michael Campbell Tinney talks like a nineteenth-century translation from the Latin. He also looks like he has stepped out of the pages of a work of fiction, probably called something like *How to Look Every Inch the English Gentleman*. In fact, Michael

Campbell Tinney looks so much like an English gentleman, in his checked trousers, his monogrammed blazer (with his own coat of arms and motto, no less) and his matching monogrammed slippers, that you know in an instant that he is an American, probably from California.

I decide to test my theory, and ask Michael where he calls home. 'I live below heaven,' he replies. For a surreal moment I think he means that he has set up home in Harrods' basement, presumably nestling between the crockery and the silverware. But he continues, 'That is really to say, as the residents say, "B.H.-land", or as most mortals call it, Beverly Hills.' Beverly Hills, *California*, I take it.

Michael Campbell Tinney takes his gourmet-dom seriously, and doesn't let a little thing like a war get in the way. Indeed, he assembled a group of like-minded gourmands in Vietnam, where he had gone 'to serve my country'. As a soldier, he was obviously a far cry from Travis Bickell or anyone who has ever featured in an Oliver Stone movie. 'When I was in Vietnam, I lived off Fortnum and Masons, Fauchon of Paris and Harrods, which despatched a box to me on a weekly basis,' says Michael. 'I was the only lieutenant flying a helicopter who had a web-belt with more than a pistol in it. I also had a leather case, which fitted on my belt, made to my specifications, so that a European fork, knife and spoon, rolled in a napkin, would be able to fit inside.' Not only that, but in order to make life just that little bit more luxurious he paid the nuns at a local Catholic convent to run up some custom-made silk sheets, pillowcases, pyjamas and dressing-gowns. Presumably all monogrammed. As Napoleon said, 'An army marches on its stomach.' However, I can't help noticing that although considerably less well fed, it was the Vietcong who eventually emerged the winners of that particular contretemps.

▲ 'Food is beautiful to look at.'
The Reverend Dr Michael Campbell Tinney enjoying the visual feast that is Harrods' fresh seafood display.

We move from the fresh seafood display, past acres of dead birds and dangling salamis, to the pastry case. A display that would grace any museum, and disgrace any weight-watcher, features delicate constructions of spun-sugar and meringue, exotic tarts and flans covered with ripe fruits and great gooey mountains of whipped-cream smothered cakes. Or *gâteaux*, as they are known in Harrods.

'Nothing is better than instant gratification,' sighs Michael, contentedly, as we stand there salivating. 'You decide what you want and you gratify your pleasure by having it now.'

I ask Michael if he knows just what it is about eating and food that attracts him so much. 'Food is beautiful to look at, it is delicious to taste and in the end that warms the heart, the entire body and gives you the strength to carry on enjoying other things that you might do.' So, apart from buying the food, what other things *does* he do that require all this strength? Does work ever rear its ugly head? Michael Campbell Tinney ponders for a nanosecond before replying, 'I indulge in things that are excellent. And it's very hard work – whether it's good travel, good food, good wine or good sex.' And what is the hierarchy of pleasure for him? 'Food is right at the top,' is the uncharacteristically succinct reply.

The next day, when I have almost fully recovered from cholesterol poisoning, I meet Michael Campbell Tinney for lunch at the Connaught Hotel, which is, as they say, 'one of London's premier eating establishments'. Today Michael is nattily outfitted in a striped shirt, and a jacket whose hand-crafted buttons spell out his name in naval signal flags. The head waiter greets us like long-lost brothers, or contributors to the *Good Hotel Guide*. 'Do you come here often?' I ask Michael. 'I come here, like most people who enjoy great food, because it's singularly excellent, without peer,' he explains. 'I, like all the people who come here frequently, appreciate the Temple of

▼ ' "Guilty" is something that man has made up. Guilt is not something that you need to worry about.'
The Reverend Dr Michael Campbell Tinney, enjoying a spot of fishing while I watch, enthralled.

Gastronomy that has been built here and that perpetuates itself every day.' I reach for my thesaurus.

We are shown to our table, in the corner of the elegant, wood-panelled dining-room. It is still early and we are virtually the only guests there. Perhaps that is why we seem to have about five waiters each. Michael basks in the refined atmosphere. 'Meals are about unions, aren't they?' he asks, without expecting a reply. 'About getting together. Like when Banquo's ghost comes to the table . . . the uninvited guest spoils the dinner party and it's horrific and he goes mad as a result.' Certainly the most novel interpretation of Shakespeare's tragedy I've yet heard. It wasn't that Macbeth was tortured by guilt because he had committed murder, he was simply pissed off because Banquo had gate-crashed his dinner party. 'Is this a dagger which I see before me? . . . But I ordered the sea bass.'

As menus the size of the Old Testament are delivered, along with a wine list bearing a striking resemblance to the original stone tablets, I become nervous that I will be exposed as an infidel in this, the Temple of Gastronomy. And is Michel Bourdin, the godhead of this particular Church, as ferocious as some of the other top chefs, some of whom, mentioning no Marco Pierre Whites, have been known to storm into the dining-room and roast guests who have dared to salt their food? I make a mental note not to ask for tomato sauce.

After receiving copious advice from the waiter and at least a dozen mouth-watering descriptions of the dishes on offer, I decide to have whatever Michael is having. After all, since he

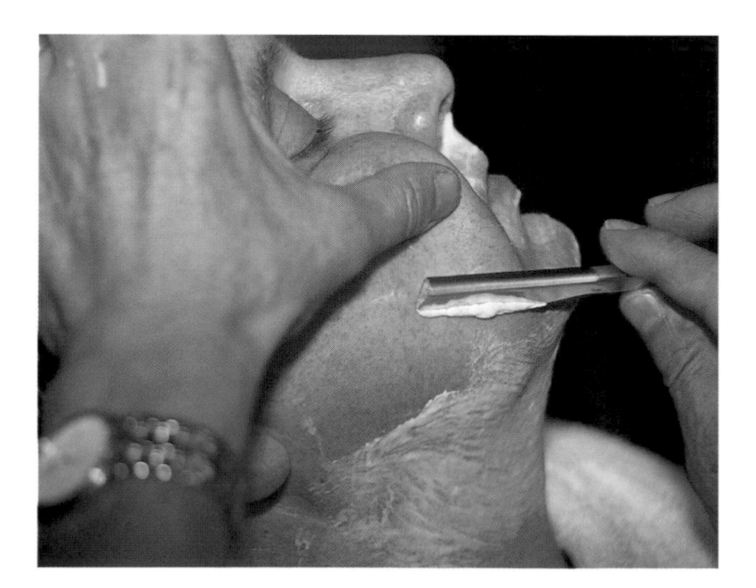

'Part of living is indulging in things. If one doesn't indulge in anything one isn't alive, one is dead.' The Reverend Dr Michael Campbell Tinney enjoying the feel of razor on throat.

'Nothing is better than instant gratification.' The Reverend Dr Michael Campbell Tinney enjoying a gratifying lunch at the Connaught.

claims to lunch in establishments such as this at least twice a week, he's the expert. 'To start with always fish,' says Michael, in danger of almost forming a comprehensible sentence. 'I think the *Zephirs de sole "tout Paris"*.' This turns out to be a plate of fish mousse served with white wine sauce and lobster sauce, so delicious that if it doesn't make you fall down on your knees and worship at the altar of fine cuisine, it might at least make you say a small benediction.

When we have almost sated our appetites, the main course arrives. Known by the Connaught as *quartiers d'agneau rôti 'forestière'*, in common parlance it would be described as 'an entire roast lamb'.

'Of all the meats, my preference would always be either for lamb or for fresh *foie gras*, which is done brilliantly here in the fashion of Normandy,' intones Michael.

'But doesn't *foie gras* involve quite a lot of cruel force-feeding of geese?' I ask Michael (my mouth full of baby lamb).

'Yes – and strangulation,' replies the Reverend, happily, as he takes a sip of the Château Giscours '82. 'Like velvet, smooth, not heady. Long-lasting. It's romantic as it goes down,' is the verdict on the wine. At least I assume that he is talking about the wine.

One dessert trolley, 'The *crème brûlée*, forever the *brûlée*', some coffee, a couple of Armagnacs and a large cigar later, we are ready for the bill. Or rather the bill is ready for us. It would take a lot of *Big Issues* to cover this lunch. The wine alone is a cool £73 per bottle. I ask Michael if it ever makes him feel guilty. He considers briefly, puffing on his Monte Cristo No. 2. '"Guilty" is something that man has made up. Guilt is not something that you need to worry about.'

As to the question of whether it's really worth that much money, Michael says, 'Was it Charles Rose who said "the quality remains long after the price is forgotten"?' Well, whoever it was that said it, you can bet it wasn't Charles Rose who was paying the bill.

Dr Campbell Tinney turns and summons the waiter : 'Would you make it a point of sending my *carte-du-garde* into the kitchen and telling him that we hope to have the pleasure of thanking him personally for such brilliant perfection. As always.' The Reverend Doctor turns back to me. 'Part of living is indulging in things. If one doesn't indulge in anything one isn't alive, one is dead. The chances are you are not going to get this in your grave.' Unless, of course, you happen to be buried at the Connaught.

WHITE DOG AND ENGLISHMAN: TOAD-TOKING IN TUCSON

White Dog – guano retriever and local high priest of toad.

People must not do things for fun. We are not here for fun. There is no reference to fun in any Act of Parliament.
A. P. Herbert, writer and politician

A little of what you fancy does you good.
Marie Lloyd, music-hall singer

Tucson, Arizona, is in the middle of the Sonoran Desert – thousands and thousands of acres of wilderness where huge stone mesas rise out of the dry red earth and the only things that provide any shade are cacti, century plants and billboards advertising Marlboro cigarettes. But despite the aridity, this desert is home to many of God's creatures, including the wild cat, the coyote, the ghila monster (a type of giant poisonous lizard) and the rattlesnake. In other words, my kinda place.

And since God, or whoever arranges these things, appears to be something of a bastard, all of these animals survive by eating each other. All that is apart from one. The Colorado River toad (*Bufo alvarius*) has no predators. This cunningly Darwinian amphibian has developed a built-in safety feature so simple yet so cunning that it deserves a Kite mark. Basically, he's poisonous. In fact, the venom of the Colorado River toad is so strong that if any coyote/wild cat/ghila monster/rattlesnake/TV presenter so much as licked him, they'd drop dead on the spot.

Now, you might very well think that this would be enough to deter the human race from going anywhere near this toad. But man is an inventive creature, and man in search of A Good Time is more inventive still. Why else would every schoolboy know that the best way to get drunk quickly and cheaply is to drink some cider through a straw and then sprint for twenty seconds? How would anyone have guessed that you could get high from that little bit of gas that comes out of the nozzle of a spray container of whipping cream if you press it very gently and sniff, or that if you run out of Rizla paper you can smoke marijuana through a hole bored in a potato? Likewise, the same dedicated team of amateur scientists and many undisclosed years of trial and error have turned up the fact that although licking the toads may be lethal – smoking them (or at least their dried venom) is one of the most powerfully hallucinogenic and mind-altering experiences known to hippie.

White Dog is the *nom de plume* (or *nom de fume*) of a toad devotee who lives in a home-made desert dwelling miles from civilization but quite close to Tucson. Originally from the colder climes of Minnesota, White Dog (aged forty-three) made his way down to the South-west twenty-two years ago in search of hallucinogenic highs. (Well, it *was* 1972, and he *was* twenty-one years old.) Sure enough, he soon became involved with a group calling itself the Peyote Way of God, and rose within their ranks to the dizzy heights of 'Courier of Sacrament', which, for some reason, I assume involved delivering Bibles on a motorbike. It was during a peyote-enhanced experience that a pale, dog-like creature appeared to him in the corner of the moon and revealed his new name. Beige Dingo, who subsequently decided to call himself White Dog, heard about toad ten years ago, when an old friend from the peyote church told him, 'This stuff's gonna scare the shit out of you.' Thus encouraged, White Dog soon managed to track down a booklet written incognito by a rogue scientist containing precise instructions about how to milk and prepare toad venom. (So next time you're looking for that book on DIY submarines or Ancient Egyptian scarab recipes, don't let the guy in the bookshop tell you it doesn't exist. Somewhere, it does.) Nowadays, White Dog is the local high priest of toad and will happily shepherd would-be pilgrims through their toad baptism. In between what he calls 'training' – experiments in expanding consciousness and spiritual awakening – he earns his living as a guano retriever (or in common parlance, 'a shit collector'). He is particularly in demand as a collector of bat shit, which is used as fertilizer. 'It's the highest form of nitrogen you can naturally get.'

As we career White Dog-wards along an unbelievably bumpy dirt track on the outskirts of Tucson, I'm almost sick with excitement at the prospect of our imminent meeting. This is because White Dog is already a bit of a celebrity – as well as having quite a following among the toad *cognoscenti* of Tucson, he's been interviewed by *Esquire* magazine, he's appeared on national TV in the US, he's written for the *New York Times*, and *Figaro* are arriving to interview him tomorrow. In fact it's nice of him to fit us into his busy schedule at all.

At first glance White Dog's house looks like a sort of white polystyrene igloo, largely because that is exactly what it is. (Well, actually it is made of polyurethane and chicken wire.) Next to the dwelling is another igloo, made out of adobe (mud and straw) which is apparently a Native American sauna or 'sweat-lodge'. Since it must be at least 100° Fahrenheit in the shade, the prospect of shutting myself into a small heated room is naturally extremely enticing.

There is no obvious doorbell, and for some reason I am finding it difficult to make myself call out, 'White Dog?' so, after a few minutes stomping around outside by the cactuses and what appears to be a large trampoline, I enter the plastic dome. It soon becomes apparent that White Dog must be accustomed to people turning up at his house unannounced, so accustomed, in fact, that I stand around in his kitchen for about half an hour before he notices me. White Dog, on the other hand, would be impossible not to notice, even for a few seconds. For one thing, he is wearing a multi-coloured Day-Glo shirt that looks like it was designed by a South Sea Islander on acid, and for another, White Dog is about six foot five inches tall, and has a full beard and a huge froth of blond dreadlocks, which cascade knottily down to his waist. Not only does this man not take two bottles into the shower, he doesn't bother to go into the shower in the first place.

My next discovery about White Dog is that he's vehemently opposed to both alcohol and tobacco, which he regards as the devil's work and won't allow in his house. Hence the immediate confiscation of my half-finished can of Budweiser. He is at great pains to explain how damaging and addictive alcohol and tobacco are, and to point out the hypocrisy of governments in condoning those money-making drugs and outlawing the innocuous ones that simply send you to the Andromeda galaxy and back. I feel like pointing out that this is not strictly true: from what I've read, it seems that the CIA make more than their fair share of money out of hard drugs too. But this might be considered flippant, and he is extremely tall. I do however pluck up the courage to ask him why he has a trampoline outside his house, and am informed that besides being used for recreational purposes, it also doubles as a spare bed. Apparently it can take up to eight comfortably. That's presumably provided you don't have a restless night, or you could wake up in a tree.

The interior of the plastic bubble house is tiny, but it seems reasonably clean and tidy. However, while availing myself of his washroom facilities, I can't help but become aware of an extremely unpleasant smell. When I mention this, as politely as

White Dog and The Polystyrene Igloos. (Sounds like a band from the early seventies.)

I can, I am informed that the odour emanates from a brace (or whatever the collective noun is for toads) of *Bufo alvarius*, which White Dog caught last night and has decided to keep in his shower. Later today he will milk them for their venom, which he will then dry and smoke in a self-devised ceremony, which we are kindly invited, and professionally obliged, to attend.

To look at the Colorado River toad, you wouldn't know it was anything special. As toads go, it's of about average ugliness. Ordinarily, it grows to a length of seven inches from mouth to anus, although locals say they have seen toads up to a foot long. What is out of the ordinary is one of the substances found in its venom. Known catchily as '5-methoxy-N, N-dimethyltrypt-amine', it is one of the most powerful psychoactive chemicals in existence. If you ever get cornered by a pharmacy student at a party he may unfortunately choose to tell you that it's a close analogue of serotonin, the main neurotransmitter in the synapse, and melatonin, a hormone produced by the pineal gland, and that this interacts with deep brain centres related to emotion and consciousness. On the other hand, if you're lucky, he may decide to discuss Warwickshire's chances in the Benson and Hedges Cup instead. Either way, 5-meo-DMT is a pretty powerful drug.

The toads, like English strawberries and débutantes, only come out in the season. In fact, they appear in the summer months when the heat and rain provide ideal breeding conditions – unlike English strawberries, but exactly like débutantes. White Dog doesn't even have to make much of an an effort to go and find them. 'I don't collect toads. They show up and I deal with them.'

The venom comes from glands on the toad's back and legs. These create a thin film of poison which permanently covers the toad's skin, although fright will cause the toad to secrete a great deal more. If done properly, milking the venom is completely harmless to the toad, providing you don't overdo it. 'You should only milk a toad twice in a season or you rob them of their natural protection. You can't keep a pet toad and squeeze it every day,' says White Dog, self-proclaimed animal lover and strict vegan. I obviously must look worried, because he continues reassuringly, 'But there are enough toads to go around and a person needs so very little that you could probably milk two or three toads and have enough for yourself for the whole year.'

Milking said toad is disgustingly similar to squeezing a spot. The viscous white venom is squeezed on to a piece of glass, then allowed to dry for a few hours or overnight. When it's attained a rubbery texture you can shave it off the glass with a razor. The flakes are now ready to smoke. And White Dog assures me that, although the venom itself is a very dangerous neurotoxin that can cause paralysis and death if taken orally (don't try

Milking the Colorado River toad (*Bufo alvarius*). Its venom contains 5-methoxy-N, N-dimethyltryptamine, one of the most powerful and difficult to pronounce psychoactive chemicals in existence.

kissing any of these toads), smoking it is 'completely safe'. But how safe is 'completely safe'? 'The effect is like having your body experience a massive adrenalin rush and such an acceleration and stuff that you're not really sure what is happening to you. It's something that, until you've smoked it, your body hasn't experienced and isn't even aware that it can survive it. There have been people who have felt very close to death on it.' So, 'safe' in the sense of 'unbelievably life-threatening', then.

As to the legal situation *vis-à-vis* toad, since its psychoactive properties have received a certain amount of publicity there has been a corresponding amount of pressure from the authorities to crack down on its use. However, as outlawing the toads themselves might lead to some rather bizarre arrests, the state of Arizona has decreed that no one may be in possession of more than ten of the creatures, and then only with the slightly strange proviso that you must own a fishing licence. This presumably means that you have to learn how to monitor the genders carefully. If any of your ten mate in the night you could be prosecuted the next morning.

White Dog doesn't own a fishing licence. 'Why would I? I don't fish.' Nor does he consider himself a frequent user. 'I do it very seldom,' he says. 'Once every few months or if I have a reason to do it I'll do it, but I don't really use it that much. In the course of eight to ten years I've done it about a hundred times, and I've gone five, six, months without smoking it.' (I've gone thirty-eight years without smoking it, but then, who's counting?) From all accounts toad-smoking is the short sharp shock of the hallucinogen family, two of its main distinguishing features being its potency and its brevity. The entire trip generally lasts ten to fifteen minutes, including seven to eight minutes of 'really accelerated activity'. Of course, this can be a distinct advantage for the busy executive. White Dog tells me: 'I smoked it once at lunchtime, laying bricks in 110 degrees. Got up after lunch, went and laid bricks for another five hours.' Try doing that after three pints of scrumpy.

But what about long-term effects, like – to pluck an example out of the air at random – brain damage? 'I don't think it dulls the senses, I think it heightens the senses, I've never been in better shape than I've been since I started smoking it. And my memory and my retention and stuff has been pretty good. I become very analytical and look at things from multiple directions before even answering a question. So for some people that may seem as if I'm spaced out. I have this problem when someone asks me a question: instead of answering it, I'll run about five or six processes through my mind to see what I really want to answer it with. I don't just want to answer yes or no, I want to try a few more things.' This is all very well, but it does lead to a style of speaking that is so slow you feel you should play some incidental music between each word.

I asked White Dog how he would rate toad in comparison to some of the other controlled substances he might have had occasion to experiment with in the course of his adult life. 'This substance is definitely different than anything I've ever taken, and I can't compare it with anything else.' Ah. So much for my idea of starting a *Michelin*-style guide for drug takers, with little symbols representing brain cell damage next to each entry.

Marijuana – dried hemp leaf. If you are a bit of a traditionalist as far as controlled substances are concerned, look no further. Unpleasant side effects may include the wearing of cheesecloth shirts.
Glue – chemical compound originally developed for the purpose of adhering two separate surfaces. Although it only acquired mass popularity in the late twentieth century, glue seems here to stay. Also highly recommended for repairing broken teapots, etc., etc.

Being with people who are taking drugs when you are not is like seeing someone receive a kissogram. You feel faintly embarrassed, slightly anxious and extremely glad it's not happening to you.

I leave White Dog's house feeling confused. Although my knowledge of the chemical components of natural psychotropic substances has positively burgeoned, and although I'm marginally more convinced that you can inhale dangerous neurotoxins without dropping down dead, I'm still in the dark as to why anyone would want to smoke toad. Where's the fun? Perhaps I'll just have to try it myself.

The Ceremony

Well, perhaps not . . . Sitting in a circle around the fire, passing round the pipe, it makes you realize how little has changed in twenty years. It's the same tie-dyed clothes, the same laid-back speech, the same insertion of the word 'man' at the end of every sentence, the same tuneless strumming of acoustic guitars and the same sense of superiority of the 'enlightened' over the 'straight'. Of course, twenty years ago we were passing around a Woodbine and a Party Seven, as smoking toad venom hadn't quite reached Purley. In fact, I'd put money on it that it still hasn't.

The wind is whistling through the cactus plants as we get ready for White Dog to begin the ceremony. There is a great deal of nervous tension, not least because there are several toad virgins present. Two of the group, a young female student and a man called Larry with long hair and a yellow T-shirt with FART printed on it, are to be initiated this very afternoon. And, despite all the protestations of harmlessness, there is a very real feeling of danger. White Dog stands up, reverentially picks up a large clay pipe in the shape of a toad and blows into it. At this point, I realize that it is not a pipe but a ceremonial whistle. Turning to each of the four points of the compass in turn, White Dog blows, producing a long, mournful, tuneless note. This done, he puts down the whistle and picks up a small, clear, crystal pipe, into which the flakes of toad venom have already been inserted. Unfortunately the wind seems to be making it difficult to light, and the orange Bic is dropped abruptly with a *sotto voce* curse as it burns White Dog's fingers. He stalks off to the house and returns some minutes later with a long-stemmed wooden pipe, which presumably is better designed for the prevailing weather conditions.

Being with people who are taking drugs when you are not is like seeing someone receive a kissogram. You feel faintly embarrassed, slightly anxious and extremely glad it's not happening to you. It's about as much fun as double maths. As it turns out the student only experiences a mild hit, but appears to lose the power of coherent speech (that is, if she ever possessed it), White Dog's friend Larry trips silently for a couple of minutes and then, raising both arms, launches into a fifteen-minute stream-of-unconsciousness burble about his 'essence' and 'being', while White Dog takes himself off to get away from the noise. When he reappears some time later it transpires that he has experienced the biggest hit – some seven or eight minutes of out-of-body consciousness.

When it is all over, they sit and grin at each other in a sort of sleepy conspiratorial way. 'So what was it like?' I venture. They grin some more. Eventually White Dog begins to speak, very, very slowly.

'All the experiences are different . . . I've had friends who have seen portholes into the past, and seen pyramids and workers around the pyramids and the mines and all these different civilizations. I've had friends who have had heat coming out of the palms of their hands, I've had friends who, and I myself, have left their body and been sitting across from themselves looking at themselves . . . I've had friends who have felt they were the toads themselves and just sat there and smiled like toads and told me they felt like them . . . I've had experiences on toad where I thought my heart was going to stop, I didn't have any blood pressure and wasn't breathing and all that you know, going into almost frozen hibernation . . .'

That's all very well, but somehow the sensations he is describing sound anything but pleasant. Is it pleasurable? Does it make you happier? White Dog considers for a long time. 'I would recommend it to people. It has opened up parts of my mind that I haven't seen before. When I have sat on earth and smoked it I've felt the earth come close to me, I've felt closer to Nature. And being close to and feeling part of Nature is a very high experience, and I can't think of anything else I would want to do on this planet, but become closer to Nature.' Somehow I was beginning to get the feeling that White Dog was quite keen on feeling close to Nature. 'It feels like you're connecting with an old friend. So it's quite a pleasurable experience,' he continues. 'I'm different since I smoked it. I just don't imagine what life would be without it.'

As we sit on the trampoline and watch the sun set over the desert, the toads begin to croak. There are many questions I ask White Dog, but even more I want to and can't. What is his real name? Could I call him White? When did he last wash his hair? If this drug is so harmless, how come there is a three-minute silence between each word he utters? And finally, if your job is collecting bat shit, what does it say on your passport?

SEX LESSONS

Caroline Aldred's Tantric Sex Class of '94 and the Institute of Higher Sexology

The orgasm has replaced the Cross as the focus of longing and the image of fulfilment.
Malcolm Muggeridge

I know it does make people happy but to me it's just like having a cup of tea.
Cynthia Payne

I am in the sitting-room in a flat in Maida Vale, but I am not sitting. My feet are firmly planted on the carpet about ten inches apart, and I am bending forward from the waist, almost touching my toes. But this is not an aerobics class. I am indulging in the rather less widely practised art of breathing through my anus. Or, rather, I am pretending to breathe through my anus as this is what I, and the seven other people in the room, have been instructed to do. Breathing through anuses is just one of the many things that, apparently, improve our sexual performance

Anal respiration – three of us taking a deep breath . . .

and make us, and our partners, very, very happy. Unless, of course, our teacher was just talking through her anus when she told us this.

The teacher in question is Caroline Aldred, a young Englishwoman who studied drama and T'ai Chi before becoming the pupil of a Tantric guru in Bali, where she studied for five years. Now the student has become the master, and the chosen subject is not geography, or netball, but 'Sex, pure and simple.' Of course, to paraphrase Oscar Wilde, sex is rarely pure and never simple. Certainly not in Oscar's case, anyway. Caroline Aldred's teachings are based on a fusion of Tantric and Taoist practices. I'm not sure exactly what that means, but for a mere £7 I can bowl up at one of Caroline's Monday-night classes and find out. And at the same time brush up on my anal respiration.

According to the experts, it is reasonable to assume that sexual fulfilment would play a large part in contributing to an individual's happiness. In a survey that asked people: 'Which leisure-time pursuit do you enjoy most?' sex received an overwhelming thumbs-up (if that's the phrase I'm looking for). Likewise, out of a sample group of two thousand British people 35 per cent of men and 26 per cent of women agreed with the statement 'Sex is far and away my greatest pleasure' while the remainder of the population were too busy screwing to fill out the questionnaire.

'If happiness can be measured quantifiably, then yes, my happiness has increased a thousand-fold because my sex is great.'

From his flat on the twenty-third floor of a high-rise block in Plumstead, self-taught, self-confessed and self-promoting 'sexologist' David Howe runs an organization he calls the Institute of Higher Sexology (presumably to distinguish it from the plain old Institute of Sexology a few floors down). According to David Howe it's not what you do, but how long you do it for that makes all the difference to you and your partner's sex life. He blames premature ejaculation on just about everything from causing unhappiness and ill health to the Third World debt and Millwall's failure to win promotion to the Premier League. Naturally, having no personal experience of this curious 'premature ejaculation' phenomenon, I am forced to ask David Howe to define it. 'All ejaculation preceding female orgasm is premature ejaculation. If you cannot make love to a woman for one to two hours and bring her naturally to orgasm with your penis, then you have got that problem,' he says emphatically. Then I make the mistake of mentioning foreplay. 'Foreplay is without doubt the sexual red herring of the twentieth century,' expounds Howe. He continues, thankfully abandoning the fish metaphor.

'The man who masters *Ejaculation Control – The Key to Female Orgasm* realizes the true Secrets of Sexual Ecstasy and becomes a Gladiator of the Bedroom. He can ravish his concupiscent lover with long erotic love-rides to as many intoxicating orgasms as she pleases . . .'
David Howe (with concupiscent lover, Linda)

'Neurotically relying on clitoral stimulation, before, during and after making love, in the frantic pursuit of female orgasm, has become the norm due to the fact that all men ejaculate too soon when making love. Thus the politics of sexual suffering marches onwards.'

I can't help noticing that anything to do with the subject of sex seems to make him very angry. 'The rhetoric of today's vibrator-wielding therapists and sex counsellors is little more than a cosy sham that unashamedly reveals the politics of feminist vengeance,' he insists. Luckily, David Howe has a solution of his own devising, based on ancient oriental principles. He calls it Orgasmic Genital Gratification (OGG) and it involves mastering something Mr Howe describes as the 'Locking Technique'. OGG is, he claims modestly, 'the most effective and potent healing balm for neurosis, biopathological antisocial behaviour, sexual deviancy, drug addiction, abuse and lack of respect between the sexes. Ejaculation control for fulfilling sexual love is the only known antidote to this chronic holocaust of sexual suffering.'

Of course, it has to be said that not everyone would endorse these (or indeed any) of his views. Sociobiologists argue (and, let's face it, when do they ever agree?) that in the early days of the human race it was of evolutionary advantage to man to deposit his semen in the female of the species as quickly as possible, or at any rate before a rival caveman or sabre-toothed tiger interrupted his coitus. Now, after thousands of years of practice, twentieth-century man can achieve orgasm in a little under two minutes. Not bad going, you might think. But the gibbon can reach the moment of ejaculation in fifteen seconds, the lemur in ten and the chimpanzee in a lightning seven seconds. The only ape to take longer than man is the orang-utan, who averages an almost endless 10.8 *minutes*. It must be spending all that time hanging out with Clint Eastwood.

However, if David Howe and articles in *Cosmopolitan* magazine are to be believed, premature ejaculation is no longer a prized skill to be proudly flaunted to attract a mate. In fact, you could even go so far as to say that it might put a few women off the idea of bearing your children. If eighties man's 'ideal mate' was a woman who screws till midnight and then turns into a pizza, then perhaps nineties woman's 'ideal mate' would be an orang-utan wearing a Keanu Reeves mask.

David and his wife, Linda, have co-written and privately published their own sex manual, which aims to provide an easy-to-follow step-by-step guide to the Locking Technique, and other 'Bedroom Secrets'. Succinctly entitled *Secrets of Sexual Ecstasy: The Oriental Bedroom Art of Ejaculation Control – The Key to Female Orgasm: The Manual* it contains 106 pages of text, a number of pen-and-ink drawings executed by Linda (stylistically *The Joy of Sex*, but without the beards) and even a gushing letter from a satisfied customer in Western Australia who apparently owns not one, but three copies: 'Your wisdom and knowledge has provided me with self-control, love and happiness. With the Locking Technique it is now possible to satisfy ten women in one night!' – Gerald B. Sadly, this book is not available in the shops. You can get it by mail order or, failing that, allow this short but pithy extract to put you off. 'The words of the famous song 'Love is a Many-Splendoured Thing' have sadly lost their meaning in the psychotic jungle of diverse sexual practices which we are encouraged to follow . . . The man who masters *Ejaculation Control – The Key to Female Orgasm* realizes the true Secrets of Sexual Ecstasy and becomes a Gladiator of the Bedroom. He can ravish his concupiscent lover with long erotic love-rides to as many intoxicating orgasms as she pleases . . .'

Time for some anal respiration.

Do not try this at home unless you are a trained flautist.

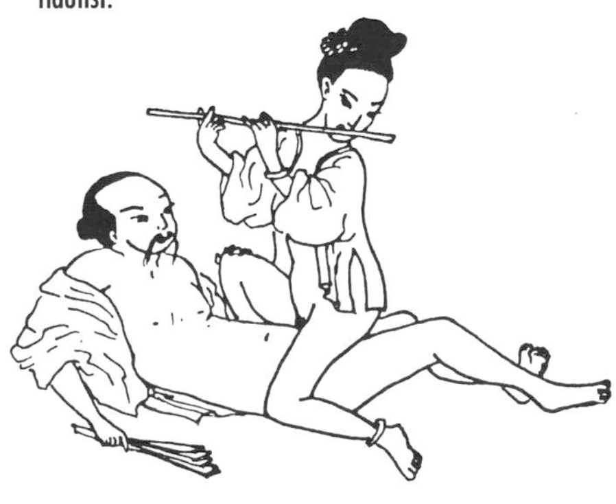

Monday arrives and I make my way to Caroline Aldred's flat in Maida Vale. Caroline has already told me over the phone that the only precautions I need to take are to wear loose-fitting clothing and refrain from eating for two hours beforehand. Inexplicably I'm feeling rather nervous. Perhaps it's because the last time anyone gave me those instructions I ended up having my tonsils out. Or maybe I'm just worried that she's going to be a female David Howe.

So, I breathe a small sigh of relief when the door of this rather posh-looking mansion flat is opened by a smiling woman looking every inch the professional (of the yoga teacher variety) in a white T-shirt and a pair of black leggings. Caroline Aldred seems as calm and cheerful as David Howe was not, although the gist of her message is the same. Most of us, it appears, just aren't very good at sex – or, at any rate, we make the mistake of viewing it as an enjoyable leisure pastime rather than as an art or even as an act of worship. For most of us in the West, sex is just 'two minutes of squelching', as Johnny Rotten once put it, although several years later, in his more mature, man-of-the-world incarnation as John Lydon, he revised it to 'three minutes of squelching'. That's unless you're a chimpanzee, of course, in which case it's seven seconds of squelching.

Caroline and her partner Jamie don't squelch at all. They 'make love' on average every day, often for several hours. Their record is apparently seventy-two hours, although Caroline tells me this marathon did involve massaging, bathing and eating (although not sleeping or watching a movie). 'It was over a three-day period – very extensive, very pleasurable.' I search Jamie's face for signs of nervous exhaustion, but, it has to be said, he's looking fairly perky.

'I'm fascinated by sex,' responds Caroline, when I ask her how she got into this line of work. 'I suppose I just want sex to be an all-over healing experience. It's about putting the sacredness back into making love, making it an act of worship.' Finally, after all these years of wondering, the expression 'missionary position' is explained. But why do people need to be taught? 'I think that the mass media is responsible for turning sex into a commodity. Our culture has become about instant gratification, which is reflected in all these fast-food restaurants. In the East it was always tradition that they were taught how to make love, because it is such a very powerful energy. These days we are very concerned about conserving the earth's energy, and our energy is just as important.' I can't help thinking that if Caroline and Jamie make love as often as they claim, they actually *are* a source

of energy. A bit of clever wiring and they could power their own windmill.

Of course, it soon turns out that Tantric sex is all about that hoary old chestnut, stopping the man ejaculating. And not just so that you can carry on for days at a time but for health reasons. Apparently how often you may safely ejaculate is determined by age (and, of course, circumstances, but no one is suggesting that you should attempt it on the bus to work every day). In order to calculate how often you can have an orgasm without wilfully squandering your *chi* or 'life energy', multiply your age by 0.2. In other words a thirty-five-year-old man can safely ejaculate once a week, a twenty-year-old every four days and a seventy-year-old once a fortnight, if he is very lucky, and still alive.

'But isn't sex without ejaculation a bit like cooking a very elaborate meal and then not eating it?' I wonder. 'No, no, no, it's like cooking a very elaborate meal and then eating it very slowly and tasting every mouthful,' replies Caroline. Well, then, what about the problem of fitting all these marathon sex sessions into a busy office schedule – I mean, how often can you get away with 'Sorry I'm late, I've been having sex for the last three days'?

Caroline says that her Tantric sex classes are all about teaching people to recognize that 'your partner is a goddess and that you are a god' (presumably no tuition necessary if you are Eric Cantona). Caroline also believes that striving to 'perfect' your sex life leads naturally to monogamy. 'It's a way of staying with one partner and being able to fulfil everything that both of you need, want, require or desire.' Either that or your partner's too shagged out to do any straying. I somehow imagine that after a few months of three-day sex sessions you would start fantasizing about lying on the sofa watching telly with a mug of tea and a chocolate Hob-nob.

However, it soon becomes obvious that not everyone feels like this. At seven o'clock prompt there is a positive stampede as the other workshop participants arrive at the flat. All of them are couples, all are suitably attired in 'comfortable' clothing of various descriptions and all seem more than ready to wash their clean linen in public. For some reason, the words New Age spring to mind, although Middle Age would probably have been more appropriate since the youngest member of the group is in her early thirties. The oldest, incidentally, was a member of King Crimson, a popular beat combo of the late 1960s.

I go into the living-room with my new classmates – Marilyn, Vince, Amanda, Jake, Yasmine, Robin and Peter. The furniture

Caroline with her gods and goddesses.

has been removed and the floor is covered with rugs and Indian bedspreads. Church candles burn inside glasses, and I am transported back two decades by the smell of joss-sticks. The shelves are festooned with ethnic craftwork – a Mexican hammock, some African wood carving and numerous artifacts from Thailand, India and other parts of the Far East, many representing Eastern gods and goddesses. The person who furnished this home has either done a lot of travelling or else spends all their money in Camden Market.

Many of them have been attending Caroline's classes for some time, and when we are instructed to start doing various yoga-type breathing exercises and generally shaking ourselves about, the others fall to it enthusiastically. However, for some reason the ability to draw air from my belly to my third eye eludes me and I am immediately the class dunce. After a while Caroline presents each of us with an orange tied to a piece of string. 'This exercise is called Tongue Kung Fu,' announces Caroline serenely. 'Remember that the tongue is a very powerful tool for love-making. It's warm and moist, it can change shape and size and with it you can direct *chi* into your lover.' I'm not entirely convinced that I would want a lover to direct *chi* into me, at least not until I've had a chance to look it up, but I comply with Caroline's instructions, dangling the orange in front of my mouth and poking at it with my tongue. (Apparently after a month or so you move on to a heavier object like a jar of pickled onions.) 'Come on, hit the orange with your tongue . . . That's right, like a viper . . . Now slap it from side to side . . . Try to hook it underneath . . .' encourages Caroline. I'm conscious of the fact that I'm beginning to dribble uncontrollably, although I think the orange is starting to enjoy itself. 'This exercise is also good because it makes you produce more saliva,' she adds. 'The Chinese believe saliva is a great vital elixir.' Yes, and they also eat ducks' feet and monkey brains . . .

After the orange we turn to the task of exercising our PC muscle (not 'politically correct' but Pubo-coccygeus). This muscle, 'located between your balls and your anus', as Caroline delicately puts it, is apparently the secret weapon in the fight against ejaculation. Develop it, learn to control it and sexual fulfilment is all yours, or at least, if you're a man, your partner's. As Caroline poetically explains it, 'A woman is a pot of water and the man is the fire underneath and it takes time for the pot of water to come to the boil. These techniques help the man keep his fire burning long enough to boil the water.'

As well as keeping your fire stoked, Caroline encourages a

Tongue Kung Fu.
'Remember that the tongue is a very powerful tool for lovemaking. It's warm and moist, it can change shape and size, and with it you can direct *chi* into your lover' . . . or your orange, depending on what you're doing.

Good practice for standing in the wall when I next play football.

certain amount of interior decorating prior to the sex act. As we lie on our backs in a circle feeling our own *chi* (i.e. with our hands cupping our genitals), she tells us, 'Make sure that your environment is completely wonderful. Whether you have sex in your bedroom or your sitting-room or your kitchen, it is really worth preparing it. Women are turned on by soft lights, soft music and soft drapy things' (as opposed to soft droopy things, which have the opposite effect). Additional tips include cutting the heads off flowers and putting them in the bath and removing the TV 'and pretty much any electrical device' from the bedroom. 'TV saps your energy.' Compared to what? Put against seventy-two hours of non-stop copulation, I'd have thought that a quick dose of Cilla Black or Jeremy Paxman would be positively relaxing. The evening climaxes – if that's the word – with us all sitting in a circle, wearing blindfolds and feeding each other. At least, I think it does. For all I know the others could have rushed off to their respective homes to have some torrid-yet-sacred sex, leaving me to be spoonfed by the cameraman.

Everyone knows that if you work out at the gym every day you can eventually get a body like Sylvester Stallone. That doesn't mean you'll get his cheque book. If you starve yourself for long enough you might look a bit like Kate Moss, but that doesn't mean Johnny Depp will wreck your hotel room. So even if you learn to swing bowling balls from your tongue and develop a PC muscle the size of a third buttock, will sex and sexual pleasure actually increase your state of happiness? 'I believe we're all in a state of happiness,' says Caroline. 'We just forget it very easily. But if happiness can be measured quantifiably, then yes, my happiness has increased a thousandfold because my sex is great.' So, no excuses, get to it! Just find some joss-sticks, some sitar music, some soft drapy things and take three days off work. Then all you'll need to complete the experiment, is a partner.

Out of a sample group of two thousand British people, 35 per cent of men and 26 per cent of women agreed with the statement 'sex is far and away my greatest pleasure'. Interestingly, none of them chose 'eating with my fingers, blindfolded'.

A DAY IN THE LIFE OF A COUCH POTATO: BRIAN TULLEY

Television is more interesting than people. If it were not, we should have people standing in the corners of our rooms.
Alan Coren

It's often been said that television is a medium, because it's neither rare nor well done.
Angus Deayton, quiz show presenter

The only thing I won't watch are those really terrible quiz programmes that we're getting lately.
Brian Tulley

Forty-three-year-old Brian Tulley is a former bus driver from Dalkeith, Edinburgh. A self-confessed couch potato, his idea of perfect happiness is spending all day every day in front of the television.

'I wake up, and turn on the television. I enjoy watching the children's programmes you get from about 8.30 a.m. onwards. Then, about five past nine, you get the old movies – you usually get two back to back, which takes you up to half-past ten. That's usually when I get up, go downstairs and switch on the telly in the lounge. At five past eleven they're now showing re-runs of *Quincey*, *Cagney and Lacey* and *Remington Steele*. That takes us up to twelve. At twelve I watch *Pebble Mill*, sometimes it's not bad, sometimes it's all right. It takes us up to the news. That's when I have a couple of biscuits, usually gingernuts, and a glass of milk. At one thirty there's *Neighbours*, then at one fifty *Going For Gold* comes on. That's when I change to another channel, I won't watch *that*. Then at quarter-past two I turn back over to BBC 1 to watch *The Rockford Files*. At three o'clock, BBC 2, there's usually some film on. If not, there's a good documentary. That takes us up to four, when the children's programmes come on again. I'm not that keen on them, however, because the presenters nowadays are all duffies. Five thirty, *Neighbours* again, then the six o'clock news. I like the main news, it's very good.

'I've got my remotes and my glass of milk and gingernuts. What more could one ask for?'

At six thirty the Scottish news comes on, that's good. Seven o'clock, depends on what day it is. Today is *Wipeout* with Paul Daniels. Oh dear, I'd like to wipe him out. At eight o'clock there's either a soap or athletics. That takes us up to the nine o'clock news. Nine thirty I might switch over to BBC 2 because they've got *Stages* – plays, which are really quite good. That takes us up to ten thirty, when you've got more sport. I wish they'd bring back some good old-fashioned variety – we've not got any on the BBC. There's people all over the country sitting around glum, they're fed up, and the BBC should bring back programmes that have got singing on them – a dancer, a comedian – and cheer up their lives for an hour. It's only an hour, after all. After that it's eleven o'clock. Tonight I'll watch *The Gator*, a movie starring Burt Reynolds, which'll take us up to one o'clock when I'll switch over to the other channel and watch the night movie.

'My average day would be sixteen or seventeen hours television viewing, unless it's really bad, in which case I'll put on Radio 2. But it has to be pretty terrible before I'll do that, although Ken Bruce isn't too bad. I also take Tina, the dog, for a walk every afternoon. I walk to the wall outside my house. I've got a big twenty-foot lead, and I take my wee portable telly, so I don't miss any of my programmes, and I sit on the wall and watch the telly while the dog walks around in a circle. I know Tina looks a bit fat. She used to be slim but when the vet . . . you know . . . she filled out. Obviously I'll get up from the sofa if I need to. I mean if you need to go, you go. But if there's a good programme on I'll cheat and use the back door and water

the plants. But first I make sure that the television's on in the kitchen, so I don't miss part of the programme.

'Of course, I couldn't really live this lifestyle without a good wife. We've been together twenty years and I wouldn't change her. We're not exactly compatible, but we get on and we've lasted longer than a lot of other people. I'm very good at DIY – though I have my own version of it. If any DIY needs to be done, I say, "Do it yourself." If something's wrong with the car, she'll go out and fix it. She does all the work – repairs, painting. She's great. I'm a good organizer, though, I tell her if she misses a bit. And she puts all my meals on a trolley in the kitchen, so that when I'm hungry I can just pull the trolley though on a string. It saves getting up off the settee. Some people might call that lazy, I call that ingenious.

'It's not like I never leave the house. I'll go out on a Saturday. I like going up to my local for a karaoke or a wee drink. Of course, first I set the video. I put it on long play, that way you get six hours out of a three-hour tape. And when I get back there's usually some late-night horror on that I can watch. I look forward to my holiday once a year at Edinburgh weekend. We always go down to Blackpool. Naturally, I make sure there's a TV and video wherever we're staying. The programmes down there are different, of course – *Prisoner Cell-Block H* is about six months ahead of ours.

'These young guys who are running and pumping and jumping, they're all dying of heart attacks at thirty or thirty-five, while I'm still alive. You can have a pleasurable day's work, lying on your settee, watching programmes, enjoying yourself.'

'You don't need to run about and play all that sport to be happy. These young guys who are running and pumping and jumping, they're all dying of heart attacks at thirty or thirty-five, while I'm still alive. You can have a pleasurable day, lying on your settee watching programmes, enjoying yourself. As for money – I've seen people with money and they're not happy, and I've seen people with no money and they're happy. We've no money but we're happy. I wouldn't change it. You don't need to be a millionaire to be happy. Sit on your couch, watch the telly, you've got the world at your feet. And your hand. Great.'

IDEAL WORLDS

Gardeners of Eden

OUNTY
Thinsulate
Thinsulate

An idealist is one who, on noticing that a rose smells better than a cabbage, concludes that it will also make better soup.
H. L. Mencken

If a woman like Eva Perón with no ideals can get that far, think how far I can go with all the ideals that I have.
Margaret Thatcher, 1980

Turn on. Tune in. Drop out.
Timothy Leary

Dropping Out was not invented in the 1960s. Throughout history, there is a long list of people who believed that since the world they lived in seemed unlikely to give them the happiness they desired, the logical alternative was to get out altogether. Space travel being largely unavailable, at least in most parts of the British Isles, their solution was to create their own ideal world, a perfect society within an imperfect society. Most were based on principles like equality, self-government and communal living, and most failed – partly because of outside pressures, partly because of basic flaws in their set-ups, but probably mainly because nobody wanted to do the washing-up.

PERFECT WORLDS: IN THEORY

Perfection has one grave defect; it is apt to be dull.
Somerset Maugham

Perhaps the most famous fictional Utopia is *Utopia.* Thomas More wasn't the first author to dream up a perfect society, but the name certainly stuck. *Utopia* – which actually means 'No place' – was written in Latin, and although you have to give the man some leeway for being born in the fifteenth century, it is still a pretty clear indication that he was a bit of a swot. Thomas More was later beheaded by Henry VIII, and although,

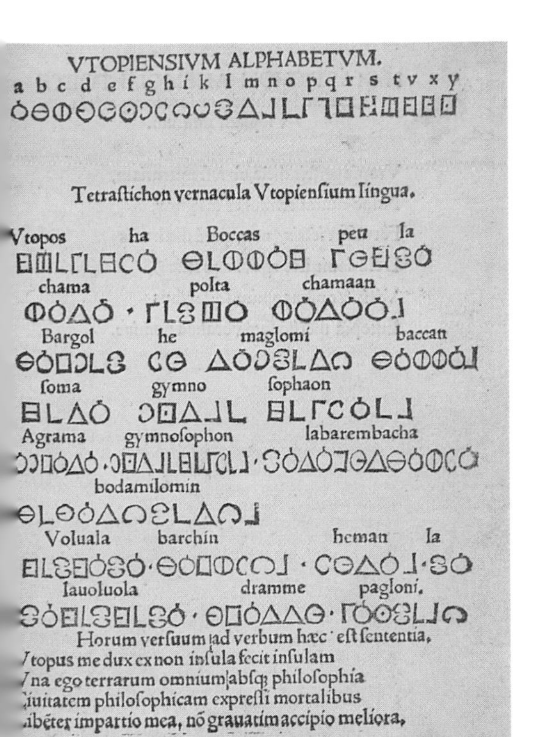
VTOPIENSIVM ALPHABETVM.
a b c d e f g h i k l m n o p q r s t v x y

Tetraſtichon vernacula Vtopienſium lingua.

Vtopos ha Boccas peu la
chama polta chamaan
Bargol he maglomi baccan
ſoma gymno ſophaon
Agrama gymnoſophon labarembacha
bodamilomin
Voluala barchin heman la
lauoluola dramme pagloni.

Horum verſuum ad verbum hæc eſt ſententia.
Vtopus me dux ex non inſula fecit inſulam
Vna ego terrarum omnium abſq; philoſophia
Ciuitatem philoſophicam expreſſi mortalibus
Libẽter impartio mea, nõ grauatim accipio meliora.

Thomas More's *Utopia*, written in Latin – a clear indication that he was a bit of a swot.

technically, this was for other reasons than swottiness, I have my suspicions. More's Utopia is in many ways a communist, or at least a welfare, state. Every inhabitant is provided with food, clothes, work, housing, education and medical treatment, which in those days probably meant free leeches. There is a rigorous penal code, especially for women, who once a month have to kneel before their husbands, confess their wrongdoings and ask to be forgiven. Reasonable enough, admittedly, but pre-marital sex for both genders is punished by compulsory celibacy for life. Adultery is punishable by slavery and repeated adultery by death. Hardly a perfect world, if you're Alan Clarke. However, before you decide that Utopia isn't the place for you, please note that Utopians are allowed to inspect their prospective spouses naked before taking the plunge into compulsory monogamy. Furthermore, although I'm not sure it would be that much of an attraction, Utopians use golden chamber pots.

One of the most famous fictional Utopias is Plato's description of the perfect state in *The Republic*, which embodies the principle of justice, and the communal ownership of goods and women, although this was some 450 years BC (Before Christ), and 2,420 years BGG (Before Germaine Greer). For the Ancient Greeks, the Elysian Fields were an underworld paradise. In the *Odyssey*, Homer stresses what nice weather there is down there, while Lucian paints it as a sort of glorified Club 18–30, with free honey and perfume, background Muzak from nightingales and self-filling wineglasses. Lucian also describes a society on the moon where they wear clothes made of flexible glass, eat smoke and think baldness very attractive. Maybe this was more 'wishful thinking' than 'Utopia'.

In Tommaso Campanella's *City of the Sun* (1623) a perfect society is largely a matter of breeding. Male adolescents can copulate freely with sterile or pregnant women, but all reproduction is government controlled. (Can you imagine a Minister for Fornication? There'd certainly be no shortage of candidates.) In Campanella's Utopia, cosmetics are illegal, to prevent one of the less good-looking women attracting one of the males. The opposite scenario is found in Francis Godwin's *The Man in the Moon* (1638) when a bishop finds a Utopian society on the moon. There he discovers a people who have no lawyers, no crime (criminal types are recognized in early childhood and instantly deported to earth) and no infidelity, for the women are so beautiful that once you have sampled one you never want another. Odd that he didn't find it necessary to make all the men beautiful too. Another Utopia in which adultery is unknown is the country of Vril-Ya, which Lord Lytton placed under the earth's crust in his 1871 novel *The Coming Race.* Here the women are seven feet tall and have such 'unalluring countenances' that extramarital relations become undesirable. Although presumably intramarital relations can't be too hot either.

But not all literary Utopias are quite so steamy. In Samuel Gott's *New Jerusalem* (1648) the secret of a happy society is education. In his perfect world, teachers get maximum salaries and their students all take down notes in shorthand. It won't surprise you to learn that Samuel Gott once worked as a teacher. In *Lost Horizon*, Shangri-La is set somewhere in the Tibetan Himalayas, yet bizarrely reminds James Hilton's hero 'very slightly of Oxford'. Probably something to do with all the snow-capped mountains and yaks. In *News From Nowhere* (1890) William Morris paints a picture of a humanist Utopia. Here poverty is extinct, and the Houses of Parliament are used to store manure (rather than produce it verbally).

Of course, writing a book about a Utopia is one thing, the genuine test of a perfect society comes when people decide to do it for real. The following have all tried and, to put it bluntly, failed. Some were battling against tremendous odds, some became gradually disillusioned as they saw their dreams fade and wither, and others just made a complete cock-up of it from the start.

'Liberté, Egalité, Décapité.'

PERFECT WORLDS: IN PRACTICE

Nothing is perfect. There are lumps in it.
James Stephens

Münzer

Münzer, sometimes called the forerunner of modern socialism, was a believer in radical reform. In the 1520s he led eight thousand peasants into battle against their sovereign, believing that this would bring on the Second Coming. Unfortunately all that happened was that the peasant army was routed, thousands were killed and Münzer himself was captured, tortured and beheaded. Not, in any real sense of the word, a success.

Bridgeman Art Library

Rousseau

Jean-Jacques became a bit of a hero for French revolutionaries after he wrote his *Social Contract* in 1762 and came up with the pithy one-liner: 'Man is born free but is everywhere in chains.' Rousseau believed that humans could achieve happiness through realizing their inner potential, which was stifled by authority and institutions. The revolutionaries had their own pretty definite ideas about how to get rid of the authorities that were stifling them, announced that 'Terror is the order of the day' and set about chopping off the heads of some of the leading members of the aristocracy.

Rousseau also inspired **Samuel Taylor Coleridge** (1772–1834) to design what he called a Pantisocracy – nothing to do with underwear, but a commune in Pennsylvania based on a system of no property. Coleridge never got to the commune and the project collapsed when he became disillusioned, following his fellow poet Robert Southey's decision to bring a servant with him. You see? It's always the washing-up that gets in the way.

The Shakers

An offshoot of Quakers, the Shakers, or to give them their more complete title, the United Society of Believers in Christ's Second Coming, were led to America in 1774. They believed in communal living so, sure enough, they set up a few communes. Some of their settlements are still left, but are now more famous for their furniture (no doubt built initially to provide them with something to sit on while waiting for Christ to arrive).

Robert Owen (1771–1858)

Owen was unusual in being both a successful businessman and one of the great British social reformers. He established a workers' commune at his mill at New Lanark near Glasgow, where he declared that his aim was to build 'a new moral world', and make lots of nice tablecloths. The factory commune, where children were sent to classes from the time they could walk to stop them 'acquiring any bad habits', became known as Happy Valley. Owen went on to found more than twenty communities in Britain and North America, but most of them only lasted two or three years, partially due to the gradual disillusionment with the social imperatives he had mooted, and partially due to the decline in the demand for tablecloths.

Charles Fourier (1772–1825)
Fourier believed that mankind could live harmoniously if freed from the evil influences of 'society'. He decided everyone should be split up into settlements of approximately one thousand five hundred inhabitants each. Everyone would live in the same building, swap jobs all the time, get paid a minimum wage and any additional profit would then be split according to factors like talent, capital investment and how much work they had done (not exactly a radical departure from existing systems). He called for marriage to be replaced by a system of licence and suggested that children should be organized into groups called Little Hordes and do the community's dirty work. Prophetically he wrote about the need to invent air-conditioning, but then he also predicted that the seas would run with lemonade. Whereas Fourier's attempts to found communities soon faltered in America and France, where they found his ideas unworkable and ridiculous, the British, rather worryingly, responded with considerable fervour. His theories even inspired town-planners to start building garden cities like Port Sunlight, Bournville and Milton Keynes. If 'inspired' is the word.

Manson Family members Susan Atkins, Patricia Krenwinkel and Leslie Van Houten visibly saddened by the prospect of a life sentence.

New England Transcendentalists
Their members included the poet Ralph Waldo Emerson, writer and critic Amos Bronson Alcott and occasionally Henry David Thoreau, also known as 'The Hermit of Walden' because he lived beside Walden Pond in a shack he had built there. They believed that through intuition, or 'Transcendental Reason', they could find a form of government beyond democracy in which the individual conscience would act as the supreme authority, forming a link with cosmic purpose (but this was after a long night down the Dog and Duck).

The Soviet Union
After the 1917 Revolution, hundreds of Westerners flocked to the Soviet Union, nicknamed 'Sugar Candy Mountain'. Some stayed and set up communes and some, like journalist Leonard Steffens, returned saying things like: 'I have been over into the future and it works.'

The Manson Family
In 1969, Charles Manson, who at thirty-five was way too old to be a hippy, and at five foot two way too short to be a heart-throb, founded the perfect society – if, of course, you were Charles Manson. At a time when communes were all the rage,

Topham Picture Source

Manson and his 'family' moved into some ranch buildings in the Californian desert to set up their own society. The commune basically consisted of a lot of young, white, middle-class girls who were instructed to do his bidding, which involved sleeping with anyone he said, usually himself, and committing crimes, including, as we know, mass murder.

Jim Jones and the People's Temple

Jones's People's Temple was an agricultural commune on four thousand acres of cleared jungle deep in the heart of Guyana. Based on racial brotherhood, socialism and a personalized Christianity, in which he himself appeared as a bit of a Christ figure (he performed healings and even claimed to have notched up a few resurrections), he described it as a 'co-operative socialist republic'. The commune attracted Utopian socialists, idealists and fair proportion of loonies.

In 1978 over nine hundred members of the community swallowed cyanide-laced Flavoraid and died. (At least the Flavoraid tasted better than usual.) A slogan painted on the wall of the commune's central hall read, 'Those who cannot remember the past are condemned to repeat it.'

The Cartwheel Movement

In 1980 a small group of people spent three months rolling a twelve-foot cartwheel a thousand miles along British roads. Their aim was first to establish a viable large-scale alternative culture where the principles of common ownership of land and houses, income sharing, non-discrimination and decision making by consensus could be practically applied, and secondly, to stop the cartwheel from falling over. However, having successfully generated lots of publicity, the group failed to reach agreement about how to actually set up this perfect new society. Eventually various small communities were formed, including one on the west coast of Scotland and one on the island of Innisfree. By 1983 the Innisfree commune had only two members (more a couple than a commune), and both have since moved on.

DEMOCRACY, DOPE AND DOG SHIT: CHRISTIANIA

Society is no comfort to one not sociable.
William Shakespeare

People who need people are the luckiest people in the world.
Barbra Streisand

A Brief, But Unnecessarily Detailed, Potted History . . .

When you first enter Christiania, it's not so much the word 'happy' as 'hippy' that tends to spring to mind.

In 1969 man walked on the moon, the Archies recorded 'Sugar Sugar', and the Danish army abandoned a twenty-two-acre barracks site in the leafy Christianshavn district of Copenhagen.

In 1970 Britain went decimal, Jimi Hendrix went to heaven and the Danish counterculture declared 'A Nordic Summer of Free Love'. A makeshift camp populated by about fifteen thousand hippies was established in the Danish countryside. Their stated aim was 'to explore and develop the possibilities of communal living', 'to enact a socio-political experiment in alternative lifestyles' and other euphemisms for having fun in tents.

In 1971 the local people of Christianshavn broke down the fence surrounding the disused barracks. Squatters moved into some of the buildings, while a few avant-garde artists started using others as studios. Hearing about this, Jacob Ludvigsen, a journalist on the underground newspaper *Hovedbladet* (*Head* magazine), wrote an article exhorting freaks everywhere to 'emigrate to Christiania on Bus No. 8' (not quite as catchy as 'Get your kicks on Route 66', but I gather it loses something in the translation), where they could found a permanent home for their alternative society. 'This is the place we're all looking for,' he concluded. In just a few months, Christiania had been colonized by over five hundred people and was one of the best-orchestrated squats in modern history.

The first settlers of the 'freetown' to set up camp in the derelict buildings merely scrawled 'occupied' on the door of their chosen dwelling, so at first sight their houses looked like a row of toilets. There was no electricity or running water, no sanitation,

no organized system of self-government – a sort of Woodstock without Jefferson Airplane. Now, twenty-four years on, Christiania is an orderly and thriving community with a permanent population of about a thousand people, not to mention two hundred cats, twenty-five horses, two pigs and a donkey called Hubert. Oh, and over three hundred dogs. The wagon-trains keep rolling, fresh homesteaders continue to arrive and although the original young pioneers of flower-power are now middle-aged parents with 2.4 children, their dream lives on. After a generation of political battles with the state and local authorities, Christiania retains its autonomy. No authorities, no laws, no violence (which arguably is a law), no hard drugs (there's another one), no private ownership and, of course, no end of dog shit.

When you first enter Christiania, it's not so much the word

'happy' as 'hippy' that tends to spring to mind. The original barracks buildings, which have been converted into homes, shops, bath houses and communal meeting areas, are colourfully painted and decorated with psychedelic murals. Cars and motorbikes are banned in the freetown, so you must either park outside or take the legendary Bus No. 8 to the main gate at Princessegrade. Day-trippers are welcomed, as long as they cycle or walk, don't bring in any hard drugs, don't litter, use the public toilets and respect the privacy of the residents. Christiania, as the local newsletter declares, is 'a visual feast for any Nature-loving anarchist'. It's one of the largest green areas in the region, and the estuary, which runs through the town, is a bird sanctuary and a known migratory stop for many species. That's provided they don't bring in any hard drugs, don't litter, use the public toilets, etc. Christiania also has several pubs, cafés, vegetarian restaurants and a bakery selling what are arguably the best Danish pastries in the country. If you choose to dine alfresco, you can expect to pick up a large canine following, but at least you won't get bitten (another Christiania law: 'Any dog that bites must go'); but guard your sandwiches, and mind where you put your feet.

After a generation of political battles with the state and local authorities, Christiania retains its autonomy. No authorities, no laws, no violence (which arguably is a law), no hard drugs (there's another one), no private ownership and, of course, no end of dog shit.

It hasn't always been so peaceful here. In fact, a battle for Christiania has been waged periodically over the last twenty-four years, on the streets of Christiania, in the courts and in the Danish parliament.

Because the land on which it sits is actually owned by the government there have been repeated attempts to clear the freetown. When the police proved themselves incapable of accomplishing this, due to the number of people living there, and the huge area over which it is spread, Christiania quickly became a political hot potato. Across the country there was widespread popular support for the commune. A Gallup poll in 1976 showed that over half the country were in favour of it – but then they said that about Neil Kinnock in 1992. However, in a desperate attempt to win votes or to discredit the opposition, successive Conservative and Social Democratic administrations have changed their policies towards the place with the regularity of underwear. (Thank goodness politicians don't behave like that in Britain over issues like the European Union, Sinn Fein, university grants, the Poll Tax, Sunday trading, VAT on fuel . . .)

In 1973 it was decreed that Christiania could stay until a better use was found for the land (to be decided by a national competition). But only three years later the government ordained that the settlement be totally cleared by 1 April. By 2 April, nothing had happened, and by 30 April everyone had forgotten about it.

There were also one or two other skirmishes along the way. In December 1974, Christianianites, dressed as Father Christmases, handed out presents to children and old people from Copenhagen's large department stores. Unfortunately they had omitted to buy the goods first, so they were soon arrested, but media coverage of Santa Clauses being dragged off in handcuffs proved unwelcome publicity for the authorities. In 1978 the government decided that a plan for the area should be produced and that Christiania should be 'normalized' (a sinister phrase), but it wasn't until 1982 that the government 'think-tank' came up with the plan. Their recommendation was that Christiania should be developed as 'an experimental city with wide frames for self-government'. This was a surprise for the residents of Christiania, who had been labouring under the impression that what they had already established bore at least a passing resemblance to 'an experimental city with wide frames for self-government'. Somewhat predictably, nothing happened.

▲ The Co-operative Workers' Meeting, having just finalized the cross-table decision on a sub-committee motion to approve the communal funding for a new sink plunger.

Meanwhile, within Christiania things evolved and got organized. Derelict buildings were repaired and renovated, new ones were built. A system for sorting and collecting rubbish was developed, old oil barrels were converted to create heaters. Gradually the town was plumbed for water and wired for electricity. A nursery, a kindergarten, a medical centre and a communal bath house were established; collectively run shops and small factories sprang up. Christiania designed its own flag, and presumably was at this stage only one step away from official recognition by the Olympic Games committee. It even started its own internal postal system, with its own post boxes and its own stamps, which generate revenue for Christiania's electricity bill. So the more letters you send, the more chance you have of being able to see to write your next letter. The artistic community in Christiania flourished: the freetown became famous for its politically charged theatre and music; it also founded its own newspaper and radio station. Like they said at Woodstock, 'It's a city out there.' Only, unlike Woodstock, it lasted slightly longer than three days.

Most significantly, a system of self-government in the freetown was established, to allow as much freedom and power to the individual as possible. In practice, this means that all decisions are taken by committee, and also that no decision can be reached unless every single person at the meeting agrees with

◀ Christiania has its own internal postal system, with its own post boxes and its own stamps, which generate revenue for its own electricity bill. So the more letters you send, the more chance you have of being able to see to write your next letter.

it. So if you like ruthlessly efficient and decisive government, don't even think of moving to Christiania.

There are eight main divisions of meetings at Christiania: the Common Meeting, the Area Meeting, the Economy Meeting, the Treasury Group (daring to be different and calling itself a 'group'), the Busy-ness Council (completely off the wall), the Co-operative Workers' Meeting, the House Meeting and the Neighbourliness Meeting. And this is, in theory, how the inhabitants' lives are governed. If they need to decide whether to buy a new washing-machine, they have a meeting. If they need to decide on a new sewage system, they have a meeting. If they need to decide whether to have a meeting, they have a meeting. And during that meeting they decide on what other things they need to have meetings about. Everyone's invited, and if just one person disagrees with the rest, his or her opinion, however loony or outlandish, is enough to ensure that no motion is carried – and that there be another meeting. Just imagine if the whole of Parliament could be dominated by just one loony extremist with some absurdly outlandish ideas . . . Well, I suppose we had thirteen years of it.

Some inhabitants of Christiania attend up to forty meetings a month. The immediate thought is that if they didn't have so many meetings, they might have more time to get things done. Surely it must be simpler to call for a quick show of hands and have done with it? If a Christianianite went to every meeting available to him, it would be a full-time occupation. 'What do you do for a living?' 'Oh, I attend meetings.' Of course, it being a free society, nobody has to go to meetings if they don't want to. And as one Christianianite put it, 'Experience has taught us only to bring up one issue at each meeting.'

Finally, in 1992, an agreement of sorts was reached between Christiania and the government of the day. Christianianites would pay a tariff for the use of water and electricity, and would agree to abide by certain planning restrictions. In exchange they could stay, subject to annual renegotiation. Of course, governments do have a habit of changing. The Christiania flag continues to fly over the *Loppebygningen* (Central Meeting Hall), but the future is by no means secure.

Christiania Today

My first impression of Christiania is made by my left foot in a large pile of dog shit. My second impression is that the place has all the communal fly-notices of a university campus and all the architectural charm of a concentration camp. Christiania seems like a place where happiness is not just possible but obligatory, part of the mandate. The dominant philosophy here is, 'You have the right to do anything you please so long as it doesn't interfere with anyone else's right to do the same.'

I am met at the main gate by my guide for the day, a tall, bald, softly spoken man by the name of Wanda (as in the fish). Wanda, who runs the commune's gay theatre company, has been heavily involved with Christiania since the beginning, and has lived there permanently since 1987. So does he think Christiania has changed much from the early days?

'It started out like a peace, love and happiness, hippies and flowers thing. That has stopped, in a way, but it's still very much based on these ideas.'

Wanda and I set out on a walking tour through some of Christiania's ten districts. As we dodge bicycles and dog shit in the *Maelkebotten* (Dandelion) District, he proudly points out landmarks like the Woodstock Café, and painted timber houses with names like the Great Bear, the Starship and Electric Ladyland. 'Looking at it, you might not think it's a paradise,' Wanda enthuses. 'But it *is* a paradise. It has such a lot of possibilities and you can enact all your ideas.'

▲ 'I never wear a watch, I don't have to inside Christiania – time is something different here.' Wanda, who was forty minutes late for his interview.

Those opposed to Christiania have often accused the people here of being a group of misfits and dole scroungers. I ask Wanda if he would like the opportunity to refute this argument. 'I would say that we are a bunch of misfits in a way, but we are trying to establish a life where it doesn't matter if you're a social misfit or not. As for welfare violations, it is true that 90 per cent of Christianianites are unemployed, so we would be on social security anyway, whether we lived in Christiania or not.' More of an endorsement than a denial, really.

We stroll past the *Fredens Ark* (Ark of Peace), the largest half-timbered house in northern Europe, formerly living space for about a hundred soldiers, now living space for about a hundred hippies. It also contains a huge room known as the *Rockmaskinen*, used for the Common Meeting and amateur dramatics, although presumably not at the same time. Beyond the *Fredens Ark* are the *Faelleskokkenet* (Communal Kitchen) and the *Grontsagen* (Greengrocer's), where you can buy organic vegetables. Although it is winter, and most of the trees are bare, there are a lot of open spaces here in the freetown, and the air is filled with the smell of growing things, albeit cold, damp growing things. Wanda says that this is another big plus for him.

'You're living in the middle of a huge city, and you're having the benefits of being in a small village, a kind of rural fantasy.' Having spent some time in Purley, I was immediately able to relate to this.

One of the great social centres of Christiania appears to be the *Badehuset* (Bath House) where grown men and women can wander in and out of showers, saunas and plunge pools, dangly bits akimbo. Such is their devotion to peace, love and sharing that they virtually debag me on the spot so I can be at one with their nakedness. The communal nudity is supposed to rid us inhibited types of our hang-ups and demystify the sight of women's bodies (and presumably men's if you are female). A kind thought, but I'm not absolutely sure I want the female form demystified. (I'd have to throw out my collection of *Amateur Photographer Monthly* for a start.) The fact that being naked in front of someone is faintly rude and unusual is a situation I'd fight to keep, not destroy. Still, I'm sure that's terribly anal, or regressive, or British. Or all three.

▼ The *Badehuset* where grown men and women wander in and out of showers, saunas and plunge pools, dangly bits akimbo, without batting an eye. That's unless they were brought up in Surrey.

Wanda also kindly shows me to the *Stenhusen* (Guest House) – aptly named, as it is a small house in which one guest can stay, consisting as it does, of one room. Still, no porters to tip, no snide receptionist, no temperamental television, no overpriced minibar, no exorbitant telephone, but then, also no bed . . . A simple mattress in a loft – what more could one want? Well, a temperamental television, an overpriced minibar, an exorbitant telephone . . . ?

If you want to be more than an overnight guest, there are two ways of getting into Christiania. Either find a job there or find a partner, or if you're really conscientious, both. (If you need some advice on getting both at the same time, just ask any Hollywood actress.) Once you're in, you're in. The only history of people being extricated is in the mid-eighties when over fifty people were thrown out for doing hard drugs. During this period Christiania was experiencing internal problems with the widespread sale and use of narcotics, and it collaborated with the Danish authorities to crack down on the dealers. Users had the choice of going into rehabilitation or being kicked out. I'm not sure who Hobson was, but I'm sure his choice can't have been much grimmer.

Hashish, on the other hand, seems to play a major part in most of their lives. It's difficult not to notice that the first two shops you come to in Christiania both sell hash exclusively. And in the first café you come to there's a notable absence of coffee. In fact, there's a notable absence of everything, as it's almost impossible to see for the smoke billowing out from pipes the size of oboes. A reporter from an American 'head' magazine writes, 'Years of toking have created customs and codes of behaviour, some smoking rituals involving the better part of the day. Christianianites take great pride in the sophistication of their hash culture, and the fortunate visitor can check out varieties provided by some of the most knowledgeable smokers in Scandinavia. The highlight is a fragrant blond poll Maroc with a rich taste and a clear high.' Unfortunately, I don't get offered any Maroc, blond, brunette or otherwise. Probably just as well, because, under Danish law, marijuana and hashish are still illegal, and from time to time, in moments of heightened boredom, the police invade the place, pick a fight with a few pushers and even arrest the occasional tourist. The dealers aren't too hard to find, as it happens, given that the first road you come to is called Pushers' Street. Sadly they stopped there, otherwise we might have Coke Crescent, Ecstasy Lane, Heroin Addicts' Alley and Cold Turkey Terrace. It certainly makes me think twice about the mainline railway station.

It is a good twenty minutes' walk to the other side of the lake, where we drop into a commune called Autogena – a sort of commune within a commune. Here, they all live together, all sleep together (although not necessarily in the penetrative sense), all share the housework and all take turns to do the cooking. A bit like being a student, but without the labels on the sausages in the fridge.

I am introduced to a Norwegian woman named Karit, who lives there with her eight-year-old son and six others. Today is her turn to cook for the commune. This area of Christiania is still not connected to any power supply, so she must prepare all the food on an old-fashioned wood-burning stove. Sensibly, she has chosen to make a salad.

▲ Today it is Karit's turn to cook for the commune. They are still not connected to any power supply, so she must prepare all the food on an old-fashioned wood-burning stove. Sensibly, she has chosen to make a salad.

Karit has lived here since the late seventies, when she was one of twenty inhabitants – somewhat of a squash for one bedroom. With true Scandinavian understatement, Karit describes having to share a bunk-bed with another couple as 'a bit embarrassing', although she says it was actually 'very embarrassing' when her parents came to visit and they walked in on said couple in the throes of rampant abandon. In those early days, Karit says, it was all a lot wilder – sex, drugs and dancing naked in the garden. Nowadays she seems to spend most of her time cooking for the kids, doing the washing-up and working in an office. And, of course, now they each have their own bedroom.

So what's so bloody good about living without electricity,

central heating and CDs, even if you have got gas lighting, a log fire and flatmates who play the bongos? What is the point in living apart from the technological advantages of the twentieth century, and among a lot of dog-shit? According to Karit it's all to do with spiritual awakening, environmental concern and learning to live with others – which may explain why she's thinking of leaving next year.

Wanda, however, has no intention of leaving Christiania, ever. 'I'm extremely happy here. I couldn't imagine any other place to stay or live, really I couldn't. If I lived in an apartment in town I would feel fenced in. Here in Christiania it is an open area, but I have a thousand neighbours. Time is something different here, too. I never wear a watch – I don't have to inside Christiania.' Most important of all, he says, is that Christiania enables you to have the freedom to do whatever you want, how and when you want and thereby remain a child (at heart) all your life. 'You could call it a prolonged childhood, somehow. It has this innocence over it – it's almost naïve, sometimes almost stupid, but it's wonderful. Where else could one do this?' he asks me. Westminster? I think.

So, dog-shit and endless meetings aside, does Christiania work? Well, a waiting list of over a thousand people testifies to some degree of success, and leaves the Garrick club in the shade. Jeremy Paxman needn't even think of applying. And the fact that it's lasted two and a half decades, despite years of outside pressure and police harassment, means that twenty-five years after Woodstock, love, peace and dropping out can still form the basis of a fundamentally happy society. Especially if you're a dachshund.

▶ Personally, I was always more of a Donny Osmond fan.

THE YELLOW ROSE OF TELFORD

Home, home on the range,
Where the deer and the antelope play;
Where seldom is heard a discouraging word
And the skies are not cloudy all day.
Brewster Higley, nineteenth century

Take me back to my home on the prairie,
Take me back to the one that I love.
Take me back to my home in Wyoming,
Take me back . . .
'Oh take him back, someone.'
Graeme Garden, twentieth century

I turn right off the A10, just north of the M25 interchange, in Hertfordshire, and follow signs to Cuffley. Following the road for about two miles, through a wooded area, past a cluster of suburban detached houses, I take a left-hand turn into a side road. This leads into the thick of the woods, deep in the heart of rural Hertfordshire. Suddenly two figures step out of the undergrowth on to the path in front of me. I can't help noticing that they are dressed as cowboys. Oak and birch overshadow low brick buildings bearing signs like 'This way to Girls' shower'. My first impression is that I've stepped into the middle of a *Carry On* film. Fifty yards further along a dirt track leading into the forest I come to a crossroads. Painted signs direct you to Justice Hill, Silver Street and Grimset. A heavily tattooed man, wearing nothing but a suede loincloth, is attacking a pile of old school desks with an axe. Good, I've come to the right place.

When the British Western Association was founded in 1973, in Birmingham (England, not Alabama), it had thirty-two members. There are now a thousand official members of the organization, which acts as an umbrella for Western clubs like the Arizona Outlaws (from High Wycombe), the Hat and Creek Cattle Company (from Hampshire) and the Gunslingers (from Milton Keynes). The BWA is itself part of the Western International Association which has branches in Belgium, Canada, the USA and South Africa.

The Three Amigos . . . of Cuffley, near Watford.

Altogether it is estimated that around three thousand Britons are involved in the Western scene and, despite what you might think, they're not all cowboys. In fact many choose to live like mountain men and trappers – the people who opened up the West in the 1820s and '30s, or soldiers from both sides of the American Civil War or, the relative newcomers on the Western scene, the Colonials – the eighteenth-century settlers of New Amsterdam and the other pre-Independence New World colonies. The Native American Indians also attract a lot of followers, but although they seem to coexist peacefully with the white man, and there have been pitifully few massacres, they tend to have their own separate organizations.

The Western and Native American societies organize many events throughout the year, ranging from Wild West shows to 'round-ups' and 'pow-wows'. Most of these gatherings take place during the summer months. The event I am visiting in Cuffley is a 'rendezvous', a camp in which the participants are supposed to recreate accurately their character's mode of living. It's open to all the different groups, although if you were a stickler for historical accuracy you might be tempted to point out that as much as a century separates the Colonials from the cowboys.

But fortunately I am not one of those sticklers so I shan't mention it.

Perhaps, two hundred years from now, scores of like-minded people will gather together during the summer months to dress up as characters from the twentieth century and attempt to recreate our lives. In one corner of the field, or whatever people have instead of fields in the twenty-second century, will be a group of suffragettes busily chaining themselves to some railings, while in a nearby copse, or whatever they have instead of trees in 2195, three families dressed as soldiers from the Second World War will be pretending to ambush a couple of middle-aged German storm-troopers. Half a mile away, a group of yuppies in double-breasted suits will pretend to talk to each other on mobile phones. It could happen. And fortunately, I won't be around to be proved wrong.

'I think a lot of people who extract the Michael out of us would like to do this sort of thing. It's just having the guts to put the clothing on and go out and wear it.'

For some of the people here in Cuffley the whole scene is just a bit of a laugh, but for many of the members it's a lot more serious. These 'authentics' *live* their characters in a full-bodied, Method acting, Robert de Niro kind of way. Why? Because it makes them happy.

In the centre of a clearing in the area designated Justice Hill stands a large teepee. Flags bearing Indian symbols fly from the apex. Outside, a blanket is spread displaying trading goods (bangles, trinkets, severed bird wings). This is the summer home of Frances Preston, a 'Native American' of Telford. Frances, a sprightly middle-aged woman clad head to toe in fringed white buckskin, beads and silver and turquoise jewellery, tells me that she was first introduced to the Indian scene about fifteen years ago. She was a divorced mother of two, still smarting from an unhappy marriage and a difficult break-up, when she saw an article in the local paper about people who owned teepees. She contacted them, thinking it would make a nice weekend break for herself, her two sons and her dog. A sort of camping trip in fancy dress.

But as soon as she had tasted the Anglo-Native American lifestyle Frances was hooked. 'I felt as though I had found myself – I felt this was me. Although I had never worn an Indian dress before it felt perfect.' Looking back at her life, Frances feels that she was predestined to find herself in this way. 'Even as a child I always had sympathy for the Indian. I hoped the cowboys lost and the Indians won.' And that was long before *Dances With Wolves.*

What had begun as a weekend pastime soon burgeoned into an obsession. 'It's a lifestyle now, because you live it and you get to know everything about the Indian way of life, the religion, the beliefs and the culture. Everything is aligned to Mother Earth and you start to live that way.' Frances says that the Indians restored her faith in human nature and believes that their values rub off on the people who decide to emulate them. She gestures across the clearing to where a woman wearing what appears to be a bonnet, a bra and a Laura Ashley skirt is cooking baked beans over an open fire. 'This lifestyle makes you much more aware of the basics. And everyone here is honest. The Indians wouldn't take from each other – they didn't steal. All right, they might borrow a few horses but basically they were honest.' That's 'borrowed' in the way Shergar was 'borrowed', of course.

Frances shows me around her teepee, which she erects entirely by herself. No mean feat, since it stands about twenty feet high, and must be accurately constructed to allow the smoke from the open fire in the centre to draw properly through the hole at the top. 'The ladies were really quite independent. They used to put their teepees up themselves because they owned them. So if they wanted to divorce their husband they would put his bow and arrows outside the teepee and when he came back from hunting he wouldn't dare step inside as he knew what the sign meant.' Still, I suppose if your husband went hunting without his bow and arrows he deserved to be divorced.

The sides of the shelter are hung with Indian symbols and fetishes which Frances makes herself: a Plains Mandala, a medicine wheel and a dream-catcher, which looks like a spider's web with some feathers hanging from it. It is supposed to trap the nightmares and only let the sweet dreams through, so perhaps video shops should rent them out with Quentin Tarantino movies. Candles and lanterns provide light, although she does carry a Calor-gas cylinder, just in case. Frances even has an Indian pipe in which she smokes a herbal mixture called kiri-kiri. She fills it and offers it to me, saying, 'When I have this in my pipe and put on Indian music, everything just drifts away.' I try it but, in true American tradition, I don't inhale.

So what do Frances and her fellow Native Americans do during the winter months? 'We repair our beadwork and teepees and make more costumes. It keeps you occupied.' Sometimes she gives talks and demonstrations of chanting and dancing to schools and old people's clubs. 'Everywhere you go, you're spreading the word. There are so many people who have said, "Oh, I didn't realize the Indians did that." People have always thought of the Hollywood image, which is the blood-thirsty savages – which they weren't.' Not that that would have made

'This takes you away from all the high pressures of the modern world. I lay in this teepee last night looking up at the moon and all I could hear was laughter from people all around. And I thought this felt like being on another planet.'
Frances Preston, a Pocohontas from Telford

Smoking kiri-kiri, a herbal mixture. 'When I have this in my pipe and put on Indian music, everything just drifts away,' says Frances . . . Particularly anyone in a ten-yard radius.

for very exciting films – Wild Bill Hickock being ambushed by a Cherokee brave and taught how to sew a buckskin moccasin.

Last year Frances visited a real Native American reservation, and even attended one of their pow-wows. She says, 'Oh, it was wonderful! Wonderful! Honestly, I thought: I could just die now – I'd be in heaven! Being a romantic I would have loved to live there in the old times, when they were free.' But in the absence of time travel she is more than content to dwell amongst the tribes of Britannica. Here she finds companionship, stimulation, challenges and a great deal of peace. 'This takes you away from all the high pressure of the modern world. I lay in this teepee last night looking up at the moon and all I could hear was laughter from people all around. And I thought this felt like being on another planet.'

Just as Frances Preston defies her name by coming, not from Lancashire, but the Midlands, Ken and Ethel Crawley are not from Sussex, but Burnley in Lancashire. Ken Crawley is the authentic's authentic. He and his wife, Ethel, in their rendezvous personae of Tricorne Ken and Mother Bear, are frontiers people, or Colonials. Even their dog, Sandy, an ancient golden retriever, is known as 'the Slug' when he's in eighteenth-century mode. Although it's unlikely he's aware of what century it is anyway.

The Crawleys first got into the scene through the Country and Western end of things. For a while they tried dressing in Western gear, but it never felt quite right. 'This is the thing,' muses Ken. 'We felt like we were dressing up, rather than wearing clothes that we were comfortable in.' When they first decided to become Colonials they thought they were the only ones, so when, during a trip to Birmingham, they discovered that there were other like-minded enthusiasts it was something of a revelation. Rather like I felt when I was given my first Donny Osmond fanzine.

To say that they are serious about the historical accuracy of what they are doing is like saying that Marco Polo was quite keen on travel. The Crawleys researched their costumes for two years before making them, and an expert at a local museum verified their authenticity. Ethel, who used to be a dressmaker, does the sewing, while Ken, who was a decorator by profession, is now in charge of leatherwork and the carving of the buttons, which are made out of wood and bone. Man-made fibres and plastic buttons are a definite no-no. Ethel generally wears a long skirt, a long waistcoat and a mob cap, while Ken, in knee breeches, a linen shirt and his long white hair in a pigtail, looks every inch the part. The part of what, I'm not quite sure, but for

anyone who says it's impossible to find a northern man who'll willingly stand up and show you a sample of his embroidery – meet Tricorne Ken. From Ethel's waist hangs an example of his work: a pouch or 'pocket' exquisitely embroidered with a grizzly bear surrounded by wild flowers.

It's not just the clothes that have to be authentic, either. The Crawleys' lodge looks like one of those museum tableaux you used to see on school trips. Constructed of heavy unbleached canvas propped up with wooden poles, it is well stocked with rum chests, lanterns, animal pelts, a water barrel and even a large jar of homemade applejack – a lethal mixture of rum and cider which, according to police and ambulance reports, I apparently like very much. Outside, smoke-blackened cooking pots hang on a pole over a wood fire. 'We use flint and steel and char-cloth and tinder to light our fires. Lighting is by candlelight. We have no torches or electrical type of lighting. It's even frowned upon if you use matches or firelighters.' In fact, quite a lot seems to be frowned upon by the true authentics. As well as matches, plastic buttons and man-made fabrics, charcoal, twentieth-century clothing, china crockery, enamel plates and Thermos flasks are

▲ 'Unfortunately they won't allow me on the M6 with a packhorse.'
Ken and Ethel Crawley a.k.a. Tricorne Ken and Mother Bear.

all no-go areas. As is the expression 'no-go areas', presumably. Sleeping bags are acceptable if they're hidden under skins and blankets, but don't even think about packing a radio. Nevertheless, a small canvas tent a few yards away from the lodge hides one of the Crawleys' few concessions to the twentieth century. A chemical toilet, for when the great outdoors just isn't great enough. They drive from venue to venue carting their belongings in a trailer, although Ken would prefer a more authentic form of transport. 'Unfortunately they won't allow me on the M6 with a packhorse.'

The Crawleys look back on the lives of their forebears with admiration. The people they are representing settled in America in the late seventeenth and first half of the eighteenth centuries, long before the cowboys of the Wild West, on land that was still a British colony. Most of them would have been soldiers, indentured labourers or trappers, moving from place to place following the bear, beaver and buffalo. Contrary to their depiction by Hollywood, these frontiersmen generally got on pretty well with the Native Americans. 'More people died from exposure than ever died from the Indians,' says Ken. 'Still, it gave John Wayne a career, I suppose.'

'Yes, it was a very hard life,' adds Ethel. 'In the winter it was so cold they never changed their clothes, although you have to realize that hygiene then was not what it is today.' Our eyes collectively swivel round to rest on the chemical toilet.

▼ Genuine frontiersman, along with authentic New England Betty Boo tattoo.

So why forsake the comforts of twentieth-century life for the comparative austerity of the eighteenth-century frontiersman? Some of us city sissies would probably starve without the convenience of twenty-four-hour petrol stations and those 7–Elevens for which we are from time to time given to thank Heaven. But the Crawleys are addicted to the outdoor life.

'There's something quite magical about a rendezvous – it's a place where people can sit and talk out in the open.' The other main attraction is the camaraderie of their fellow authentics. 'They are more like a family than just friends. If anybody gets into difficulty, they're there, they help,' says Ethel.

Ken agrees wholeheartedly. 'Today people are feared of leaving their property, but here, in this type of life, we can't lock anything away, we've got to trust one another, and we can. There's very few places in the world where you can, but among the authentic people we don't lose things.'

As for people who think it's just, well, a little eccentric to refer to yourselves as 'the authentic people' and go around dressed in eighteenth-century costume, Ken says, 'I think a lot of people who extract the Michael out of us would like to do this sort of thing. It's just having the guts to put the clothing on and go out and wear it. Anyway, I don't think it's any different from wearing a uniform. For example, twenty-two men running after a bag of wind with thousands of people watching them. What is a football strip but a costume to play a game in?' So if Arsenal run out next season in leather breeches and ten-gallon hats, you'll know who to thank.

They are keen to distinguish themselves from the fly-by-night fancy-dress brigade, who might turn up to one rendezvous as a cowboy and as a mountain man to the next. 'To us, we call it "playing at it". They haven't found what they really want. They're pinching bits off everyone 'cos they think it looks great. To me, they are frowned upon. Once we put the clothes on we're not playing a part, we're living it . . . it's a strange feeling, it's hard to describe to people – but once you've done this it becomes part and parcel of your life. I'm proud of being or representing what I am representing.'

So have they found the secret of happiness, here in the twentieth-century frontierland of Cuffley, Herts? 'We have found what we have been looking for, if you like, for many years. I think we are all looking for something as we go through life, aren't we? We feel that we have found it now.'

It is almost dusk. A group of mountain men are trooping back from a field where they have been holding a knife-throwing competition. Ken leans on his walking stick and gazes up at the trees. My eye alights on an empty Diet Coke can nestling against the trunk. 'We do believe in destiny: there's a path for you to follow, and you'll follow it, whether you want to or not. When we are putting on the clothes there is nothing strange about putting them on. This was the thing, and it was a pleasure making them.'

Ethel nods enthusiastically. 'When we go through a gate into a field we leave all our cares and woes and worries behind us, and we live in fantasy land.'

'Although it's not a fantasy to us,' adds Ken. 'We've made this our reality. To us it's a quiet way of life. It'll give us up before we give it up, I think.'

Night is falling in the forest. Outside the tents and teepees, lamps are twinkling and the air is filled with the sickly sweet smell of woodsmoke. Soon the dream-catchers will be doing their stuff, but meanwhile the woods are full of the sound of voices raised in laughter, as cowboys, Indians, mountain men and frontiers people cluster together, not under the stars, but under the twentieth-century roof of the local pub.

▼ 'More people died from exposure than ever died from the Indians. Still, it gave John Wayne a career, I suppose.'

THE KING OF PERCY ISLAND: ANDREW MARTIN

I am monarch of all I survey,
My right there is none to dispute;
From the centre all round to the sea
I am lord of the fowl and the brute.
O solitude! where are the charms
That sages have seen in thy face?
Better dwell in the midst of alarms,
Than reign in this horrible place.
William Cowper

In solitude
What happiness? Who can enjoy alone,
Or all enjoying, what contentment find?
John Milton

I vant to be alone.
Greta Garbo

I first learned of Andrew Martin through some old newspaper clippings. The papers had picked up the story of a man who had been living totally alone on a desert island off the coast of Australia since 1964. Now, you might think that anyone who would choose to live completely alone on a desert island was either a misanthropist or mad. Or both. You might also think that if he wasn't mad to begin with, after thirty years of this kind of life, he would, at the very least, be pretty bloody eccentric. And, quite frankly, you wouldn't be far wrong.

A Brief Biography (or Baby Bio)

Andrew Martin went to Eton, which, some might say, accounts for a lot. But although he says that in retrospect he had dreamed of living in a place like Percy Island since he was a tiny boy, the way that he came to be here was pure chance. Like many a good British eccentric before him, he had a conventional upbringing in North Devon. After he finished school, his intention was to go into farming or forestry, but first came National Service. During his time in the army he rose to the dizzy heights of corporal before being demoted. 'Unfortunately I told an officer what I thought of him, so I was back to square one.' To Andrew's great disappointment, the war finished a few months after he was called up so he never got a chance to see active service. After leaving the army, Andrew married and had a child, but he still yearned for adventure. When his sister went to live in Japan, Andrew seized the opportunity to travel to the Far East to visit her. It was to be, as he puts it 'a short break'. In reality it turned out to be one of the largest breaks this side of Steve Davis.

Three months later, Andrew found himself on the docks in Singapore, looking for a passage back to England. 'I was bored to tears and there was a boat on the wharf going to Fremantle so I got on. That's how I came to Australia, pure chance.' Once in Australia, he caught sight of some yachts moored in the harbour and was instantly attracted. 'I said: "Well, go and change your life. Buy a boat and charter it round the Pacific." Of course I knew nothing about sailing or navigation or anything like that.'

'This view, everything running free, knowing that I can walk around, muster the sheep, shoot the goats, this is what makes my heart beat. It *sends* me, as they say.'

Sure enough, Andrew bought a boat and went to Sydney, where a friend had offered to teach him how to sail. Together they sailed to the Whitsunday Islands where, one day, they happened to drop anchor at Percy Island. At the time it was inhabited by a sheep farmer and his family and they just happened to mention to Andrew that they were thinking of selling it. 'Out of pure curiosity, not thinking of buying an island, I said, "How much?" And it seemed to me such a plum at such a low price.' The asking price was £15,000, coincidentally the value of Andrew's new boat. The deal was done, and thus Andrew Martin became King of Percy Island, lord of all he surveyed. Originally he planned to keep the island for a few months, then sell it at a profit. 'My head said, "Go and make some money on it," but my heart said, "You'll never leave." Thirty years later he is still here, and even though he could probably sell Percy Island to a property developer for anywhere between fifteen and twenty million pounds, Andrew isn't interested. 'It's too good to sell to some developer or rich man who's just going to treat it like a vanity plaything. It's invaluable, like the most precious jewel in the world.' (Incidentally, in case you were wondering, his wife divorced him.)

The Visit

It isn't the easiest thing in the world to set up a meeting with someone who has no telephone and only gets his mail delivered every three months. But eventually one of our bottles did wash up on the shores of Percy Island, and Andrew Martin invited us to visit him. His only stipulations, which at the time seemed delightfully hospitable, were that the crew and and I stayed on the island, and that, since we would be his guests, we weren't to bring any of our own provisions.

For anyone curious or insane enough to want to know how to get to Percy (as it is known to its friends), the nearest island with an airstrip is a place called Hamilton Island, which is itself a three-hour flight from Brisbane. I arrive at Hamilton to find myself in the middle of what the travel industry describes as 'an integrated resort complex', that is to say, everything on the island – restaurants, villas, beach bars, hotels, etc. – is all owned by the same company. The advantage is that you can sign for anything you buy, every drink and meal that you consume, and have it added to one central bill which you only see when you leave. The disadvantage is that you can sign for anything you buy, every drink and meal that you consume, and have it added to one central bill which you only see when you leave.

The crew and the helicopter aren't due until the next day, so I opt to spend my night on Hamilton Island in something called a 'bure' which, as far as I can make out, is a cross between a chalet and a retirement home. After lying by the pool looking pale and uninteresting for an hour or so, I decide to pop into Romeo's Romantic Restaurant for a seafood salad. In true Aussie style this turns out to comprise an entire aquarium of marine life, a hillock of mayonnaise and one lettuce leaf. Delicious, although not especially romantic.

After a deep and blissful slumber, disturbed only by the lapping of gentle waves against the shore, a couple having a screaming row outside my door and the efficient amplification system of a nearby discothèque, I rise unrefreshed, and raring to go back to bed.

The helicopter ride to Percy Island is almost the highlight of the trip. (The real highlight is the trip home.) The white coral of the reefs shines through the clear water like a set of teeth, and the hundreds of tiny islands are like morsels of broccoli stuck between them. However, as we near Percy a sudden storm blows up and my first sight of the island is through blinding rain. So blinding, in fact, that we almost land at the next-door island by mistake.

'Gibraltar, Hong Kong and Percy Island still belong to Britain – but don't tell the Australians.'
Andrew Martin

When the helijet eventually manages to touch down on one of Percy's glorious sandy beaches, Andrew Martin is there to greet us, wearing only flip-flops and what appears to be a pair of pink satin underpants, although on closer (but not too close) inspection they turn out to be a pair of skimpy, early-seventies-style swimming trunks. Despite a limp, caused by a bad tumble a few years ago, he looks fit and well for his age, 'sixty-six or sixty-seven, I can't quite remember', and he retains the voice and demeanour of an Old Etonian as he welcomes us to 'the last outpost of the British Empire'.

Percy Island is only ten square miles, but that can seem awfully big when you're carrying suitcases uphill, over uneven terrain and through the dense foliage of a tropical rainforest. It is a forty-five-minute trek up to Andrew's homestead, a ramshackle 1920s house on high ground about a mile and a half from the beach. The clearing around the house is teeming with livestock: three dogs, chickens, geese, peacocks, geckos and cockroaches. Rather less welcome is the news, gleefully delivered by my host, that the entire island is swarming with poisonous snakes. Seeing my alarm, he adds that the only ones I am likely to encounter are the whipsnakes and the constrictors, which hang in the nearby gum trees in the hope of snaffling a goose egg or two.

I quickly step on to the wooden veranda, only to come face to face (or face to mandibles) with a spider the size of an antelope. Andrew confesses that he himself has always had a phobia about spiders – something of a drawback, considering his chosen lifestyle. Apparently when he first lived here, he would actually sleep outside if he caught sight of a spider inside the house. So didn't it make him have second thoughts about living here? 'I couldn't face myself if I was driven out by a spider. Out of the house, yes, but not out of the island.' So how does he cope?' 'Oh, within five or six years I began to get used to them.' I guess after five or six years you can get used to anything, but I make a mental note not to stay here that long. In fact, I keep my fingers crossed that the helicopter won't forget to pick me up in two days' time.

An ambitious and somewhat optimistic estate agent might describe Andrew's house as a 'characterful property with plenty of scope for improvement, many original features'. My description would be 'rickety wooden shack with a tin roof that appears to be propped up by a tree'. Although it has four bedrooms, Andrew has opted to sleep on the veranda, probably because it's one of the coolest parts of the house. The temperatures on Percy are usually in the mid-eighties, but in the summer they can go much higher, with the humidity at 100 per cent.

The house is furnished in an eclectic fashion, ranging from novice DIY enthusiast to some fairly decent-looking antiques. I ask Andrew how he came to acquire it, and he replies, 'Don't tell anyone, but to be honest, we're pirates.' It turns out that he is quite partial to lifting bits and pieces from abandoned houses on some of the nearby islands. The police even came out once 'to make enquiries', but he sent them away with a flea in their ear, saying that *they* had committed the crime in leaving good furniture to rot unused. Anyway, since when did a bit of looting ever do any harm? As Attila the Hun might have said.

In terms of mod-cons Andrew wants for nothing. Well, except for a washing machine, air-conditioning, a telephone and a bathroom. He does have a TV, though. It runs off electricity generated by a solar panel he fitted three years ago, with which he also powers a small electric flour mill, which he presumably uses when in need of small electric flour. So has he become a fan of *Home and Away*? 'I will only watch the BBC,' sniffs Andrew. 'I watch the news, current affairs programmes and I'm a big fan of *The Two Ronnies*.' Yes, that's what thirty years on a desert island can do for you. The only BBC programmes he can't stand are those presented by David Attenborough. 'His beliefs are

▶ **In terms of mod-cons, Andrew wants for nothing. And sure enough, that's what he's got.**

▶ **Use Timotei – and you too can have a receding hairline.**

totally stupid and cause immense harm.' Apparently Andrew takes great exception to the fact that Sir David believes in evolution. Andrew thinks the theory of evolution is rubbish, although he grudgingly concedes, 'He is very, very good with animals – I wouldn't go and sleep with gorillas, would you?' I avoid the obvious response.

We sit down to a dinner of goat spaghetti, accompanied by bread and rancid butter, all washed down with some of Andrew's home-made island mead, which rather worryingly is kept in a large bottle marked Bleach. Andrew seems to be watching me closely during the meal as though waiting to pounce on any hesitation or lack of enthusiasm in my chewing and swallowing. Or maybe there is a genuine possibility that I am drinking bleach. I'm sure that if I had been starved for two weeks before coming to the island it would have tasted delicious, but on balance the seafood salad was rather more appetizing and somehow less 'goaty'.

Afterwards I realize that on my tour of the house I haven't come across anything closely resembling a bathroom or lavatory. Sure enough, when I broach the subject, Andrew leads me out of the house and across the dark yard to a small shack containing a toilet. I take one look, wait till he has gone and pee in the bushes as I nervously scan the trees for boa constrictors. Then it's off to my allotted room, where I sleep fitfully, dreaming of loud discothèques and seafood salads smothered in mayonnaise.

Over a breakfast of toast with rancid butter, Andrew is working his way through a two-foot stack of *Guardians.* He has a subscription, but the papers only get delivered every three months with the mail. So, twelve weeks of ignorance is followed by a few days of being fantastically well informed. Rather frustrating during the football season, I should imagine. Andrew also belongs to a book club, and has a fairly bizarre collection of literature, including *Sex and History* and *Thatcher: The Downing Street Years.* I ask Andrew if he is a fan of the ex-Prime Minister. 'When she isn't banging on about politics or economics,' is the puzzling reply. After all, with the exception of Rolf Harris's 'Two Little Boys', when does she ever talk about anything else? As I sip my coffee and goat's milk, I idly wonder what will be on the menu tonight. Andrew announces that we are off to shoot a goat. No need to wonder any longer.

We set off on our hunt, Andrew kitted out in the same skimpy bathers as yesterday, and carrying a .303 rifle slung over one shoulder. We climb through the shade of coconut palms and

Percy Island Goat Cuisine

All recipes serve 1 to 20 (depending on how much of it you are able to keep down).

GOAT STEW

Ingredients:
Goat
Anything else you can find

Catch, kill, skin and cut up goat into large chunks. Remove testicles (the goat's) and throw to dogs. Add other ingredients, and boil for several hours. Serve with as much of anything else as possible, so as to smother taste.

GOAT RISOTTO

Ingredients:
Goat
Rice

Catch, kill, skin and cut up goat into large chunks. Fry goat pieces till chewable and add to cooked rice. Serve, and spend rest of night on the lavatory – or before eating simply throw the lot down the toilet, thereby missing out the middle-man.

GOAT SPAGHETTI

Ingredients:
Goat
Spaghetti

Catch, kill, skin and cut up goat into large chunks. Boil for several hours, add spaghetti and a dollop of rancid butter.
Salt and pepper to kill taste.
Serve to unsuspecting television presenter.

If you would like to try out any more Percy Island recipes, please send a stamped addressed envelope to:

Goat, Goat and More Goat, PO Box 234, Mackay, Queensland, Australia.

eucalyptus to more open country where the sun beats down and the earth is a bright ochre. All the livestock on the island roam about quite freely, although few of them are native to Percy. There is a handful of cattle and a few sheep although, strangely for someone who blithely shoots goats and cattle, Andrew developed an aversion to killing the sheep and let most of them die out naturally. One can't help wondering what the sheep did to secure such a special place in his heart. In 1967 Andrew brought half a dozen kangaroos to the island. Ten years later, they numbered around a thousand. However, three years ago a spell of wet weather drastically reduced the population, and since then many of those that didn't die from exposure have got it in the neck from Andrew's rifle. He sells their skins to some of the yachtsmen who stop at Percy, and sometimes even makes bagpipes out of the pelts. As we climb up Dead Sheep Hill, presumably soon to be Dead Goat Hill, Andrew declares, 'This view, everything running free, knowing that I can walk around, muster the sheep, shoot the goats, this is what makes my heart beat. It *sends* me, as they say.' Well, as they said in 1964, anyway.

We spot the herd of goats. They spot us and start running. It appears there is something to be said for evolution, after all. One–nil to Charles Darwin and Sir David Attenborough. Andrew lifts his rifle and fires three times. 'Got him,' he says, with great satisfaction. One–all.

Back at the homestead, Andrew sets about skinning the goat with vigour and a large knife. With a couple of deft, wince-inducing swipes, Andrew cuts off the goat's testicles and tosses

▲ Andrew in the process of being stung twenty-nine times. The Goat in Honey was delicious, though.

◄ One of Andrew Martin's main sources of revenue is his hives, both from selling the honey itself and the mead that he makes from it. Luckily he doesn't have to rely on his skill as a poet to earn a living.

them to his Labradors. 'They love those,' he remarks casually. I suppose that's what they mean by 'the dogs' bollocks'. By the time Andrew has finishing skinning, disembowelling and dissecting the unfortunate billy goat, I am seriously considering becoming a vegan. 'The way I look at it,' says Andrew, 'it's not unkind. This is just part of life.' Well, not as far as *that* goat's concerned, it isn't.

Next it's time to don our bee-keeping suits and go and collect some honey. Although Andrew is mainly self-sufficient, he still needs a certain amount of money for things like kerosene, tools, books about Mrs Thatcher, etc. One of his main sources of revenue is from his hives, both from selling the honey itself and the mead that he makes from it. We waddle over to the hives, which look suspiciously like old wooden filing cabinets, and while I keep a discreet and circumspect distance, Andrew lifts the lids and removes some of the combs, doing a strange jerky dance as he does so. It later transpires that the reason for this sudden unchoreographed routine is that Andrew got stung twenty-nine times in the process. Apparently the bees were angry because of the wind.

The next day we set off across the island to the lagoon where the 'yachties' moor their boats, last night's Goat Supreme still lying heavy in my stomach. Percy can get as many as a thousand of these visitors every year, an international brigade of boat enthusiasts who tour the islands, occasionally dropping anchor and coming ashore for a day or two. Andrew has constructed an A-frame building on the beach, made from the timber of an old squash court in Mackay. Here, he lays out an array of Percy Island produce: mead, honey, goat and kangaroo skins, tropical fruit and fresh vegetables from his garden. (No wool, you'll notice.) Sometimes he even provides barbecues for the yachties – goat kebabs, presumably. The yachties in their turn leave

'Today's Premier League results are as follows . . .'

◀ The yachties who visit the island leave painted signs. Any sign which doesn't meet with Andrew's approval is taken down. Unfortunately there is no one to do the same for Andrew's own signs.

▼ Exactly what I've been worrying about.

painted signs (e.g. 'There is no time to stop and stare', 'The Hills are alive . . .' and 'Eric Clapton is God'), which are dotted all round the island. Any sign which doesn't meet with Andrew's approval is taken down. Everyone is welcome to stay on Percy, as long as they don't 'misbehave'. 'I suppose I run this island fairly toughly according to some people,' says Andrew. 'I've asked a few to leave.' Somehow I get the feeling I'm going to be the next.

▶ Maybe he *is* God – he certainly seems to be omnipresent.

Andrew Martin says he didn't choose to live alone. 'It just happened that way', although he admits that he does have 'a low tolerance for man's laws'. Furthermore, although the island is picture-postcard beautiful, his isn't the idyllic life of a Bounty ad, lying on a palm-fringed beach sipping cocktails while the waves lap against the shore. (Apart from anything else, the sharks, stone fish and sea snakes make swimming dangerous.) Life on Percy is unremittingly tough, and Andrew has to work harder than most people to maintain his self-sufficiency. Whatever brings him happiness, it isn't lounging about all day drinking Malibu and getting a sun-tan. 'No, that would be an unbelievable nightmare,' he says at the suggestion. 'There's no fulfilment in that kind of life.'

We sit on the beach waiting for the helicopter to arrive and carry me back to the mainland and the creature comforts for which I'm already pining. A thunderstorm is brewing and, if the weather doesn't hold, it means staying another night on the island. With relief bordering on hysteria, I hear the sound of chopper blades. Soon Percy Island is just another splodge of broccoli below us. We may be leaving a paradise, but to me it feels like being delivered from hell.

QUINTESSA
BRIGADOON
PERCY
ERIC CLAPTON
IS GOD
BOTANY BAY

AFTERWORDS

At this start of this book I asked many questions about happiness. Searching questions like 'Happiness, what is it?', and 'If I find happiness, am I allowed to keep it, or do I have to hand it in at the nearest police station?' Now, many months and many weary miles later, I can safely say that I have learned everything there is to know about the subject at hand. That is, 'everything' in the 'sod all' sense of the word.

That is not to say that many of the people featured in this book have not themselves found ways of attaining this contented state of mind. Or heart. Or soul. Or wherever happiness does, in fact, lie. Some of them seem almost indecently happy. In fact, if I had to award prizes for 'Happiest Interviewee in a Book Accompanying a BBC 1 Television Series About Happiness', I'd unhesitatingly give joint first place to the Langs (Love) and Charles Gray (Money). Even so, what makes them happy would not necessarily make anyone else happy. One man's meat is some unfortunate cow's bottom, as they say.

So was it all a waste of effort? Not quite. I may have had to trek halfway around the world to find it, but find it I did. The answer, if you want to be happy, is not to trek halfway around the world looking for happiness. And in case you are in any doubt as to what I mean, no, there will not be a sequel. That is, until the BBC ask me to start work on their forthcoming production, *In Search of Caribbean Beaches.*

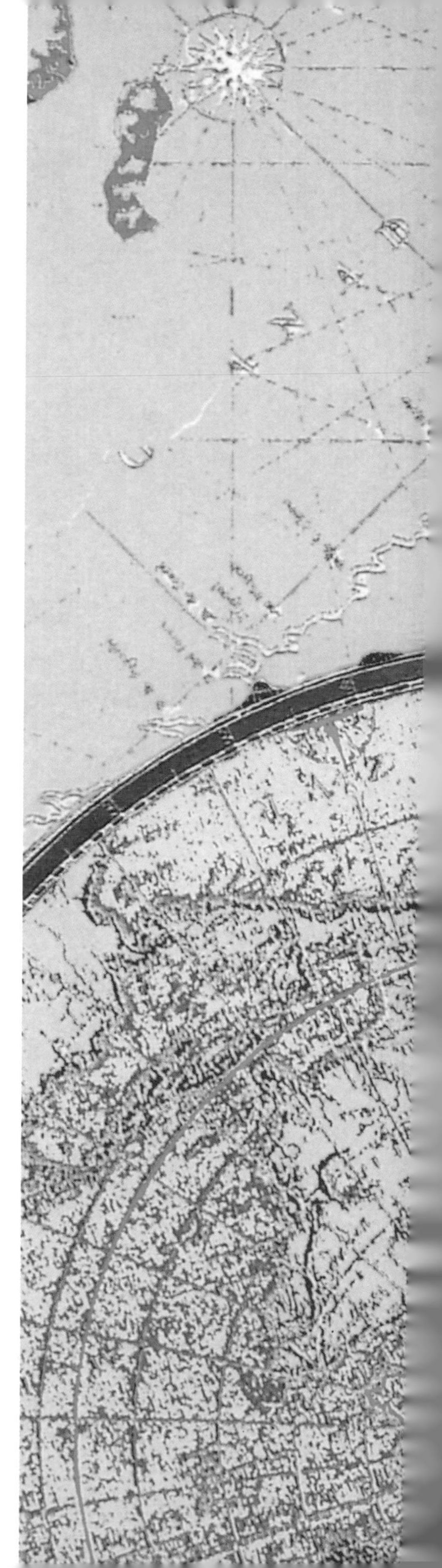

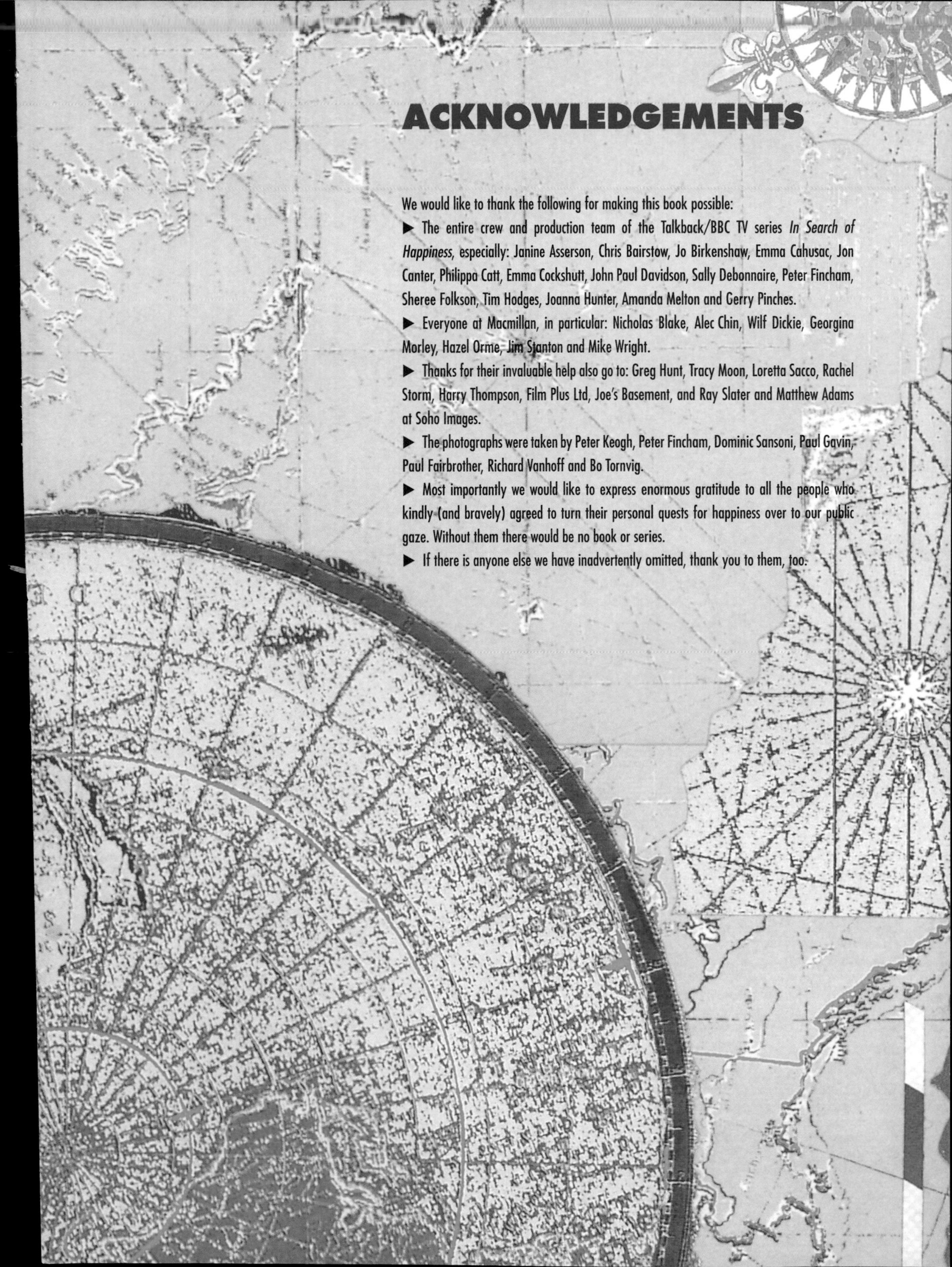

ACKNOWLEDGEMENTS

We would like to thank the following for making this book possible:

▶ The entire crew and production team of the Talkback/BBC TV series *In Search of Happiness*, especially: Janine Asserson, Chris Bairstow, Jo Birkenshaw, Emma Cahusac, Jon Canter, Philippa Catt, Emma Cockshutt, John Paul Davidson, Sally Debonnaire, Peter Fincham, Sheree Folkson, Tim Hodges, Joanna Hunter, Amanda Melton and Gerry Pinches.

▶ Everyone at Macmillan, in particular: Nicholas Blake, Alec Chin, Wilf Dickie, Georgina Morley, Hazel Orme, Jim Stanton and Mike Wright.

▶ Thanks for their invaluable help also go to: Greg Hunt, Tracy Moon, Loretta Sacco, Rachel Storm, Harry Thompson, Film Plus Ltd, Joe's Basement, and Ray Slater and Matthew Adams at Soho Images.

▶ The photographs were taken by Peter Keogh, Peter Fincham, Dominic Sansoni, Paul Gavin, Paul Fairbrother, Richard Vanhoff and Bo Tornvig.

▶ Most importantly we would like to express enormous gratitude to all the people who kindly (and bravely) agreed to turn their personal quests for happiness over to our public gaze. Without them there would be no book or series.

▶ If there is anyone else we have inadvertently omitted, thank you to them, too.